POE POE POE POE POE POE POE

Poe Poe Poe Poe

'...much of Madness, and more of Sin And
Horror the soul of the plot!'
—LIGEIA

'Poor Hoffman, this going mad of a friend comes
straight home to every man who feels his soul
within him. For in all of us lodges the same fuel
to light the same fire. And he who has never felt,
momentarily, what madness is, has but a
mouthful of brains.''
—HERMAN MELVILLE

'Keep the imagination sane.'
—NATHANIEL HAWTHORNE,
TO HIS WIFE, SOPHIA

DANIEL HOFFMAN

Poe Poe Poe

PARAGON HOUSE  NEW YORK

First Paragon House edition, 1990
Published in the United States by

Paragon House
90 Fifth Avenue
New York, NY 10011

Acknowledgment is made for use of the following
material:

The London Magazine for 'Send-Ups,' from the
January 1970 issue.

The Southern Review for 'The Remarriage of Ligeia's
Husband,' from the January 1972 issue. Copyright
© 1972 issue. Copyright © 1972 by the Louisiana
State University.

Library of Congress Cataloging-in-Publication Data

Hoffman, Daniel, 1923–
  Poe Poe Poe Poe Poe Poe Poe / Daniel Hoffman.
— 1st Paragon House ed.
      p.   cm.
  Reprint. Originally published: Garden City, N.Y. :
Doubleday, 1972.
  ISBN 1-55778-274-1
  1. Poe, Edgar Allan, 1809–1849—Criticism and
interpretation.   I. Title.
PS2638.H57   1990
818'.309—dc20   89-38304
                                           CIP

Manufactured in the United States of America
10   9   8   7   6   5   4   3   2   1

Contents

Preface

What, another book on Poe!

Who needs it? Don't we already have a book called *Poe: A Critical Study*? And another titled *Edgar Allan Poe as Literary Critic*? Yes, and *Poe the Detective*, and *The French Face of Edgar Poe*, and *Poe's Literary Battles*, and *Poe and the British Magazine Tradition*, and *Edgar Poe the Poet*, and *The Mind of Poe*, not to mention a shelf of monographs on Poe and Baudelaire, Poe and E. T. A. Hoffmann, Poe and the Bible, Poe in Spanish literature, *The Origins of Poe's Critical Theory*, and the like; plus several biographies—some factual, others psychiatric, in which Poe as analysand is diagnosed, and his work treated, as cases of psychic impotence or compensatory aggression or prenatal consciousness of parental sexuality—as well as a couple of anthologies of chapters from most of the foregoing plus contemporaneous reviews of Poe and cullings from recent issues of the scholarly journals. Why, you may well wonder, would anyone offer yet another book on so well-documented a subject as the poetry, the tales, the critical theory, the life, the works, and the spell of Edgar Allan Poe?

Many books, many Poes. Edgar Allan Poe was always complex, inspired, limited, pretentious, uncompromising, banal. This was acknowledged as long ago as in his own time. James Russell Lowell, in *A Fable for Critics*, said it first:

> Here comes Poe with his Raven, like Barnaby Rudge,
> Three fifths of him genius, two fifths sheer fudge.

In criticism it is usually assumed that to be worthy of scholarly attention an author is, by common consent, a sheer genius. Or perhaps, sheer fudge. But Poe was a deeply, tragically divided man. We can't get his genius without his fudge, or his fudge without his genius. Nor is it a foregone conclusion which is which.

Henry James, however, thought it was. He acknowledged Poe as both a 'genius' and a 'charlatan,' but James never expatiated on what was genius-like in Poe. (He called Poe's criticism 'the most complete and exquisite specimen of *provincialism* ever prepared for the edification of men.') As for the charlatanry, James opined that 'It seems to us that to take him with more than a certain degree of seriousness is to lack seriousness one's self.' I have heeded that advice, although I'd like to think I'm not as much put off as was Henry James at discovering myself the butt of some of Edgar's hoaxes. It seems to us that Henry was perhaps a little lacking in that lack of seriousness sometimes necessary for a higher seriousness, the understanding of a man of genius whose genius is not lacking in charlatanry.

Seventy years after James, in 1948, T. S. Eliot, himself, one thinks, capable of a greater lack of seriousness than his predecessor, offered a view more serious though hardly more commendatory of Poe. Eliot proposed to explain why Poe's appeal is primarily to readers 'at the period of life when they were just emerging from childhood':

> That Poe had a powerful intellect is undeniable: but it seems to me the intellect of a highly gifted young person before puberty. The forms which his lively curiosity takes are those in which a pre-adolescent mentality delights: wonders of nature and of mechanics and of the supernatural, cryptograms and cyphers, puzzles and labyrinths, mechanical chess-players and wild flights of speculation. The variety and ardour of his curiosity delight and dazzle, yet in the end the eccentricity and lack of coherence of his interests tire.

Like all of Eliot's criticism, this is scrupulous; but nevertheless it's not quite just. For the fact is—I believe it to be

a fact, I've written what turns out to be this book to prove
it—while Edgar Poe's views may well strike us as eccentric,
nothing could be further from the mark than to call them
lacking in coherence. From Eliot's point of view there could
be no coherence where there was eccentricity of interest, since
coherence demanded commitment to the centrality of the
culture of Christendom. That seems plausible enough, but
not for Poe; for, as Allen Tate has brilliantly shown, the
entire Christian ethical tradition was quite beyond the
periphery of Poe's interests. It does not necessarily follow,
however, that Poe's interests are incoherent. And Eliot himself points out (as I shall have occasion to point out too)
how central to modern literature is Poe's image of the poet
as a conscious manipulator of his craft. There's a view
that's *quite* coherent; only trouble is, it's only about three-
fifths true. Like most of what is true in Poe.

Reading and re-reading Poe, I found myself wishing to do
justice to the actual experience of reading Poe, of reading him
again and again over half a lifetime. Like Eliot's hypotheti-
cal reader, I really began to read Poe when just emerging
from childhood. Then one was entranced by such ideas as
secret codes, hypnotism, closed systems of self-consistent
thought. That was the time of life when one couldn't help
but surrender to the insistent clangor of a rhythm, the gong-
like resonances of rhyme. Who could but thrill, then, with
an *inexplicable eagerness*, to each successive paragraph in
tales of unimaginable terror—to motifs of premature entombment, of motiveless malignancy, the murder of beloved persons, the relentless self-exposure of the criminal who revels
in his guilt as he had revelled in his revenge? Returning to
the *loci* of these pubescent shocks and thrills, returning from
both occasional choice and repeated obligation—as is the
lot of a teacher of American literature—I found that what I
first had found in Poe remained, but, even more to my surprise, there was often a complexity of implication, a plumb-
ing of the abyss of human nature, and a strange webwork of
consistency among the poems and tales. Much, much more
than the shuddering boy had ever dreamed of.

I started to write a sketch of Poe as he appeared—and changed—to me over the years, to bring out the full range of emotion his work stirs in the reader. This Poe who can frighten a boy out of his pajamas is the author whose vision of the artist has burned like a smoking flare into the unconscious of Baudelaire, of Mallarmé, of Valéry. The inventor of such seemingly trivial popular amusements as the detective story and the science fiction tale is also the systematic philosopher of the Absolute Autonomy of Art. The poet whose vision of Beauty is mournful, ethereal, otherworldly has strewn his tales with bold and impositious hoaxes upon his readers. I have tried to render the full effect of the work of this wild, eccentric, audacious, tortured, horror-haunted, sorrowing, beauty-loving Edgar Allan Poe, so as to comprehend and demonstrate the sources of his imaginative power.

That power is evident to some degree in everything he wrote, but in much of the work—two-fifths, I would guess— he can avail himself of only a fraction of that power, or use it only in distorted and uncertain ways. Since each of his writings is a comment upon and extension of the rest of his *œuvre*, my enterprise involves a rather full exploration of that *œuvre*. But it is not my purpose to propose Olympian judgments of Poe; instead I would rather respond to his qualities as they really affect me, as I believe they really affect any other reader who puts himself in the way of Poe's vision.

For these reasons I've introduced, as a surrogate for all of Poe's readers, an *homme moyen sensuel*, called 'I,' whose circumstances, however disparate from those of Poe, demonstrate the powers of Poe's work, and its occasional failures of power, to stir the imagination, the passions, and the mind. These are the powers which Poe designed his work to exercise upon us. If the responses of the 'I' who speaks in this book are not always the same to the same poems and tales, that is because what Poe (or any author of comparable durability) says to us is not a message unchanged by the circumstances in which we read him. One of the fictions of conventional criticism which I would overturn with fact is the notion of there being only one permissible and authoritative 'meaning' in a work of literature.

Many readers are put off from Poe by the *décor* of his writings—the settings of his tales and poems, the often grotesque style of his prose, what Aldous Huxley objected to as the vulgarity of his verse. His excrescent Gothic conventions which are often on the verge, if not over the verge, of self-parody, seem willfully remote from any possible reality. It is, however, a function of Poe's theories of both poetry and fiction that so many mannerisms be interposed between reality and the reader. It is my hope, in writing sometimes personally about one reader's relationship to Poe's work, to suggest how Poe's artifices—the images and patterns in his Arabesques, the strange diction of his poems and tales—are intensifications of the realities they seem to avoid. Poe has exerted a force upon later readers and writers quite disproportionate to the weight of his slender stock of verses and the brevity of his tales. Although the characters in his tales are without exception fantastic personages, they must touch some deep, responsive nerve hidden in ourselves. Whose image do we see in Poe's insane criminals, in his detectives with their superhuman intelligence, in his protagonists driven by mysterious obsessions or passively suffering equally mysterious adventures? As Thoreau replied to a correspondent who complained about Whitman's animality, of whose experiences has he the power to remind us?

Edgar Poe led the most luckless life of any writer. His only talent was for suffering. His genius was to make of his own sufferings the paradigms of our fate elaborated with such energy and intelligence in his writings. Through the miraculous paradoxes of his art, we are rewarded in his greatest tales with the joy of recognition: This is a part of ourselves, of our own reality, which would have remained inarticulate and unacknowledged but for him. I can understand the tribute paid to Poe by François Truffaut in his film, *Fahrenheit 451*, based on the book by Poe's epigone, Ray Bradbury. In this futuristic science-fiction (a genre in which Poe pioneered), technology becomes the repressive instrument of the fascist police, and the ownership of books a treasonable crime. The hero escapes to an underground commune of rebel humanists, each of whom has committed to memory the entire text of one book, thus preserving our culture from extirpation. Bradbury's hero had memorized Ecclesiastes, but Truffaut substitutes an even more appropriate title. The text his hero offers as his passport to freedom is *Tales of Mystery and Imagination* by Edgar Allan Poe.

Acknowledgments

This book was begun with the aid of a Research Fellowship from the American Council of Learned Societies and a sabbatical leave in 1966–67 from the University of Pennsylvania. I owe thanks to these patrons not only for their generosity and their patience but for their tolerance of a book which has turned out so differently from the study I thought I was going to write. On my return to the University, the opportunity of giving seminars to graduate students in the work of Poe provided a stimulating and rigorous forum for the working out of some of the interpretations in these pages.

It is my good fortune that several friends have read earlier versions of some or all of these chapters. Richard Wilbur increased the debts I owe his essays on Poe by reading mine; I thank him for his encouragement of this enterprise as well as for his forbearance of our differing points of view. Alfred Kazin, too, shared his interest in Poe by reading my first drafts; I am obliged to him for several valuable suggestions. My colleagues at the University of Pennsylvania, Philip Rieff and Robert Regan, heartened me with encouragement and protected me from errors. To Richard Howard I am especially grateful for his unstinting reassurance, over several years, that such a book as this was worth the writing, and for his belief that my way of approaching Poe's work is feasible. Anne Freedgood, Editor of Doubleday Anchor Books, gave my MS. the blessing of her skilled direction. Had I been able to take advantage of all the suggestions offered by these first readers, this would have been a better book.

My discussion of Poe's *Eureka* has been broadened by readings in physics suggested by Dean William E. Stephens of the University of Pennsylvania. Many of my obligations to the criticism and scholarship of Poe's works are mentioned in my text. I have found particularly helpful the synoptic essays on Poe by, among others, Harry Levin, F. O. Matthiessen, and Patrick Quinn, all of whose work helps the reader to comprehend the interrelationships among Poe's writings. Most valuable for my purposes were the discussions of Poe by poets from Baudelaire to Tate, Eliot, Auden, and Wilbur. Most of the individual essays mentioned in the text may be found in two recent anthologies of Poe Criticism: *The Recognition of Edgar Allan Poe*, edited by Eric Carlson, and *Poe: A Collection of Critical Essays*, edited by Robert Regan.

I am indebted to the librarians of the British Museum, the Library of the Royal Borough of Kensington, the University of London, Swarthmore College, and the University of Pennsylvania.

The text of Poe's poems is taken from Thomas O. Mabbott's edition of *The Poems* (volume I of *Collected Works*, Cambridge, The Belknap Press, 1969); for Poe's prose I have relied on the Virginia Edition of *Collected Works of Edgar Allan Poe*, edited by James A. Harrison (17 volumes, New York, Crowell, 1902), and *The Letters of Edgar Allan Poe*, edited by John Ward Ostrom (2 volumes, Cambridge, Harvard University Press, 1948).

To my wife and children, who endured the writing of this book, I am indebted beyond the power of words to say.

London, Cape Rosier,   DANIEL HOFFMAN
Swarthmore, Penna.
May 1971

Several factual errors in the first edition were brought to my attention by Clifton Waller Barrett, John Hollander, Philip Van Doren Stern, and John H. Yohalem. I am grateful for their corrections. Needless to say, for any misstatements that may remain, I alone am responsible.

D.H.

August 1972

'I can afford to wait a century for readers when God himself has waited six thousand years for an observer.'

Kepler, writing in 1619, quoted by
Pundita in 2848, quoted by Poe in 1848.

I

Poe Poe Poe Poe Poe Poe Poe

Across the flyleaf of my old *Commemorative Edition of the Works of Edgar Allan Poe in Ten Volumes, Volume I* (the only one I owned), a strong hand had written, 'I hate Poe,' and signed my name. That hand was mine. I remember pressing the pencil so hard that the writing came through in reverse, a hieroglyph in secret code across the phrenological features of the author's daguerreotype. And I held the book up to the mirror, seeing Poe's image in my hand and the image of his image in the image of my hand, my adolescent hatred inscribed both backwards and forwards across his forehead.

I was haunted by Poe long before I defaced his daguerreotype. How could I but be haunted, for did not I, a member of the Debating Team and the Cross-Country Squad, a serious student of chemistry and Intermediate French, long for nothing better, nothing more, than, with Poe,

> To muse for long unwearied hours, with my attention riveted to some frivolous device on the margin or in the typography of a book; to become absorbed, for the better part of a summer's day, in a quaint shadow falling aslant upon the tapestry or upon the floor; to lose myself, for an entire night, in watching the steady flame of a lamp, or the embers of a fire; to dream away whole days over the perfume of a flower; to repeat, monotonously, some

common word, until the sound, by dint of frequent repetition, ceased to convey any idea whatsoever to the mind . . .

And, my attention caught, diverted, hypnotized, so that even
the intensity of 'Berenice' faded momentarily from my mind,
what word repeated itself with the monotony of water dripping on a rock but the name, the very name, of the author
who had so irremediably seduced my spirit from all pur-
posive goals to follow some unknown, indefinite pleasure:
Poe Poe Poe Poe Poe Poe Poe, the name resounded, soon
becoming not a name at all but now a note, a tone struck
upon some inward anvil of my being, one syllable in a chord
I strained to hear, an ineffable harmony plucked from some
sphere beyond the meshes of our common feelings.

Poe's portrait, like his name, haunted my dreams and
waking dreams. How shall I describe his demeanor?

> A cadaverousness of complexion; an eye large, liquid, and
> luminous beyond comparison; lips somewhat thin and very
> pallid, but of a surpassingly beautiful curve; a nose of a
> delicate Hebrew model, but with a breadth of nostril un-
> usual in similar formations; a finely moulded chin, speaking,
> in its want of prominence, of a want of moral energy; hair
> of a more than web-like softness and tenuity;—these fea-
> tures, with an inordinate expansion above the regions of
> the temple, made up altogether a countenance not easily
> to be forgotten. . . . I could not, even with effort, con-
> nect its Arabesque expression with any idea of simple
> humanity.

How better describe Poe's demeanor than in his words, for
Edgar Poe, too, had mused upon his image in a glass—with
not the usual, or expected, vanity of an *uninstructed* self-
flattery. Poe was, or rather made himself become, an adept
in the science of phrenology, of which he wrote (reviewing a
treatise on this subject in March, 1836), that among its uses,
the 'most direct, and, perhaps, most salutary, is that of *self-
examination and self-knowledge*,' through which individuals
may obtain 'a perfectly accurate estimate of their own moral
capabilities.' Since Poe had the aforementioned bulging

forehead, how reassuring to him must have been 'the opinion of Gall, that a skull which is large, which is elevated or high above the ears, and in which the head is well developed and thrown forward, so as to be nearly perpendicular to the base, may be presumed to lodge a brain of greater power (whatever may be its propensities) than a skull deficient in such proportion.'

Poe of course was neither so vain nor so naïf as to publish the description of that 'countenance not easily to be forgotten' as of himself. No, I have copied out those sentences from his curious tale, 'The Fall of the House of Usher,' where the cadaverous yet 'surpassingly beautiful' features are attributed to Roderick Usher, that man of supersensual perceptions and more-than-human sufferings, who, despite the abundance of his natural gifts and an estate beyond all dreams of riches, goes weirdly mad and inters his sister living in the tomb. His is the countenance which Poe—if we assume the narrator of Poe's story to be a voice that speaks with Poe's voice— 'could not, even with effort, connect its Arabesque expression with any idea of simple humanity.'

No more could I so connect Poe's strange expression as his portrait stared at the mirror-image of his portrait in my hand. I did not then know it to be true, but at the moment a seal was set upon my own endeavors; for whatever else I should attempt of willed accomplishment or of the surrender of the will to the imperious seekings of the soul induced by seeming indolence, I would not rest until my own brain, of whatever power in my own thrusting temples, try to comprehend the propensities of Poe's intelligence, that is to say, to understand, as fully as I was moved by, his strange, haunted, tawdry, inexorable, remote yet inescapable Art. Since Poe is not a piece of simple humanity the intellectual devices of his work are neither transparent nor commonplace. But I am wandering from the reveries induced by the repetition of his name . . .

Poe's features—the bulging forehead, the beautifully curved lip, the studiedly disarranged dandyism of those curled black locks, the insouciance of that loosely flung

cravat—haunted me from a realm where a man, however self-
tortured or by the world abused, could look like *that*. My
world seemed carefully to have sealed up all the chinks and
crannies through which a soul so tortured, a self so suffering,
could invoke upon my head its curious spells of woe. My
world, at fifteen, was New Rochelle, New York, a city once
a citadel for Huguenots fleeing the barbarous devices of the
mailed men of Cardinal Richelieu; perhaps, for them, 'The
Pit and the Pendulum' would have been the mere report of
a reality rather than a masochist's dream. Through New
Rochelle Edgar Poe himself may well have walked, perhaps
on Forest Avenue across our tulip bed and lawn, during that
season of his direst misery after his wife Virginia died, when
he trod the weary miles from his unheated cottage in Fordham to visit—but let me quote Professor Mabbott, editor of
the Belknap Press of Harvard University edition of Poe's
Collected Works, Volume I, *The Poems* (Cambridge,
1969):

> The impulse finally came to compose a version of 'Ula-
> lume' after a walk to Mamaroneck, New York, on the
> mainland a dozen miles from Fordham. There he saw the
> private cemetery of the Guion family, of Revolutionary
> stock. The tomb of Thomas Guion is approached by an
> avenue of pine trees, which gave Poe his setting. I heard
> the story myself from a lady resident of Mamaroneck over
> twenty years ago, and it is still told locally.

Over twenty years before 1969 would have been during my
time in New Rochelle, and I too had heard the tale—but
surely in a more authoritative version: It was Virginia whose
grave was situated in Mamaroneck, or in Port Chester . . .
and to walk from Fordham to either of these destinations,
one *has* to go right through New Rochelle, where 'The skies
they were ashen and sober; / The leaves they were crisped
and sere / . . . It was down by the dark tarn of Auber, / In
the ghoul haunted woodland of Weir.'
    Yes, Poe must have trudged through New Rochelle. But
I guess I was the only citizen of that city or scholar in her
schools who ever gave the matter a thought. Civic pride, his-

torical priority, pointed to other lights in the past of that
dormitory suburb of New York. It was still proudly reported
that in antebellum days New Rochelle had been a center of
French culture (not a Huguenot left by my time), and that
Southern planters often sent their daughters to live with the
elegant families of La Nouvelle Rochelle as an alternative to
the Grand Tour or a winter in Paris. Why any should have
considered this alternative satisfactory I never thought to ask.
But however close the cultural interchange between my home
town and Poe's Virginia a century earlier, I could think of
nowhere on earth that seemed more alien to me than the
American South.

And what did I know of the American South, I who had
not yet gone as far south as Washington, D.C., nor would
until the pilgrimage thither of the Senior Class? Imagination
provides what knowledge lacks, imagination fed, in the event,
by shibboleth and *idées reçues*. The South: Plantation and
cabin. Colonels and slaves. Ladies in the leisure of their
farthingales, and black women in the sweat of their labor-
stained bandannas. Songs of Stephen Foster. Ebony spirituals
from the slave quarter. Lazy banjo-pickin' strummed across
the river. The wailing work-chants of the black—in those days
we said Negro—suffering singing cotton-picking hands, over-
seen by a whip-wielding white on horseback, moustache curling on his lip. A South made out of *Uncle Tom's Cabin* and
Gone with the Wind, a landscape of faëry, based on reports
of the real which a century's time and a hundred ulterior
motives had *slightly* distorted. And it was from the benighted
customs and deplorable prejudices of this region, his own,
that Poe had made his aesthetic absolutes. For who could
succumb to the temptation, as he went on to describe it in
'Berenice,' the temptation

> to lose all sense of motion or physical existence, by means
> of absolute bodily quiescence long and obstinately perse-
> vered in,

or the other means, aforementioned, of suspending the workaday faculties, the rational mind, the desires and skills of

6

POE POE POE POE POE POE POE

getting and spending—who, I say, could succumb to the lure
of this suspension of both belief and disbelief, this suspension of all *activity*, save a member of a class as privileged
as Egaeus, Berenice's lover; or the nameless husband of
Ligeia; or Roderick Usher; or the prince Mentoni (in 'The
Assignation')? Ah, but to share with them the contemplation
of the unknowable indefinite infinite, the essence of beauty
—although the reader who persists in sharing their contempla-
tions ends, not with the tranquil bliss of beatitude, but in
a state of disordered excitation in which his fitful bliss is
intermingled with terrors unplumbed hitherto, with horrors
unsuspected yet unexpectedly *enjoyed*. Such luxuriousness,
such indulgence of the sensibility, seemed to me the un-
earned prerogative of an aristocracy. And much as I longed,
in reading Poe's poems at this time, for the lost bliss of
'Annabel Lee,' much as I sighed for Israfel's heavenly lyre,
yea, even dreamt on Helen, when I read Poe's 'Philosophy
of Composition' and 'The Poetic Principle' a fierce and lurid
war raged within my breast between Indefinite Beauty and
Moral Imperative.

Moral Imperative. The Duty of Social Man. The Individual as a Contributing Part to the Life of the Community.
This was the earnest high-minded vision spread before my
classmates in high school, and if no heed was taken of the
pilgrimage across its grounds of the bereaved Poe a century
earlier, who among us didn't know that across Woodrow
Wilson Boulevard from the school, over the moat and bridge,
on the other side of North Avenue, was the Thomas Paine
House? In this shingled bungalow, maintained by the State,
the focal interest was a rusted crease along the doorjamb
where one of the local farmers had scored a near-miss on the
detested atheist who lived there on his Congressional pension in 1810. The Tom Paine memorial was crucial to my
sensibility then, since Paine, interpreted as an evangel of
Reason's rightness, was echoed and applied to daily life and
studies by my persuasive teachers at New Rochelle High.
(It's true that the quotations facing North Avenue are en-
graved from *The Rights of Man*, while those from *The Age*

of Reason were scraped and hidden by a rear hedge of barberry; but no matter . . .) All the civics teachers I ever had at New Rochelle never tired of quoting Tom Paine, whose house, as I've said, was just across the moat that rippled in the wind before the castellated walls of the school. For the philanstery of learning and the arts in our old Huguenot city had been conceived on the model of a Norman castle large enough for two thousand inhabitants, and built in the shape of a hollow pentagon.

This ducal schoolhouse looms in my memories like the Gothic châteaux in Poe's stories—the Hungarian castle in 'Metzengerstein,' the Venetian palace in 'The Assignation,' the pentagonal abbey refurbished with such saracenal abandon by Ligeia's husband—perhaps above all the House of Usher, with its air 'of an excessive antiquity,' on which 'the eye of a scrutinizing observer might have discerned a barely perceptible fissure, which, extending from the roof of the building in front, made its way down the wall in a zigzag direction, until it became lost in the sullen waters of the tarn.' In dreams I have often confused that desolate manse with its secreted guilt and terrible doom—why did Roderick Usher put his sister living in the tomb?—with the architectural *fantaisie* in which my college preparation was performed.

I see myself seated at a desk in a large study hall, turning the pages of a heavy book. It is a familiar book, an anthology of short stories used in Miss Newell's English class, but I cannot recall its title or its editor's name. I am reading a story in which I feel myself becoming the trapped victim who is the hero, or the nonhero, of the tale. For some reason he has ventured to climb a tower on which there is a huge clock—it is the clock tower of our high school—and he emerges from the clockworks to look out through a window in the face of the clock. As his head comes through this window, the minute hand of the clock lurches forward with the force of a scimitar, pinioning me by the neck. My one cheek is crushed against the face of the clock. The sword-edge of the minute-hand is biting into my neck. My eyes bulge out with the strain, the pain. Another minute strikes, the edge bites deeper, the blood pounds furiously and trickles down my chin, dripping with a horrible spat, spat, on to the pavement far below. Another minute strikes—my right eye pulses out of my head and falls with a sickening *phht* to the sidewalk. There it rolls like a marble, then comes to rest, looking up at my left eye looking down at it. I am at once the suffering victim and a separate person, observing the entire scene as from a window of an adjacent building. I see myself pinioned, one-eyed, bleeding, the clock about to strike another minute, the minute-hand about to cut clear through the neck-cord. Then in a lurch of horror and relief I am awake, shuddering and drenched in a sweat like dew.

Where could I have read so terrifying a tale, so horrifying a predicament, so inescapable a servitude to the inexorable movements of time, but in the work of Edgar Allan Poe? For years my waking hours were troubled by the search, as were my sleeping hours by the memory, as I combed the pages of the tales of Poe I owned. How many times have I re-read 'The Pit and the Pendulum' in the fascinated hope that I had somewhere overlooked a page, a paragraph—perhaps only a phrase—which was the source of that terrible dream! It was surely not in Poe's weird love stories, his tales of intellectual rape and the violation of bodies by the spirits of departed earlier lovers, that such a ghastly scene was enacted. Nor did it appear in his tales of murder: neither the madman killer of the black cat, nor the lunatic whose malfaisance is revealed by the tell-tale heart, nor even the avenger who walled up his enemy alive in the wine-cellar, had to do with towers, clocks, murderous minute hands. I read and re-read the detective stories, thinking perhaps Monsieur Dupin, or Legrand, who deciphered the pirate's map with the aid of the gold bug, might, in an aside, have let slip some allusion to the loss of an eye by means of a clock-hand's blade. But nowhere did this bizarre motif appear.

One day a few years ago, at a country auction in a barn, I found myself the only bidder on a box of books. The auctioneer, with his wheedling palaver and homey jokes, had softened up the crowd to overbid the value of battered

crockery and dented furniture, of defective kitchen equipment and rain-damaged rugs, but neither his hoary anecdotes
nor the imperious summons of his gavel could induce any
but myself to venture a bid on an unopened box of assorted
books, sight unseen. I got the lot for three dollars. There,
among a stack of old *National Geographics*, bound, and A
Tour of the Holy Land, three novels by Gertrude Atherton
and *The Lives of Famous Temperance Workers*, I found a
complete set—all seventeen volumes—of the Virginia edition
of the *Works of Edgar Allan Poe*. There it was—the whole
shebang—poems, tales, reviews, articles, newspaper fillers, introduction to *The Conchologist's First Book*, treatises on poetics and cryptography, studies of furniture, architecture,
Stonehenge, Poe's *Marginalia*, his *Eureka!* I have been des-
ultorily reading all this ever since.

A few months ago I was diverted to come on his spoof,
'How to Write a *Blackwood's* Article'—for Poe has his droll,
as well as his horrible and ethereal, moments. This one is a
little—well, to be sure, most of Poe's drollery is at least a
little—labored, a sententious analysis of the kinds of preten-
sion which *Blackwood's* imposed on its readers. At the end
he proposes, in a spirit of pure send-up, to write a piece for
Blackwood's to his own formula. I should say that Poe here
adopts the persona of Miss Psyche Zenobia, a lady of
Philadelphia who is visiting Edinburgh accompanied by her
lap-dog and her Negro servant Pompey, a dwarf three feet
tall. In the ensuing tale, 'A Predicament,' Miss Zenobia relates how she climbed the clock tower of a cathedral,
stepped on Pompey's back to peer through an aperture in the
'cabalistic-looking machinery,' and discovered that 'the huge,
glittering, scimitar-like minute-hand of the clock had, in
the course of its hourly revolution, *descended upon my
neck.* . . .' In the spirit of merry satire, Miss Zenobia tells
how her saucy eye fell out, then how her *other* eye joined
the first, and then at last the hand cut off her head, with
amusing complications since both head and body each
thought itself the real Psyche. Well, at last my search was
over. And I have not had that dreaded dream since.

Instead, on nights when I cannot fall into my usual sleep, I find myself thinking of 'A Predicament.' I wonder at the way my dream transposed that tale of Poe's. Instead of a humorous female caricature, the figure in my dream was *me*. True, her name was 'Psyche,' and I, not being as agile as Poe, may not so readily personify my psyche as he did his. But the tone of 'A Predicament' is grotesque exaggeration, while the spirit of my dream was unmitigated terror. Yet isn't Poe making a parodic jest out of a real fear, a horror too pressing to be stated without the release of bizarre comedy? Sick comedy, really. I remember now when it was that I wrote 'I hate Poe' across the flyleaf of my book. It was after reading 'A Predicament.' No sooner had I read the tale than I began to dream the dream. Perhaps already then, at the age of fifteen, I knew that the ultimate enemy of our happiness is Time.

And I remember now when it was that I determined to write this down, this meditation on the propensities of Poe's mind, the scope of his Art, the sources of his claims on us and the nature of our responses to those claims. It was when I re-read 'A Predicament,' and wondered why so buffoonish a satire, so grotesque a caricature, should have had the power to haunt my mind for years, the power to transform itself into the serious thing of which Poe's tale was a parody. What is that original thing? And what is that power of transformation, working from the real to the fantastic, from the fantastic to the real? These truths, in all their strangeness, were unknown to me, reading 'A Predicament' in school.

That school, with its castellated walls, its pentagonal corridors, its turrets containing the spiral stairs that led to gray mansard roofs indented with *mâchicoulis*, the oaken floors of that house of learning across the divided tarn where I first read the adventures of Roderick Usher, is no more. I think back sometimes to the touching faith in reason imparted to my civics class, to the earnest advocacy of such right causes as Lend Lease espoused by our debating team, and the knowledge that the temple of such reasonableness has vanished brings an ache I can't explain. Like the prince's palace in

'Metzengerstein,' like the king's castle in 'Hop-Frog,' the entire structure seemed one night last year to leap into the sky
upon the breath of the flames that consumed it. I would have
stood by the bridge at North Avenue to marvel at that smoky
pyre, had I been there. The firemen's apparatus was as useless as their courage was unavailing to bring the holocaust
under control. Once ignited, the schoolhouse seemed to have
been made of tinder and powder. No human force could save
it from destruction. It will cost the town millions to replace;
meanwhile those thousands of students must be quartered in
the basements of church annexes and in disused supermar-
kets. How did this catastrophe strike with such unexpected
swiftness and horror into the life of the sleeping city? One
backward boy, failing the elements of algebra—that mental
simulacrum of the invisible movements of the universe—was
so wroth against the facts of failure being forever on file in
the principal's office that, in the dark hour before the dawn,
he broke into the school, escaping the vigilance of the aged
night watchman, and, pouring kerosene over the file cabinet,
struck a single match and escaped into the night. Wishing
to obliterate but one sheet of paper which recorded his own
failure, some perversity within his soul caused him to light a
pyre destroying all the records of his successful contemporaries and predecessors, and reducing the entire site of his
ignominy and their success to a smouldering heap of ashes.
So the facts were ultimately determined. But Poe had
foreseen this too, in his description of the Imp of the Perverse, that 'overwhelming tendency to do wrong for the
wrong's sake . . . It is a radical, a primitive impulse . . .'

> The impulse increases to a wish, the wish to a desire, the
> desire to an uncontrollable longing, and the longing (to
> the deep regret and mortification of the speaker, and in
> defiance of all consequences) is indulged.

The impulse to do what? The primitive urge is an unfathomable *desire for vertiginous self-destruction,* a merging
of the self with the dizzying extinction of the self:

> We stand upon the brink of a precipice. We peer into
> the abyss—we grow sick and dizzy. Our first impulse is

to shrink from the danger. Unaccountably we remain. By slow degrees our sickness and dizziness and horror become merged in a cloud of unnameable feeling. . . . out of this our cloud upon the precipice's edge there grows into palpability, a shape . . . a thought, although a fearful one, and one which chills the very marrow of our bones with the fierceness of the delight of its horror. It is merely the idea of what would be our sensations during the sweeping precipitancy of a fall from such a height. And this fall— this rushing annihilation—for the very reason that it involves that one most ghastly and loathsome of all the most ghastly and loathsome images of death and suffering which has ever presented itself to our imagination—for this very cause we now the most vividly desire it.

And in this irremediable predicament, self-induced, self-sought, self-appalling, 'because our reason violently deters us from the brink, *therefore* do we the most impetuously approach it.' We are literally torn apart, our feelings imperiously propelling us toward an annihilation which our intellect fully recognizes and is powerless to avert. Whether that destruction be literally the plummeting into a precipitous depth, or the analogical fall from the security of a conventional life into the terrors attendant upon perversity enacted —whatever the *form* of the fall of man, it is the result of *man's own nature*.

Poe's fallen creatures are indeed twice self-doomed, doubly victims of their Imp of the Perverse. First their spirit of perversity compels them to commit atrocious and unreasonable crimes—to torture the cat, to murder the wife, to terrify and kill the benevolent old man. The second, equally gratuitous act of perversity is, after having committed the Perfect Crime (all the more perfect for its gratuitousness), inexorably to incriminate oneself by leading the policeman to the exact spot where the victim is entombed. What else can happen then but that other self, which the Imp of the Perverse, usually itself submerged, has now repressed, must come wailing out of the wallboards into the conscious world again. Now the still living cat yowls its terrible revelation and the guilty heart resounds its tale.

Edgar Poe, however grotesque your tarns and castles, your spectral lovers and premature entombments, however ethereally lifeless the tintinnabulation of your rhymes, you yourself spelled out in *Marginalia* the reason for the authority which your strange imaginings wield over me, as over all your readers—over T. S. Eliot even, who, seeming to share so little of your fated avoidance of history, religion, culture, yet must confess that 'One cannot be sure that one's own writing has *not* been influenced by Poe.' All, you said, that a man need do 'to revolutionize, at one effort, the universal world of human thought, . . . is to write and publish a very little book. Its title should be simple—a few plain words— "My Heart Laid Bare." But—this little book must be *true to its title.*'

Because you so succeeded, in your poems and tales, in your rigorous *esthétique* and your equally scrupulous cosmology, because you laid bare with your art what your art concealed, whether you dreamed as poet, or conceived of the thought of the suprarational detective, or imagined the sufferings of the immutably doomed and the unassuagably bereaved and suffering man, because you looked into your heart and did not flinch to record what, in defiance of all custom and sanction and social contract, revealed itself to you, your great contemporary across the sea could acknowledge in you his *semblable*, his *frère*. He must acclaim you for the courage with which you 'imperturbably affirmed the natural wickedness of man . . . a mysterious force which modern philosophy does not wish to take into consideration. . . . This primitive, irresistible force is natural Perversity, which makes man constantly and simultaneously a murderer and a suicide, an assassin and a hangman.' And Baudelaire, recognizing in you the voice of the injured and the damned, acknowledged also that your view of Imagination was as sublime as your view of experience was appalling. For Poe, he wrote, 'Imagination is an almost divine faculty which perceives immediately and without philosophical methods the inner and secret relations of things, the correspondences and the analogies.'

Poe—I will apostrophize him no longer—required a *sembla-*

ble to be understood on his own terms in his own country. With characteristic ill luck, he had not only a set of ideals quite inimical to the earnest and pragmatic values of ante-bellum America, ideals, unlike those of the transcendental-ists, which absolutely divided Art from life, Beauty from Truth and Goodness; he had also a tetchy disposition, a prickly knack of alienating his would-be friends and a genius for picking quarrels with those he could least afford to of-fend, like his carping accusations of plagiarism against Long-fellow or his unfortunate dealings with the editors and pub-lishers of the magazines he worked for, or his managing to be drunk on the one occasion when James Russell Lowell (who had praised his work and exchanged cordial letters) called to see him.

Most of all, his own Imp of the Perverse so arranged the history of his career that his literary executor was his most invidious enemy, the Reverend Rufus W. Griswold. This man, an ex-minister, a busybody of letters, an incessant an-thologist and publicizer, a failed poetaster fattening on the writings of others as does a moth eating Gobelin tapestries, went to extraordinary pains, after Poe's death, to present the deceased writer in a manner designed to make his name a household word for the dissolute, immoral, recklessly de-bauched. Griswold falsified the facts of Poe's life, and he revised the texts of Poe's letters, always with this calumnious end in view.

It took the detective work of Arthur Hobson Quinn—by curious coincidence a predecessor of mine in the American literature faculty at the University of Pennsylvania—to re-veal, by publishing Poe's original letters alongside Griswold's cadenzas upon them, the extent to which the editor had li-belled the poet in his charge. W. H. Auden has observed,

> That one man should dislike another and speak maliciously of him after his death would be natural enough, but to take so much trouble, to blacken a reputation so subtly, presupposes a sustained hatred which is always fascinating because the capacity for sustaining emotion of any kind is rare, and, in this instance, particularly so since no reason-able cause for it has yet been found.

But, as Baudelaire said, *à propos* the Imp of the Perverse, Poe adds,

> with a remarkably satanic subtlety, the impossibility of finding an adequate rational motive for certain wicked and perilous actions could lead us to consider them as the result of the suggestions of the Devil, if experience and history did not teach us that God often draws from them the establishment of order and the punishment of scoundrels;—*after having used the same scoundrels as accomplices!*

In God's own mysterious fashion, Griswold became an instrument for establishing an order. Perhaps, for Poe's work to have won its present high regard, it was *necessary* that poor Poe be so badly abused by Griswold's poisonous pen. (The scoundrel's punishment is this: he is now known everywhere, if known at all, as the maligner of a helpless genius; whereas had he done his job honestly, he'd have won his proper modest niche among the footnotes by which the nearly forgotten are saved from total oblivion.) His motive, however, may not be as inscrutable as Auden supposes, for surely this failed preacher-cum-poetaster-turned-editor was absolutely consumed with envy at the sight of a genuine man of letters, a truly individual and distinguished poet and critic, an original literary philosopher—the mockery of it, the cruel presence of his own impossible ambition personified. Personified as a *victim*: a man so incompetent in worldly affairs that despite his genius he had no talent not to starve; a poet so committed to his own vision of art that he had not the prudence to protect that vision from the charge of the greatest immorality. Not merely the immorality of his alleged personal habits— Griswold didn't hesitate to impute to Poe the opium-taking, laudanum addiction, drunkenness, and madness that Poe made the attributes of characters in his tales. No, the greater immorality, that which may have been the mainspring of Griswold's malignity, was Poe's insistence that Art provides the only path to beatitude, dismissing religion as a vapid illusion. Poe sometimes speaks of God, but never of Christ.

He imagines, creates, enacts a religion without a church, a faith with no other Gospel than his own *Tales of the Grotesque and Arabesque,* his *Poems,* his *Eureka.* Poe's universe has no need of the Reverend Griswold's conventional ideas, nor of the faith in which Griswold was certified a preacher. It is a world of atoms, of material particles, of energy, in which the nearest man can come to the unity that is God is through his disembodied thought. If we give Griswold credit for being serious in his Christian profession, even without the added meed of envy for a genius in the art at which he was himself a mere scribbler, he would have found, in Poe, the very person of the Anti-Christ. And so he treated the character of his legatee.

All the more mysterious, as God moves in His ways, that the two American poets who restored Poe, more than did any others, to the place which his sublime vision of imagination deserves, are the very ones who tried, more than any others, to reverse the tendency, stronger in our day than in Poe's, to make Art a substitute for Christianity. Allen Tate, in his essay 'The Angelic Imagination,' anatomizes the dangers of Poe's sublime vision: having separated feeling from both will and intellect, Poe anticipates the special hell of modern man; Poe endows imagination with Godlike power, but 'Since he refuses to see nature, he is doomed to see nothing.' Yet the 'nothing' that Poe sees is, in Tate's demonstration, an epitome of our own condition—ahistorical, unfaithed, deracinated, suffering.

Not only did T. S. Eliot write a magisterial appreciation of Poe's influence upon Baudelaire, Mallarmé and Valéry, from which I have quoted an aperçu appropriate to Poe's influence on himself; not only that, but at the climax of 'Little Gidding,' Eliot's last great poem, where he imagines himself, in the London air raid, as being addressed and guided by the 'peregrine, composite ghost'—the ghost of Virgil, the ghost of Yeats—that spirit quotes (in translation) a line from Mallarmé's famous tribute to Poe, 'To purify the dialect of the tribe.' *Donner un sens plus pur aux mots de la tribu:* This is the poet's task, its accomplishment his only means of being true to his gift, to his obligation to his time.

But did *Poe* really give a purer meaning to the words of the tribe?

II

'O! Nothing Earthly . . .'

November 1956. I am brooding on the poems of Edgar Poe in Dijon, living with my wife and two babies in the only *maison bourgeoise* in a farm village three kilometres beyond the end of the bus line. All the other houses in Saint Apollinaire are attached to barns and have cows in the front yard, but our yard is given to a garden, the beds crowded between pebbled walks. It's getting chill. There's hoarfrost on the beet fields and morning mists hang from Madame Pagès' pear tree. Ever since my compatriot John Foster Dulles halted the Franco-Israeli conquest of Suez last month, oil, coal, rice, and soap have been in short supply. I spend every other day scouring the coal yards of Dijon along the rail line—have become an expert scrounger, putting to unwonted practice the vocabulary lists memorized while reading *Lettres de Mon Moulin*. Also others words, newly heard and remembered. I can distinguish by their shapes and brand-marks the pressed coal briquets from Belgium, Germany, Italy, Poland. I buy wherever I can, hauling fifty-kilo sacks on the floor of my Anglia. I've built a coalbin in Mme Pagès' garage. It's cold. Today is the Fête des Fulbrights, the presentation of new American books to the Faculté des Lettres, the visit by the American Consul and the Fulbright Commissioner from Paris, the speeches of welcome and acceptance. Then my lecture, on the poet whose work is set for examination this year for the *agrégé*: Edgarpoe.

So, in Saint Apollinaire, surrounded by the sounds of low-
ing cattle in the barns and crowing cocks on the dunghills
beside the lavage, with the medieval church down one road,
the Renaissance château down the other, I spend the morning
re-reading the poems of Edgarpoe. Now it is time. The lecture hall in the old Faculté is filled to the ceiling—all my
students, and scores of teachers of la littérature Américaine
in lycées from as far out in the hinterland as Besançon. Here,
in Dijon, they have walked through narrow alleys and crooked
streets bordered by Roman walls and overhung by swollen
Renaissance balconies, walked beneath roofs upheld by flam-
boyant caryatids, and entered the gloomy gateway of the
Faculté. They have climbed the treadworn stairs into the
dim lecture chamber to hear le Professeur Visitant Chargé
avec l'Enseignement des Etudes Américaines, himself said
to be a poet, speak of Edgarpoe.

They are poised in a tiered semicircle around me, strain-
ing to hear my English words, ready for my American accent
to fall flatly on their ears. I commence. 'I cannot read the
poems of Edgarpoe without feeling a sensation—of pain.' A
gasp clutches the breath of my auditors. 'No poet in the
English tongue who is still read with reverence has committed
such gaffes against the genius of our language, nor has written
lines of comparable banality.' An indignant murmuration
surges around the amphitheatre. 'It cannot even be said of
Poe that when he is at his worst he is awful in a manner peculiarly his own—need he have been Edgar Poe to write, in
'Al Aaraaf,'

> O! nothing earthly save the thrill
> Of melody in woodland rill—

or, in 'The City in the Sea,'

> Where the good and the bad and the worst and the best
> Have gone to their eternal rest . . .

or, from 'The Sleeper,' a line as tasteless as 'Soft may the
worms about her creep!'; or so vulgar a rhythm as that in
'Lenore,' 'A dirge for her that doubly died in that she died

so young.' Did it require a poet of Poe's sublimity, or a critic
as fastidious in the matter of the prosody of his contemporaries, to contrive such a rhyme (in 'Ulalume') as mated
'kissed her' with 'vista,' or such sustained banality as in this
stanza from 'Israfel'—

> Yes, Heaven is thine: but this
>   Is a world of sweets and sours;
> Our flowers are merely—flowers,
>   And the shadow of thy perfect bliss
>   Is the sunshine of ours.

or such evanescent balderdash as in the lines,

> And softly through the forest bars
>   Light lovely shapes, on glossy plumes,
> Float ever in, like wingèd stars,
>   Amid the purpling glooms—

None of these passages would be out of place in the 'Poet's
Corner' of a weekly rural newspaper in my native country.
In fact that's probably where the last quatrain I've quoted
first appeared, for it is not by Poe at all, but by a justly forgotten poetess named Mrs. Amelia Welby. I mention her,
and quote her lines, because Poe himself applauded her
poem as 'one that would do honor to any one living or dead,'
citing the passage about glossy plumes and purpling glooms
as 'unquestionably, the finest in the poem.' A poet of such
faulty taste would well be capable of writing, in his own
poem, such bathos as

> Save only thee and me. (Oh, Heaven!—oh, God!
> How my heart beats in coupling those two words!)

or committing to print a description so gross and literal as

> seraphs sob at vermin fangs
>   In human gore imbued.

What claims, I asked, have such thumping doggerel, such
sentimental clichés, on our serious attention?

Ah well, you can't take away from the French, already on

short rations of rice and soap and enduring a *pénurie d'es-sence*, their reverence for Baudelaire's spiritual brother. Half-way through my lecture I recognized it as a piece of Poesque arrogance, a catastrophe inspired by some perverse imp of my own. For despite his blatant faults, Poe's poems do have a gaudy grandeur. Although marred by all the vulgarities and overwearied rhymes I have quoted and then some, when one has read 'The City in the Sea' or 'Ulalume' or 'Annabel Lee,' one has had an experience he does not forget.

All this—the power of Edgarpoe—came back to me when I avidly read the mad adventures of Humbert Humbert, who seduced and was ravished by his twelve-year-old beloved in plain view of several hundred thousand *voyeurs* like myself:

> Did she have a precursor? [Humbert asks on the very first page.] She did, indeed she did. In point of fact there might have been no Lolita at all had I not loved, one sum-mer, a certain initial girl-child. In a princedom by the sea.

Humbert, whose mother had died when he was three (Poe's mother died when he was *two*), lived, a petted darling, on the grounds of his father's Riviera Hotel. It was there that he fell wildly, unrelievedly, in love with that 'initial girl-child.' Her name? A maiden there lived whom you may know by the name of Annabel. Name of Annabel Leigh.

Annabel Leigh, the archetypal lost love of the pubescent motherless boy in a princedom by the sea. They snatched a moment, a moment beyond her family's vigilant protection, a moment in a cave beside the sea, where they awkwardly groped for one another's pleasure-parts, tormented to a de-licious frenzy by each 'incomplete contact,' until, at last,

> I was on my knees, and on the point of possessing my darling, when two bearded bathers, the old man of the sea and his brother, came out of the sea with exclamations of ribald encouragement, and four months later she died of typhus in Corfu.

And Humbert Humbert spent the rest of his life looking for her—'that mimosa grove—the haze of stars, the tingle, the flame, the honey-dew, and the ache remained with me, and that little girl with her seaside limbs and ardent tongue haunted me ever since—until at last, twenty-four years later, I broke her spell by incarnating her in another.'

By incarnating her in another! Ah, Humbert, Humbert, had *you* re-read the works of Edgarpoe you might have found some other, some less dangerous means to break her spell! For you might have remembered not only the mellifluous rhythms and melodious periods of 'Annabel Lee' but also the terrors, the horrors, the eerie and immitigable sufferings recorded by the narrator of 'Ligeia,' the tale of one who, like yourself, assuaged his aching longing for a lost love by reincarnating her in another—or did she reincarnate herself in the dying body of his second wife, thus exercising her awful claim upon his devotion? Whoever did what, 'Ligeia' should be a cautionary tale to any like Humbert Humbert, who tries to assuage the pain of a lost childhood love (in a kingdom by the sea) by incarnating her into another. It won't work. That other won't, simply won't, be just as was the initial child-love. She will exercise her own claims, live in the satiation of her own lusts, wrap you, Humbert, whoever you are, wrap you around her little finger, ride you, the lovely little witch that she is, to your doom.

> For the moon never beams, without bringing me dreams
> Of the beautiful Annabel Lee;
> And the stars never rise, but I feel the bright eyes
> Of the beautiful Annabel Lee:—
> And so, all the night-tide, I lie down by the side
> Of my darling—my darling—my life and my bride,
> In the sepulchre there by the sea—
> In her tomb by the sounding sea.

To be the lover, or the would-be lover, of Annabel Lee, or Annabel Leigh, is a fate not easily avoided. On the one hand you end up yearning to lie down by her side in a sepulchre: necrophilia! On the other, you can't get her, can't get *at* her, can't consummate all those exacerbated urgings which you and she began to feel and which you haven't ever

since ceased feeling, so you *incarnate* her in another. That
way, *Lolita*. But Poe had been there, too.

Edgar Allan Poe wears all the medals of the sufferings
his poems record and celebrate and revel in. The intensity of
his sufferings is the badge of his honor. The garish light by
which his verses flicker, the weird, wild, and wonderstruck
helplessness of the personages in his tales, these are the expressions of a possessed and demonic writer, hatched from
the one egg he has put in his haunted basket.

And what were these sufferings? Who doesn't know them,
who can't infer them from the first perusal of his verses!
The details are *peculiar*, the specific instances of a special
type of woe accumulate upon the defenseless head of a little
orphaned boy with a repetitious savagery which makes inescapable the conclusion that Fate itself had an obsessional
interest in inflicting upon poor Edgar Poe one particular
species of human woe. As though by intensifying that one
suffering, he could be made to write of it in paradigms of
all the lesser losses which the rest of mankind must endure.
But what a capricious choice Fate made as the vessel through
which its mordant yet exalted dithyrambs would be poured.

Fate waited, to enact this particular purpose, until a troupe
of itinerant thespians was cast up on the shores of penury,
'at liberty,' in Boston, Massachusetts, in the dead of winter,
1809. On January nineteenth of that year a son was delivered
of Elizabeth Arnold Poe. The father, David Poe, Jr., was,
like his wife a treader of the boards. An indifferent actor, it
would appear, thought to be of Irish descent, and, by all
evidence, addicted to the bottle. Not a very stable or responsible fellow, David Poe, Jr., although his father had been
an honorary Quartermaster General in the Continental Army
during the Revolution. Elizabeth Arnold Poe was very much
more popular, more versatile, more successful on the stage
than her nearly ne'er-do-well husband. She'd been bred to
the theatre by her mother, an actress of some repute in England before her emigration, with her little daughter, to these
States. So Eddie was born into that most precarious profession, the art of feigning. And within a year his bibulous father

had disappeared. Simply vanished, leaving the young and
beautiful Elizabeth, with her great moody eyes brimming, to
look after little Eddie and his elder brother William Henry
and his younger sister Rosalie. Alas, Rosalie proved, when
grown, to be mentally retarded; she plays no part in Edgar's
development. Nor does his brother, who was raised by grand-
parents in Baltimore after the mother's death.

The mother's death! Mother, with her infants in her care,
still had to provide for her family, still had to follow her
profession, trudging from one provincial town to another for
one-week or one-night stands, developing a cough, a paroxys-
mic seizure, at last, in 1811, in Richmond, Virginia, spitting
blood. In Mrs. Osborne's boarding house. There, in her single
room, with her infant son beside her, Mrs. Poe lay dying,
attended in her misery by the charitable solicitation of several good ladies of that gracious city. Edgar was two years
old, watching his beautiful mother die of consumption, or,
as they called it in those days, phthisis. Spitting blood.

One of those good, kind ladies whose heart was touched by
the sufferings of the unfortunate Mrs. Poe was the childless
wife of an ambitious tobacco merchant. On Mrs. Poe's death,
Frances Allan took little Edgar into her own household and
raised him as her son. Her husband, John Allan, was not
quite so precipitate—his part in the chronicle of Edgar's woes
is complicated, and I'll defer its recital till a more appropriate page of this, my chronicle of Poe's life and work and
reputation and influence and how Edgarpoe wormed his
way into my guts and gizzard and haunted my brain and laid
a spell upon my soul which this long harangue is an attempt
to exorcise.

Of John Allan I will now say but this: he did not adopt
Edgar Poe, the infant son of wandering actors so fortuitously
thrust beneath his eaves. If there is a villain in Poe's destiny,
a malign person insinuated into his fortune by the machina-
tions of that evil fairy who always spoils the christening party,
it may have been his nonadoptive guardian. For John Allan
reared the boy in full expectations of becoming his heir and
gave him half a claim on the rights and privileges accorded

in the antebellum South to a would-be gentleman. (Actually, Allan, a merchant in that cotton kingdom ruled by baronial planters, was himself a pretender to those airs and graces.) But at the crucial moment, he cast Edgar adrift without a cent, without a foster-father's blessing, to make his own way in a profession still more precarious than the ill-starred career of his true parents: the profession of a Poet.

By that time, the kindhearted and beautiful Mrs. Allan, too, had died. Had died, like Elizabeth Arnold Poe before her, of consumption.

I skip a few chapters in the Life of Poe, skip over to his twenty-seventh year. He has been in and out of the army—yes, the United States Army—he has been in and out of the U. S. Military Academy, for Poe is our only great writer to have tried for a commission at West Point. He has been a magazine writer, has published two volumes of verse at his own expense, has won a fifty dollar prize from the Baltimore *Saturday Visiter* for his story 'MS. Found in a Bottle,' has become editor of the *Southern Literary Messenger*, and has married Miss Virginia Clemm of Baltimore.

Arthur Hobson Quinn, whose magisterial biography is still the authoritative source for all facts and figures about Edgar Allan Poe, finds it *not unusual* that a man of twenty-seven marries a girl of fourteen, his first cousin. Or that all throughout their married life he called her 'Sis,' or that her mother, his aunt Mrs. Clemm, lived with the couple, kept house for them, and was addressed by the husband, Edgar, as 'Mother.' Dr. Quinn exercised great ingenuity in recapitulating, *inter alia*, the complete dramatic career of Poe's grandmother, and in ascertaining precisely in which room at 2230½ East Main Street, Richmond, Elizabeth Poe died. But to questions like the propriety of Edgar Poe's marriage to a scarcely nubile girl half his age, and his close blood relation at that, Quinn's powers of detection were not attracted.

On the other hand perhaps too much has been made of these rather odd circumstances by Joseph Wood Krutch and Marie Bonaparte.

What should I make of them? Right now I'll make little,

merely mention the facts as facts, and complete this factual recital (carefully edited to emphasize certain effects—for as Poe advises, all must be bent toward unity of effect).

The effect toward which I'm trying to unify these sometimes intractable events is, well, it's the effect which is *suggested* by the next relevant fact: nine years later, in 1847, Virginia Poe—I forgot to say that Virginia had a beautiful voice, was trained as a singer—Virginia burst a blood vessel *in her throat,* and in a matter of months she sank into consumptive pallor, feebleness, much spitting of blood, and, at last, the surcease of an early death.

Virginia was twenty-three, the age when many young women are about to be married. She had been nine years a bride, yet, if Poe's posthumous psychoanalysts, Drs. Krutch and Bonaparte, are to be given credence, she died a virgin and a maid:

> . . . a maiden there lived whom you may know
> By the name of Annabel Lee;

> And so, all the night-tide, I lie down by the side
> Of my darling—my darling—my life and my bride,
>   In the sepulchre there by the sea—
>   In her tomb by the sounding sea

They so conclude, not, I must say in defense of their ratiocinative analysis of Poe's life, on the evidence of his poems. They examine his life, his circumstances, his whole personality, and conclude that he was psychically impotent.

That seems an impertinence, doesn't it? I mean, there's something rather tasteless in hypothesizing about the sexual relations of a man who died over a century ago. None of our business, that.

What is our business, though, is not what Poe did or couldn't do in the dark womb of his conjugal bed, but *what he wrote.* And that, of course, brings us around once again to what he lived, what he suffered. Whether he could get it up or not (the evidence of the tales is pretty one-sided), you don't have to have a certificate from Dr. Freud to recognize

Poe's sad and crippling obsession; he put into his writing an intense energy as great as that which a libidinous seducer would have expended upon the breaching of a thousand virgins. Poe was born to suffer, to thrill to the exquisite torment of those sufferings, to transmute them by his symbolistic imagination into paradigms of man's divided nature, of man's heroic efforts to escape his fate.

But you might not guess all this from a poem like 'Annabel Lee.'

I mean, would you be likely to hail, as an expression of imaginative *power*, Poe's sad, musical ballad of a lost love?

Poe, who had lost his three great loves—his mother, his foster-mother, his bride—all in the same way, all wasting on their sick-beds, all spitting blood, choking, all pathetically grasping and gasping for breath, while he, the infant son, the boy, the bridegroom, can but sit beside his beloveds in helpless anguish, watching them sink, sink, sink, and slip away until their pain-wracked seizures at last are stilled by their last, wakeless sleep.

How could such a boy, such a man, but ask, What are we born for? 'What is beauty, saith my sufferings then?' cries Tamberlaine in Marlowe's play (Part 1, v ii 97). One *poète maudit*, killed in a tavern brawl, speaks across the centuries to his *semblable*. Edgar Allan Poe, aged eighteen, chooses as *his* theme, for the title poem of his first book ('by a Bostonian'), *Tamerlane!*

Tamerlane, 243 lines of *Tamerlane* (as finally revised, in 1845), 'by a Bostonian,' aged nineteen, recently rusticated from the University of Virginia for debts to his landlord, tailor, gambling companions, etc., etc.

In exile.

But, in this free country, exiled from what?

From childhood. From mother and from foster-mother. From all his dreams of temporal power and social supremacy, his dreams of an inheritance and his hopes of a college education and a secure place in society. At nineteen.

All that is left to this headstrong and penurious youth are his dreams, his vain imaginings, which he spells out in chiming, rhyming lines. Edgar has no recourse but to become the hero of his own imagination.

In 1827 that seemed a likely course. Not so much the hero of *The Prelude*, but—Byron. *There's* a hero for the age! Byron, with his romantic black locks, his brow streaked by the howling blasts of the tempest—how very like Byron is Poe, in Walt Whitman's dream, half a century later; the dream of Whitman, the only American poet who attended the dedication, in Baltimore, of that monument at Poe's grave for which Mallarmé had written his sonnet 'Au tombeau d'Edgar Poe.' Whitman had dreamed of Poe rushing toward the grave—

In a dream I once had, I saw a vessel on the sea, at midnight, in a storm. It was no great full-rigg'd ship, nor majestic steamer, steering firmly through the gale, but seemed one of those superb little schooner yachts I had often seen lying anchor'd, rocking so jauntily, in the waters around New York, or up Long Island Sound—now flying uncontroll'd with torn sails and broken spars through the wild sleet and winds and waves of the night. On the deck was a slender, slight, beautiful figure, a dim man, apparently enjoying all the terror, the murk, and the dislocation of which he was the centre and the victim. That figure of my lurid dream might stand for Edgar Poe, his spirit, his fortunes, and his poems—themselves all lurid dreams.

Walt, perspicuous, magnanimous old man—how wisely he chose as *an image of the poems* a tableau which could have been drawn *only from the tales!* There is no poem of Poe's in which a figure, a dim Edgar, is hurtling toward destruction aboard a schooner-yacht; but wait until we come to 'A Descent into the Maelstrom,' 'MS. Found in a Bottle,' and *Narrative of Arthur Gordon Pym!* Wise old Walt, who conceived, as his tribute to Poe, his only real rival as the nineteenth century's Literatus, a perfect put-down: The poetry is in Poe's *prose*.

Neither Walt Whitman nor anyone else would have dreamed such a dream about Poe were he only, or chiefly,

the author of 'Tamerlane.' That's a poem nobody today
would be likely to read for pleasure. The students in my Poe
seminar read it—they *had* to—and were convinced that, during that week in the fall semester, they were the only ten
souls in the entire nation so occupied. Plodding through the
243 lines of Tamerlane's lament, they read the confessional
monologue of the Tartar peasant who left his native cottage
to conquer the world, then returned intending to marry his
beloved, but—guess what—found that she had died. As Richard Wilbur points out in his notes to the Laurel edition of
Poe's poems, 'It is not that Tamerlane has made an erroneous
choice between Love and Ambition: it is that Time has inevitably estranged him from his boyhood and from the visionary capacity to possess, through Psyche, "the world, and
all it did contain." The fundamental contrast is between two
kinds of power: the despotic imaginative power of the child,
and the adult's struggle for actual worldly power. The first is
judged ideal or "holy," the second earthly or evil.'
    Like all of Wilbur's comments on Poe's poems, this is both
sensitive and accurate. But Wilbur forbears to judge the
poems; he is content to describe them and to relate their
images to one another. I'll be more temerarious and assert
that 'Tamerlane' is a poem nobody would read unless he
had to, one which is valuable chiefly for what it suggests about
the young Poe's reading and for demonstrating his limitations. He'd been reading Byron and Milton and was already
mapping out the very special and peculiar territory in which
his poetic faculty could function. But in 'Tamerlane' he drew
a huge overdraught on his poetic account. Who would read
'Tamerlane' today, but a graduate student in Professor Hoffman's Poe seminar? Or Professor Hoffman? Yet, when I
checked the early (1827) version (*Complete Works*, VII,
127–39) I found who else had been reading 'Tamerlane':
in strophe XIII, 'I pass'd from out the matted bower / Where
in a deep, still slumber lay / My Ada . . .' whose name does
not appear in the later version. But this is the Ada whose
name *does* appear (it was Byron's daughter's middle name),
indeed is the title of, a novel, a prodigious creation of an

anti-world, by Vladimir Nabokov, author of the pseudony-
mous Humbert Humbert's confessions and a confirmed, nay,
an obsessional, reader—or should I say devotee, or enchantee
—of Edgar Poe.

Why this modern creator of an anti-world should be—
would *have* to be—in thrall to Poe isn't very clear from 'Tamerlane,' but in Poe's next major (that is to say, large) poem
it all comes clear. I mean in 'Al Aaraaf.'

But first, what went wrong in 'Tamerlane'? Poe was trying
to do too many things at once: tell a narrative, project an
epic, dramatize the conflict between earthly and spiritual
power. His diction is more appropriate to lyric verse, his story
remains static, his hero speaks to no respondent. Poe hadn't
yet discovered exactly which *form* was required by his theme.

How could it be otherwise? He was only eighteen. Every
week I have a bull session called a class with half a dozen
student poets and would-be poets of just that age. The very
best of them are likely to change their styles, meters, dic-
tions, forms, stance, subjects, personae, three or four times a
semester. A young poet must discover who he is, he must
create himself as a poet. Even a genius must do this. It's a
painful process, splitting your own skin and squeezing your
soul and body out of it, even, sometimes, before you know the
shape or color of the new self you are going to become. Poe,
like any young man teaching himself to be a poet, made a
couple of false starts.

But even in false starts there's a gain, an increment, an
increase in technical skill and the uncovering of a part of
one's own *donnée.* That's one gain. Another is the recognition of what *won't* be carried over into the next self-image of
the poetic persona. So even losses are gains.

The poet discovers his self by creating it. However much
tempted was Edgar Poe to imagine himself as puissant as
Tamerlane, and to imagine Tamerlane as powerless in the
coils of time as himself, he came much closer to defining the
essential *Moi* who speaks in his best poems in a confessional
meditation, first published in *Scribner's Magazine* in 1875,
a quarter century after his death, but signed and dated 'E A.

Poe. Baltimore, March 17, 1829.' Nobody knows why Poe
never included it in his books of verse—or rather, in his book;
for, like Whitman, though on a very minuscule scale indeed,
Poe's poetical productions comprised a single *œuvre* which
was added to in each of the successive volumes he issued
between 1827 and 1845. Perhaps the copy which came to
Scribner's was unique, and not having that copy in his possession, Poe had lost the poem. But no. He'd have written it
down again, with his prodigious powers of memory and concentration. Maybe 'Alone' cut a little too near the bone for
Poe, whose poems and tales are an elaborate repertoire of
masks: Poe Poe Poe Poe Poe . . . We'll meet him as Hoaxiepoe, as Inimitable Edgar the Variety Artist, as Horror-
Haunted Edgar, as . . . but I'm getting ahead of myself here.
'Alone':

> From childhood's hour I have not been
> As others were—I have not seen
> As others saw—I could not bring
> My passions from a common spring—
> From the same source I have not taken
> My sorrow—I could not awaken
> My heart to joy at the same tone—
> And all I lov'd—*I* lov'd alone—
> *Then*—in my childhood, in the dawn
> Of a most stormy life—was drawn
> From ev'ry depth of good and ill
> The mystery which binds me still—
> From the torrent, or the fountain—
> From the red cliff of the mountain—
> From the sun that round me roll'd
> In its autumn tint of gold—
> From the lightning in the sky
> As it pass'd me flying by—
> From the thunder and the storm—
> And the cloud that took the form
> When the rest of Heaven was blue
> Of a demon in my view—

Although there are echoes here of Byron's *Manfred* (ii ii
50–56), this is Edgarpoe's own work, his own destiny, his

own woe: The Alienated Poet come-to-life. Not alienated by the neglect of a materialist bourgeois society—that *is* the case of course, though here he doesn't complain of it—but alienated because of the fated specialness of his own nature. Edgarpoe is a marked man, one of the Chosen. Chosen to enjoy what others cannot even sense, chosen to suffer what others know not, to love whom he loves in an isolation as complete as that in which he feels suffering and joy. All this, because of 'The mystery which binds me still.'

The poem is nearly a success, for though it begins with the tone and the commonplace diction of a song of Thomas Hood's or Tom Moore's, it modulates, by the end, to the intensity of early William Blake. The openness of diction is not as unusual for Poe as one would think, if one were accustomed only to the rhodomontade of 'The Raven,' 'Ulalume,' and 'Lenore.' Poe was quite able to write with clarity, indeed the language here is so ordinary it dips into the banal. But the last six lines redeem the poem from that. 'A demon in my view.' Poe really *was* a haunted man, and as a poet, in verse or prose, he had the power to haunt his readers.

I think of Edgar Allan Poe at nineteen, author of these poems and others I've still to re-read, making his bid for Fame and Immortality and Recognition and who knows what else by publishing his slender store of verses at his own cost—at his own cost who could scarcely afford the next night's lodging. Those humiliating letters he had to write to John Allan, the nonsire who had already cast him off, pleading for money, as gift, as loan, on any terms, money to publish, money with which to buy a suit, a shirt, pay the landlord, the grocer, the printer. How much self-abasement can a boy stand, how much abuse of the ego can he bear?

Richmond Monday [19 March, 1827]
Sir,
     After my treatment on yesterday and what passed between us this morning, I can hardly think you will be surprised at the contents of this letter. My determination

is at length taken—to leave your house and indeavor to
find some place in this wide world, where I will be treated
—not as *you* have treated me . . . my resolution is unal-
terable. . . .

. . . Send my trunk &c to the Court-house Tavern, send
me I entreat you some money immediately—as I am in the
greatest necessity—If you fail to comply with my request—
I tremble for the consequence

Yours &c
Edgar A Poe

It depends upon yourself if hereafter you see or hear from
m.

So distraught he left off the second letter in the word *me*.
The next day Poe writes to Allan again:

Dear Sir,
Be so good as to send me my trunk with my clothes—I
wrote to you on yesterday explaining my reasons for leaving . . . I am in the greatest necessity, not having tasted
food since Yesterday morning. I have no where to sleep
at night but roam about the Streets . . . I beseech you
as you wish not your prediction concerning me to be fulfilled—to send me without delay my trunk containing my
clothes, and to lend if you will not give me as much money
as will defray the expence of my passage to Boston ($12)
and a little to support me. . . .

The following December, now in the army at Fort Moultrie,
Poe writes:

I only beg you to remember that you yourself cherished
the cause of my leaving your family—Ambition. If it has
not taken the channel you wished it, it is not the less certain of its object. Richmond & the U. States were too narrow a sphere & the world shall be my theatre—

One can only imagine with what apoplexy Allan read this
page, in which the ungrateful young whippersnapper he had
fed and clothed like a member of his own family has the
impudence to flaunt his insane ambition—and to revel in that

allusion to the *theatre*, as though his proper parentage were
something to brag up and down the market square!—

> . . . There never was any period of my life when my bosom
> swelled with a deeper satisfaction, of myself & (except
> in the injury which I may have done to your feelings)—of
> my conduct—My father do not throw me aside as *degraded*
> I will be an honor to your name.

This letter pled with Allan to obtain Edgar's discharge from
the army. Like his other pleas, before and after, it was
ignored.

Such are a few of the sufferings which Edgar bore alone.

We have not done with his relationship to John Allan,
who seems gratuitously to have dealt his helpless charge one
blow after another. Or were his blows gratuitous? For Allan
must have known that Poe knew of his infidelities to his wife.
Yet Allan had a case, too, for Edgar was surely the least
sympathetic boy in Richmond for him to have in his own
household—headstrong, insubordinate, self-willed, forever
making outrageous demands. Poor Edgar.

Where did we leave him? Down from the university, out
from his enlistment, then a cadet and again pleading with
'Pa' to secure his release; that aid not forthcoming, Edgar
is dismissed from the U.S.M.A. for being on sick call instead
of on duty. And now he has published his second volume of
verse—it's 1829, in Baltimore—*Al Aaraaf, Tamerlane, and
Minor Poems.* Edgar is twenty years old.

What can we expect in the way of poems from a twenty-
year-old genius? He will write poems conceived within the
conventions of his age, and some of those poems will outlast
the conventions within which they were conceived, while
others will fade with the changing of taste and fashion. A
poet has to start somewhere, he must plunge into the swim
at the moment when he becomes aware of his own ambition.
For Poe, that moment came during the notoriety of Byron
and Shelley, during the popularity of such third-team min-
nesingers as Tom Moore and Thomas Hood, and during the
influence on the best poets of the critical ideas of Coleridge.

What would you expect but that the verse of a twenty-year-old, even a genius, would be a hodgepodge of these and other influences?

Poe's genius announces itself in startling ways. More by his renunciations than by his achievements. His special genius was the kind that rules out, on principle, most of the subjects and themes that other poets spend lifetimes trying to deal with. For Poe, such *materia poetica* as physical love, the influence of the natural world upon human sensibility, and human history simply aren't on the page. Not in poetry.

What's left, then? A narrowing concentric circle of concern. Poe ends by asserting that poetry itself must be devoted to the presentation of a single subject. Yet even while foretelling these extreme exclusions, 'Al Aaraaf' is very ambitious —too ambitious. It is Poe's most ambitious failure.

Before I sink in its ethereal vapors, let me quickly say which were those poems of Poe's that do transcend the conventions of his time. 'Alone' is one of these. So are 'Romance,' and 'The City in the Sea,' and 'Dream-Land.' These are all lyric soliloquys. His other successful genres are the brief lyric ('To Helen,' 'To One in Paradise,' 'Israfel'), the sonnet ('Sonnet—To Science,' 'To My Mother'), and the literary ballad ('Lenore,' 'Ulalume,' 'For Annie,' and 'The Raven'). Some of these poems transcend their time without being good poems; they may be terrible poems, but they are, undeniably, unforgettable. Some of them are very good indeed. Still, that's not much of an output for a genius who confessed 'With me poetry has been not a purpose, but a passion.' One hidden thread in this inquiry, a thread I will seize and draw taut at the right instant, will sew up the answer to the query, What went wrong with Poe's passion for poetry? Why did he dry up, and leave one of the teeniest bodies of verse of any poet the world has applauded for over a century?

But now, the ethereal vapors of 'Al Aaraaf.' What a piece of machinery is this! 'Al Aaraaf' exhibits extreme symptoms of what Poe was later to attack—after he had convinced himself that he could not write this way—as 'the Epic mania.'

This piece reads like the first two of a dozen, or a score, of cantos in a Great Poem of Cosmological Revelation. But Eddie ran out of gas.

'Al Aaraaf' is the best he ever did in the line of Jumbo Productions. Fractured though it is, we have here a far more convincing imaginative experience and a much more adept show of versification than in either of his other two elephantine failures, 'Tamerlane' and 'Scenes from Politian.' (A word about 'Politian': this is a sketch for a Jacobean tragedy, using the same plot—fixated love, madness—as that in Simm's *Beauchampe*, Chivers's *Conrad and Eudora*, Charles Fenno Hoffman's novel *Greyslaer*, and Robert Penn Warren's poem *Brother to Dragons*. Poe's 'Politian,' however, is no better than the least of these: an inflated, ill-managed costume drama set in Rome.)

In 'Al Aaraaf' Poe finds a different way to evade dealing with the actual world from such efforts at archaic history as 'Tamerlane' and 'Politian.' He escapes into an imaginary future—well, it's not specified as future, so let's call it an imaginary time out of time—in which an apocalyptic vision may be vouchsafed to his supernatural protagonists.

So Edgar takes over the very machinery of epic which Toqueville six years later would deny the American poet because the American people no longer believed, or wished to believe, in the past, in gods, or in the intermediary creatures between Heaven and earth—be they angels, spirits, or merely (as in *The Rape of the Lock*) parodic sylphs. What the American public believed or wished to believe never cut any ice for Edgar. This lad not yet old enough to vote against President Jackson has his own vision of truth, of cosmological truth. He had been reading Milton and Shelley and Tom Moore, and let the reader who dares, follow, and be compelled to believe as Poe believes. For 'Al Aaraaf' is a wild mishmash of things strayed, stolen, or transformed from *Paradise Lost*, from *Queen Mab*, and from Moore's *The Loves of the Angels*. Poe undertakes to believe, to write, and to live as a poet-prophet, delivering the Word—not from Ararat or Sinai or Calvary, but from that remote star which he alone has seen. Al Aaraaf, Poe's note informs us, is 'A star . . . discovered by Tico Brahe which appeared suddenly in the heavens—attained, in a few days, a brilliancy approaching that of Jupiter—then as suddenly disappeared, and has never been seen since.' This distant realm of beauty fading from our sight Poe describes, in another note; 'With the Arabians there is a medium between Heaven and Hell, where men suffer no punishment, but yet do not attain that tranquil and even happiness which they suppose to be characteristic of heavenly enjoyment.' Thus Poe circumvents both mundane reality and Christian cosmology. 'Kubla Khan,' 'Lalla Rookh,' and the Brighton Pavilion attest to the lure of Arabian Nights felt by the Romantics. Poe is making the Arabic scene too, but he is making that scene his own.

As he makes his own his borrowings from Milton, Shelley, and Moore. For 'Al Aaraaf' is puzzlingly original. It is a fable about the wholly aesthetic conception of ideality and of an afterlife in which participation in that ideality is possible. The cosmological scope of this production as well as the grand effect of some of its lines bears the mark of Milton (however little like Milton is the theology). Another of Poe's models seems to me to be Shelley's *Queen Mab*. As with *Paradise Lost*, the differences are just as revealing as the similarities.

Both 'Al Aaraaf' and *Queen Mab* take place in an imaginary landscape, in both there is a Spirit named Ianthe, and truths unknown on earth are revealed. But where Shelley's poem is one of rebellion—of specific rebellion against the tyrannies of an oppressive class system; against war-mongering kings; against God, Christ, and the Church—Poe in 'Al Aaraaf' doesn't deign to attack any such abuses. Instead he writes as though the real world were completely irrelevant. His poem is devoted to the evanescent terrain of the ideal, and the only resemblance to human life on Al Aaraaf is the presence, among certain of its inhabitants, of that impure passion, love. Poe's poem is a cosmological legend, a breathing-into-being of a realm of the ideal, to which he consigns the existence of *the idea* of the lost sculptures of our Classical antiquity. From such snippets of Christianity, Neoplatonism, and his own imperious designs, Poe constructs his non-Christian, nonplatonic star.

Much too ambitious. Yet the young Poe was already able to handle complex conceptions in his verse, and to vary the texture of that verse. In Part I the normative line is first, octosyllabic couplets, then pentameter couplets, with the interposition at lines 82–117 of a lyrical interlude in alternately rhymed trimeter-dimeters. Part II consists of pentameter couplets with the interposition at lines 68–155 of another lyric, this time in anapestic dimeters:

> Ligeia! Ligeia!
>   My beautiful one!
> Whose harshest idea
>   Will to melody run . . .

The whole opus runs to 422 melodious lines, more than four times the length Poe later decided was admissible in a true poem. Part I introduces Al Aaraaf, where there is 'nothing earthly save the ray / (Thrown back from flowers) of Beauty's eye.' This world, ruled over by Nesace, contains both the originals and the departed spirits of all earthly beauties. By a trick of synaesthesia, we attend

> Fair flowers, and fairy! to whose care is given
> To bear the Goddess' song, in odors, up to Heaven.

She sings her song (the first lyrical interlude), and then

> She stirr'd not—breath'd not—for a voice was there
> How solemnly pervading the calm air!
> A sound of silence on the startled ear
> Which dreamy poets name "the music of the sphere."

From this eloquent silence speaks 'the eternal voice of God,' commanding Nesace, in couplets of Miltonic grandeur,

> What tho' in worlds which own a single sun
> The sands of Time grow dimmer as they run,
> Yet thine is my resplendency, so given
> To bear my secrets thro' the upper Heaven.

Leave tenantless thy crystal home, and fly
With all thy train, athwart the moony sky—
Apart—like fire-flies in Sicilian night
And wing to other worlds another light!
Divulge the secrets of thy embassy
To the proud orbs that twinkle—and so be
To ev'ry heart a barrier and a ban
Lest the stars totter in the guilt of man!

Nesace has already defined her embassy, in her hymn to
Heaven:

And here, in thought, to thee—
In thought that can alone
Ascend thy empire and so be
A partner of thy throne—
By winged Fantasy,
My embassy is given,
Till secrecy shall knowledge be
In the environs of Heaven.

Thus the divine mission of Nesace, the agent of Beauty, is
the revelation of her secret knowledge 'in thought that can
alone . . . By winged Fantasy' ascend the throne of God.
This thought can only be the creative imagination of the
artist or the poet, earthly creators of beauty.

The message of 'Al Aaraaf' is so evanescent, its language
so opaque, that the argument is difficult to follow. If this be
an epic, it is an epic without an epic hero; if it be legend, it
is the legend of no people. Indeed there is not a living person
in the poem—so far its only characters are a fairy, Nesace,
and the voice of God. Poe is his own myth-maker. What relation there may be between his conception of 'Al Aaraaf'
and the beliefs of Christians, Arabs, or any other sect is completely accidental. Poe's 'myth' in 'Al Aaraaf' is about as
cloudy and as self-determined as that of Shelley in *Queen
Mab* and of Keats in *Endymion*. Indeed, Poe is writing his
screed across the heavens in the manner of these greater English poets a decade before him. There is not one word in 'Al
Aaraaf' by which a reader, unfamiliar with its authorship,

could infer it to have been written in Baltimore, by an American.

The second canto gives no better clue to the author's nationality than did the first:

> High on a mountain of enamell'd head—
> Such as the drowsy shepherd on his bed
> Of giant pasturage . . .

This is the world of Romance, of pastoral, actually a world as yet unknown, for we are on Al Aaraaf, where

> A dome, by linked light from Heaven let down,
> Sat gently on these columns as a crown . . .

—an image reminiscent of Shelley's 'dome of many colored glass.' On these columns are sculpted the lost 'Achaian statues,' and

> Friezes from Tadmor and Persepolis—
> From Balbec, and the stilly, clear abyss
> Of beautiful Gomorrah! O, the wave
> Is now upon thee—but too late to save!

This demonic suggestion of the flooded city prefigures Poe's later poem, 'The City in the Sea.' So far, in Part II, we have been given a spiritual *tableau vivant*. This sets the scene for the return of Nesace, who sings her second hymn. This time she invokes the divine spirit of harmonious correspondence of idea with ideal:

> Ligeia! wherever
>   Thy image may be,
> No magic shall sever
>   Thy music from thee.

Nesace urges, in anticipation of the last hundred lines of the poem,

> And true love caresses—
>   O! leave them apart!
> They are light on the tresses,
>   But lead on the heart.

For the divine throne to which Ligeia, the spirit of ideal beauty, may ascend, does not tolerate earthly passion. This is Poe's hymn to intellectual beauty, the attainment of which requires the abnegation of the dross of our flesh, our world, our life, our loves.

Not until line 174 of Canto II do we find anyone like a person in the poem, and what pass for persons prove to be the risen ghost of Michelangelo and the fallen spirit of one of Nesace's minions, Ianthe. There they are, on that distant star, doomed not to know true Heaven because they love one another. The last hundred lines of the poem speak of their unavailing love; the passage concludes as it began 'They fell: for Heaven to them no hope imparts / Who hear not for the beating of their hearts.' This couplet holds the germ of half of Poe's other poems and of his best-known tales.

The Angelo-Ianthe episode has very much the look of an original cadenza upon an ancient theme, one much favored by other Romantic poets before and after Poe. The motif is the love between a supernatural being and a mortal; always a bad show, since either the goddess loses her gleam and sinks into mere mortality (Undine); or the lover must be made an immortal too (Endymion) and so is translated out of this life altogether; or the punishment of the gods is visited upon the lover—as an evil transformation or a curse—for his hubris in desiring to ravish a lady so far out of his class (Actaeon; Tithonus; Yeats's *At the Hawk's Well*).

But Poe works it out still another way. In 'Al Aaraaf' *both* lovers lose. Angelo isn't actually a man, he is a ghost or spirit of a man—in fact the spirit of the man who was the world's greatest lover and creator of beauty, the incarnate Artist's ghost. As such, in Poe's cosmology he is only demidivine and semimortal, for such a spirit is not conducted directly into Heaven.

Ianthe, too, although a nymph, is not fully spiritualized. Enough of Earth's grossness and the mortality of flesh pertains to her that she may undo her equivocal status among the higher beings by succumbing to *passion*. In Poe's aes-

thetic universe, any creature who feels the stirrings of his
heart is thereby damned.

Any such representation of a romance between an earthling
and a spiritling is bound to run certain procedural risks, not
the least of which is sheer incredibility. It must have galled
Poe, who followed the state of his own reputation with the
care of a speculator reading the daily tickertape, that a
decade after 'Al Aaraaf' had appeared—and nearly disappeared, so little was it noticed—the most touted poem
written by an American was Joseph Rodman Drake's 'The
Culprit Fay.' This piece of paltry frivolity Jacksonian America could safely extol, since it made no serious challenge to
the premises of a go-ahead, materialistic society but offered
merely the safe diversion of a pretty and fanciful story. Not
to wonder that Poe slashed 'The Culprit Fay' in his review
in April, 1836, of a posthumous edition of Drake's poems.
What may be surprising to some, however, is the tone of light
irony and easy humor with which he outlines the defects of
'The Culprit Fay,' defects which we may be sure his own
ambitious poem had successfully avoided:

> We are bidden, in the first place, and in a tone of senti-
> ment and language adapted to the loftiest breathings of
> the Muse, to imagine a race of Fairies in the vicinity of
> West Point. We are told, with a grave air, of their camp,
> of their king, and especially of their sentry, who is a wood-
> tick. We are informed that an Ouphe of about an inch
> in height has committed a deadly sin in falling in love
> with a mortal maiden, who may, very possibly, be six feet
> in her stockings. The consequence to the Ouphe is—what?
> Why, that he has 'dyed his wings,' 'broken his elfin chain,'
> and 'quenched his flame-wood lamp.' And he is therefore
> sentenced to what? To catch a spark from the tail of a fall-
> ing star, and a drop of water from the belly of a sturgeon.
> What are his equipment for the first adventure? An acorn-
> helmet, a thistle-down plume, a butterfly cloak, a ladybug
> shield, cockleseed spurs, and a fire-fly horse. How does he
> ride to the second? On the back of a bull-frog.

And so forth. Poe continues for half a page his catalogues of these twee fancies, then adds,

> Such are the puerilities we daily find ourselves called upon to admire, as among the loftiest efforts of the human mind, and which not to assign a rank with the proud trophies of the matured and vigorous genius of England, is to prove ourselves at once a fool, a maligner, and no patriot.

To dispraise an American poet took courage; to raise above the Muse's temple the Union Jack on a higher staff than that of Old Glory took even more. To sink forever the specious repute of the ridiculous 'Culprit Fay' Poe cites, not his own superior practice in 'Al Aaraaf,' but Shelley's invocation of Queen Mab:

> It will be seen that the Fairy of Shelley is not a mere compound of incongruous natural objects, inartistically put together, and unaccompanied by any *moral* sentiment—but a being, in the illustration of whose nature some physical elements are used collaterally as adjuncts, while the main conception springs immediately, *or thus apparently springs,* from the brain of the poet, enveloped in the moral sentiments of grace, of color, of motion—of the beautiful, of the mystical, of the august, in short of *the ideal.*

Poe is of course making clear the distinction between Fancy, such as Drake's, and Imagination, such as Shelley's —and, by implication, his own. He has brought into the criticism of American poetry the division of these lower and higher imaginative faculties first proposed by Coleridge, distinctions which will become very important in his own criticism, though to be sure he wields them in ways and toward ends which would have surprised Coleridge himself perhaps more than they would have pleased him.

Coleridge, proposing Imagination as the esemplastic power, had further distinguished between the primary and the secondary imagination. 'The primary IMAGINATION I hold to be the living Power and prime Agent of all human Perception, and as a repetition in the finite mind of the eternal act of creation in the infinite I AM.' The secondary imagination he defined as 'an echo of the former, co-existing with the conscious will,' like the primary in kind but differing in degree and in the manner of its operation. The secondary imagination, says Coleridge, 'dissolves, diffuses, dissipates in order to re-create. . . . It is essentially *vital*, even as all objects (as objects) are essentially fixed and dead.' The lower order of thought is Fancy, which 'has no other counters to play with but fixities and definites,' and is thus 'a mode of Memory emancipated from the order of time and space.'

May I be forgiven for summarizing this familiar doctrine from *Biographia Literaria*, Chapter XIII. The point I want to make about 'Al Aaraaf' and about Poe's poetry in general is, Poe tries to operate *only* in the realm of the *primary* imagination, arrogating to his own creative powers the 'repetition in the finite mind of the eternal act of creation in the infinite I AM.' Even the secondary imagination is too impure for Poe, since it accepts the world of dead objects in order to visualize, idealize and unify. In 'Al Aaraaf' Poe had to depend upon his own imaginative distortions, through synaesthesia, of common objects (like flowers, stars, and meteors) in order to make tangible his wholly imaginary world. So his flowers sing hymns, his silences speak, the twilight murmurs as it falls (II, 40–41). Even so, the irreality of Al Aaraaf is conceived in terms of the objects and sensations of the earth to which it is designed as a preferable alternative. In certain of his later poems, Poe creates a landscape which is further supposed to be an evidence of the primary imagination, because so little like *any* sensible objects, because apprehended by no sensations already known to the reader. This is a course at once heroic and hazardous for a poet, since it debars from his art practically all of the experiences of mankind and makes his poetry completely self-defining, self-limiting, solipsistic.

As though the primary imagination were a self-begotten, self-renewing power, independent of human relationships, carrying out its imperious directives with the same independence and autonomy as does the infinite I AM.

Poe, poor Edgarpoe, the penniless orphan, the abandoned

and lovelorn boy, cognizant of his impotence in the affairs of
men and the love of women, conceives himself as a self-
begotten deity, the infinite I AM made finite, given a habi-
tation and a name. Name of Edgar Allan Poe.

This reads indeed like psychotic behavior. And it is not
surprising that Poe's psychiatric critics, like Krutch and Mme
Bonaparte, have declared him psychotic and insane. As for
me, I too am a psychiatric critic of sorts, and I hereby expound another doctrine. Edgar Poe was both insane and sane,
but sane mostly, especially sane when writing his poems, his
criticism, and his tales. For these are composed not, as he
would have dearly hoped, out of the disinterested stirrings
of the primary imagination alone; they are composed out of
the sufferings and wounds of his bruised and beaten yet resilient ego, his ego that had the extraordinary power of
dipping, slipping, ripping down into his unconscious and,
while not surrendering its willed control of the shape and
form of what he wrote, yet depending for its content—always
for its latent content, sometimes even for its manifest content—upon the id. The work of Idgar I AM Poet.

For such a youth the power of fancy is beneath contempt,
the power of secondary imagination is but secondary. He
must aim beyond the known stars, for Al Aaraaf. Out of the
extremity of his own miserable life he imagined a life as little
like our life as can be the life of spirit like our raw sufferings. His principles are aesthetic—that is to say, he pursues
the pleasure principle until, like Freud, indeed, anticipating
Freud (as we shall see in *Eureka*), he goes beyond the
pleasure principle. One side of his art is the effort to create
the ineffable, the bower of unutterable delight. But the road
thither is terrifying, frightening, for, like the lover of a spirit,
Edgarpoe must put in direst jeopardy the only life he knows
—this one, miserable as it is—in his quest for a realm of being more sublime. Therefore delight and terror are everywhere mingled in a weird harmony in Poe's writings.

This heroic abandon of the poet to live by imagination
alone, this insistent effort to create a contra-world, has made
Poe the hero of symbolist writers and readers from Baudelaire

until our own time. The absolute autonomy of imagination is not a tenable doctrine, but it sounds like a siren's song in the mind of Nabokov, as it tempted Wallace Stevens, and, through Baudelaire, a line of great French poets running from Mallarmé and Verlaine to Yves Bonnefoy.

But what, in fact, did Poe accomplish? I've placed a heavy load of historical influence upon poor Eddie's shoulders, all because of 'Al Aaraaf.' The brief poems with which he prefaced and followed 'Al Aaraaf' help to clarify the urgency in 'Al Aaraaf' to escape from this world. The prefatory poem is 'Sonnet—To Science'; the coda, 'Romance.'

What else would a young poet in 1827 try his hand at besides an Epic Poem of Cosmic Revelation? What else but a sonnet! To write a good sonnet you usually have to have climbed over the bones of your fourteen apprentice sonnets, each good line putting paid to the ghost of a failed poem. It's a devilish difficult form, the sonnet, though it always seems, in a good one, to be so simple, so logical. Edgar must have burned his apprentice sonnets, for the earliest one we have from him is 'Sonnet—To Science,' a poem worthy to appear beside the great sonnets of Wordsworth, Shelley and Keats—to say nothing of Sidney, Shakespeare, Milton, et al.—as in fact it does appear, in *The Penguin Book of Sonnets*, where I first read it. In 1945. Surrounded, as it then was, by more familiar Romantic masterpieces—'To Ozymandias,' 'When I have fears that I may cease to be'—how could one help but take Poe's lone sonnet as an outcry against the antipoetic materialism of the modern scientific age, the utilitarian logic which drives imagination 'To seek a shelter in some happier star?'

Of course we read into the poems we read the needs we need those poems to serve. And when I first read Poe's sonnet, that was my need. It's true, I could have read 'Sonnet—To Science' in that first volume—*The Poems*—of Poe's work in which I had scribbled an inscription, having endured a troubled sleep after reading 'A Predicament.' But I had

bought that book to own other poems in it—'To Helen' and
'The Raven' and—I confess it—'The Bells.' At fifteen one is
ready, one *needs*, to be swept away by the sheer tintinnabulation of a poetry of sound, of incantatory spells, a poetry of
hypnagogic trance which will possess one's whole consciousness with a tomtom and a chime. Sonnets march to a different drummer, one I wasn't ready then to heed. But when
on a weekend pass, in Cincinnati, in a bookshop, stealing
forty-eight hours from my quasi-scientific military assign-
ment, I was ready for the disciplined argument of a sonnet
and especially for the seeming rejection, in Poe's sonnet, of
Science which preyed upon the world and drove Imagination
into exile. In those days I was writing abstracts of aeronautical
literature—articles, captured documents, tech reports on aero-
foil design, strength of materials, power plants, super-
chargers, injection pumps. Sometimes a single word, or the
design on the edge of a page would snag my attention, and
I'd start up half an hour later from a trance in which I had
been hypnotized by the meaningless repetition of injection-
pump, injection-pump, injection-pump. Start up guiltily, for
it was my duty that had been neglected, and I had no poem
to show for my dereliction. Being thus entrapped by
science, stifled by technology, manacled by duty, you can
imagine how I longed for the guiltless indulgence of my wayward and indolent imaginative faculties. Such was *my* need,
when I first read Poe's 'Sonnet—To Science':

Science! true daughter of Old Time thou art!
    Who alterest all things with thy peering eyes.
Why preyest thou thus upon the poet's heart,
    Vulture, whose wings are dull realities?
How should he love thee? or how deem thee wise,
    Who wouldst not leave him in his wandering
To seek for treasure in the jewelled skies,
    Albeit he soared with an undaunted wing?
Hast thou not dragged Diana from her car?
    And driven the Hamadryad from the wood
To seek a shelter in some happier star?

Hast thou not torn the Naiad from her flood,
The Elfin from the green grass, and from me
The summer dream beneath the tamarind tree?

Ah well, I'd never actually seen a tamarind tree (had Edgar
seen one?), but I'd had summer dreams, and now, thanks to
duty, to science, to the Cartesian spirit which had dis-
enchanted the magic casements of imagination by congealing
the world of appearances into a realm of fixities, exact
measurements, concrete objects, facts, causalities—my summer dreams had vanished as the Milky Way before the light
of a wintry sun. Neither Edgar Poe nor I had, at this time,
any of Whitman's hospitality and amplitude regarding
science. We couldn't and wouldn't say, with Walt,

Hurrah for positive science! long live exact demonstration!
. . . .
This is the lexicographer, this the chemist, this made a
    grammar of old cartouches. . . .
This is the geologist, this works with the scalpel, and this
    is a mathematician.

Gentlemen, to you the first honors always!
Your facts are useful, and yet they are not my dwelling.
I but enter them to an area of my dwelling.

'An area of my dwelling.' Walt Whitman is still dwelling on this earth, and so the discoveries of geologists and
chemists are useful to him. But where was the area of Edgarpoe's dwelling?

Al Aaraaf. A somewhere other. Since Imagination has been
driven from the glades and groves of this earth, it must seek
its proper home 'in some happier star,' not on earth at all,
not at all in this life. There, on Al Aaraaf, among the spirits
of the vanished beauties of both the Parthenon and Gomor-
rah, alongside still greater beauties never yet experienced
here. So Poe's poem is really not concerned primarily, as I
was when I first read it, with merely fretting against the
dominance of the Cartesian mind. Its first concern is to insist upon the necessity of Imagination creating its own
world.

And the real enemy in 'Sonnet—To Science' isn't even science. It's 'Old Time,' whose 'true daughter' Science is. For Time is the father who has hatched the vulture-like Science, therefore Time, too, plucks at the carrion of things, feeding upon the dead body of this world. Science is thus imagined as the monstrous offspring of a monstrous parent, the second generation of the original sin against Beauty and Imagination. That original sin is personified as Time.

And Edgarpoe longs, longs, desperately longs to return to that paradisal time before Time began or was begotten, before that original sin. Longs to return there, even if it kills him.

The image of vulture Time appears again in 'Romance,' this time in opposition to another bird image, that of Romance itself—

> Romance, who loves to nod and sing
> With drowsy head and folded wing,
> Among the green leaves as they shake
> Far down within some shadowy lake,
> To me a painted paroquet
> Hath been—a most familiar bird—
> Taught me my alphabet to say—
> To lisp my very earliest word
> While in the wild wood I did lie,
> A child—with a most knowing eye.

In this first stanza Poe has summoned an image at once autonomous and archetypal, a *reflection* of a *shadowy, painted* bird—thus already at two or three removes from reality. That bird is one which, when tamed, can speak. And from it he learned 'my alphabet to say.' This is a tellingly compact symbol of the source, within the 'most knowing eye' of his own infantine being, of the very art by which he depicts it.

This power he had 'While in the wild wood I did lie, / A child,' but, as the second stanza makes clear, 'Romance is a poem lamenting the loss of that power, and invoking the recurrence of imaginative vision:

> Of late, eternal Condor years
> So shake the very Heaven on high
> With tumult as they thunder by,
> I have no time for idle cares
> Through gazing on the unquiet sky.

The tumult of the Condor years breaks up the calm tranquillity in which the paroquet taught the dreaming child its ABCs.

> And when an hour with calmer wings
> Its down upon my spirit flings—
> That little time with lyre and rhyme
> To while away—forbidden things!
> My heart would feel to be a crime
> Unless it trembled with the strings.

The consistency of the poem is flawed in the end, as the governing metaphor undergoes an illogical transformation, from bird to lyre. The threatening, tumultuous Condor years may be fitfully evaded under the 'calmer wings' of 'an hour,'—a species of bird not specified, but one which flings its down upon the poet's spirit. In the Cartesian world, described in 'Sonnet—To Science,' from which Imagination has been banished, 'with lyre and rhyme' to while away that brief hour are now 'forbidden things.' Yet the poet's heart speaks the truth of its own nature and would transgress another, higher law 'Unless it trembled with the strings.' If we bridge the mixed metaphor, what the poem tells us is that the true language of the heart is the alphabet taught it in childhood by the dream-image of 'Romance, who loves to nod and sing, / With drowsy head and folded wing.' Dreams, then, are more ideal and beautiful than the tumultuous realities beneath the condor wings of the passing years.

The imaginative authority of dreams will be explored in such poems as 'Dream-Land' and 'The City in the Sea'; but first let's follow another image from 'Romance,' the trembling of the strings which the poet feels vibrating with a music like his own heart's beat.

This is the music of 'the angel Israfel, whose heart-strings are a lute, and who has the sweetest voice of all God's creatures,' an epigraph which Poe, incorrectly, attributed to the Koran. As Killis Campbell pointed out many years ago, the quotation itself is incorrect too: it seems adapted from a phrase in George Sale's *Preliminary Discourse* to an edition of the Koran (1764) which read, 'the angel Israfil, who has the most melodious voice of all God's creatures.' Of course what's lacking is the most telling part of the epigraph— *whose heart-strings are a lute.* But another epigraph of Poe's supplies the missing phrase. His most terrifying tale of horror, the one in which Roderick Usher buries his twin sister alive, is prefaced with a couplet from Béranger (who actually wrote 'Mon coeur . . .'):

> Son coeur est un luth suspendu;
> Sitôt qu'on le touche il résonne.

This suspended lute is of course an Aeolian harp, that favorite image of the Romantics for the songs made by the breath—that is, the spirit—of Nature herself. But Poe's songs are not those of Nature, they are songs of the spirit which has successfully escaped its bondage to Nature, realm of mortality, suffering, and corruption. How it is that the wind-harp hung above the House of Usher corresponds to the lute-like heart of the Arabian angel Israfel is one of the mysteries in Poe's work it would take a detective like Monsieur Dupin to solve. Perhaps I'll yet untangle it.

Israfel's lyre! Poe would, if he could, have always smitten those angelic strings. Poetry, to him, is *song;* and this one option bends his verses on its stave, making inaccessible to Edgarpoe all those other marvellous effects attained by Romantic poets from Wordsworth to Williams, the poets for whom poetry is *speech.* No, it's song, song, song, as in Shelley's lyrics, in Byron's 'Hebrew Melodies,' in the Songs and Anacreontics of Moore. It was the ear, the taste, the craving of the age, this conscious confusion between the music of rhyme, the music of melody, the music of music, the music of the spheres. Ideality, that perfect beauty on which Poe gazed with such longing, that perfect beauty he

attempted to imitate and enshrine in his verses, is for him
attainable, if at all, through the effects of musicality of sound
and indefiniteness of meaning. The nearest Edgarpoe gets to
that heavenly music in 'Israfel' is in the first and the last
stanzas:

> In Heaven a spirit doth dwell
>   'Whose heart-strings are a lute;'
> None sings, so wildly well
> As the angel Israfel,
> And the giddy stars (so legends tell)
> Ceasing their hymns, attend the spell
>   Of his voice, all mute.
>
>   .   .   .   .   .   .
>
> If I could dwell
> Where Israfel
>   Hath dwelt, and he where I,
> He might not sing so wildly well
>   A mortal melody,
> While a bolder note than this might swell
> From my lyre within the sky.

When Edgarpoe has really set his lyre within the sky he
is capable of a lovely music, a lyrical movement, a fortuitous
lilt of chiming sounds. The lyrical interludes in 'Al Aaraaf'
are quite delicately managed, the brevity of their trimeter/
dimeter lines hastening the reappearance of the rhyme
sounds, and those sounds invariably mating soft and mellifluous syllables with one another. Occasionally Edgarpoe
strikes on the lute-strings of his heart a few chords which
sound as sweetly as do any struck by Shelley or Byron. Who
cannot but be charmed by the melodiousness of rhyme and
alliteration, the lulling lilt, and the indefiniteness of meaning imposed by a syntax purposely inconclusive, of the last
stanza in 'To One in Paradise':

> And all my days are trances,
>   And all my nightly dreams
> Are where thy grey eye glances,
>   And where thy footstep gleams—
> In what ethereal dances,
>   By what eternal streams.

You wouldn't think the author of such a lovely lyric could be the perpetrator of those walloping bloomers, those resounding clichés, those lines of tawdry vulgarity, with which I tried to shock my audience of Poe-worshippers at Dijon into a realization that their angelic *semblable* was, at times, incapable of sublimity. The wild vagaries in tone and execution between a poem like 'To One in Paradise' and a set of verses like 'Eulalie—A Song'; or even the divagations in finesse among the stanzas in 'Israfel' I've just quoted and those which Poe insisted upon interposing between them, suggest that Poe had, at best, *a very uneven ear*. It may suggest, too, that his poems weren't as totally committed to the strains of the wind-harp in his heart as he would like us to think. What else then, besides singing the angelic tones of the soul, is his poetry trying to do?

Or, to put it differently, what, in fact, is his soul trying to sing on that harp, which is his heart within the sky? In 'Al Aaraaf' his soul is revealing a tableau of the Great Good Place and, in Part II, a fable of the exile from Heaven of the artist who allows passion to divert him from the quest for ideality. In 'Israfel' and 'To One in Paradise' Poe actually sings a lyric, a song. But even in these melodious lines he is also *telling a story*—a truncated story, true, but there is the seed of a narrative: How I, Edgar Allan Poe, would exchange my mortal melodies, if I but could, for the immortal strains of Israfel, and in 'To One in Paradise,' the song in fact conveys the rudiments of a story: 'Thou wast that all to me, love, / For which my soul did pine. . . .' It's the same old story. The lament for the departed beloved. As indeed the title might have tipped us off.

All of Poe's poems are at the same time committed to the conception of poetry-as-song and of poetry-as-narrative. Each of his poems is the metrical account of an action. The common denominator of this action in the poems, the archetype of their plot, is this: Someone goes somewhere. The Imagination goes to a happier star; the 'thou' who 'wast all to me' goes to Paradise; I the Poet go to Heaven as Israfel perhaps comes down to earth. The highest common denominator

among these poems is they are all poems of journeys, and
the journeys are all quests. The Journey and the Quest!
Those Great Archetypes!

Whither journey we, and for what are we questing?

Two poems announce our destinations: 'The City in the
Sea' and 'Dream-Land.' Maybe the one is the other? Both
are *tales dreamed and sung*: the strains Romance has plucked
upon the poet's lyre. In these dream-poems the function of
rhythmic regularity is primarily to induce in the reader that
trance-like helplessness which Richard Wilbur has called the
hypnagogic state. It is exactly the same use of meter that
Yeats, half a century later, described in his essay, 'The
Symbolism of Poetry' (1900). The meter favored for this
purpose is the octosyllabic couplet, perhaps because so employed by Coleridge in 'The Pains of Sleep.' It's a meter
that will dull the mind with its metronomic insistence and
its lack of either the quickened music of trimeter rhymes or
the sinewy movement of caesura-filled pentameters. Once the
dream mood is established, once the reader has been
mesmerized and has suspended his workaday rational
faculties, the imagery of the poem takes command of both
the dreamer's and the reader's minds, and the meter can also
be commanded by the imagery—commanded to indulge itself in the freer movement, the more lively displacement of
stresses, by which we distinguish a flexible rhythm from a
mechanistic meter.

Poe has a really dreadful poem on the same dream-subject
as his two good ones. If we compare 'The Sleeper' to
'Dream-Land' or 'The City in the Sea,' the difference between his meter and his rhythm, between his originality and
his balderdash, becomes clear. How long are we going to stay
with a poem that begins,

> At midnight, in the month of June,
> I stand beneath the mystic moon.
> An opiate vapor, dewy, dim,
> Exhales from out her golden rim . . .

If we stick around for a few more lines, we have to rhyme
musicálly with *valley*. This language is as dead as the meter.
Yet the vision the poem is trying to evoke was, I don't doubt,
as genuine for Poe as that in 'The City in the Sea':

> Lo! Death has reared himself a throne
> In a strange city lying alone
> Far down within the dim West. . . .

What a beginning! That first 'Lo!' makes a spondee when
followed by *Death*, and in the next line metrical distortion
places the heaviest accents right where they belong, on the
adjacent syllables *stránge cíty*. This distortion of iambs into
spondees recurs twice in the next line—*Fár dówn . . . dím
Wést*. The only words to receive vocal stress are the operative
words which determine the meaning.

But the next couplet nearly blows it:

> Where the good and the bad and the worst and the best
> Have gone to their eternal rest.

What a string of banal clichés—the worst line in the poem.
But I forgive it, for the rest of the poem really does create
the weird wild sunken scene promised in the title.

If we went aloft in 'Al Aaraaf,' 'Sonnet—To Science,' and
'Israfel,' this time the trip we take heads the other way: beneath the sea. Yet both noplaces are the home of the shades
of the dead. Here we are, among 'Time-eaten towers that
tremble not,' where 'melancholy waters lie,' where 'No rays
from holy heaven come down,' but the light—ah, the light!—
comes

> from out the lurid sea
> Streams up the turrets silently—
> Gleams up the pinnacles far and free
> Up domes—up spires—up kingly halls—
> Up fanes—up Babylon-like walls—
> Up shadowy long-forgotten bowers
> Of sculptured ivy and stone flowers—
> Up many and many a marvellous shrine
> Whose wreathéd friezes intertwine
> The viol, the violet, and the vine.

This is a venue outside of Nature, where, we would expect, light would 'from holy heaven come down.' Instead, a weird light clambers up, up, up, encompassing the entire city which, with its domes and fanes, its friezes and bowers, is as opulent as Xanadu. The unearthly light reveals the images— the sculptured artifices—of music (the viol), of natural beauty (the violet), and of that intoxication (the vine) in which we recognize music as a simulacrum of the ideal beauty of nature. I'm divided between admiration for this stanza's astonishing creation of an unreal reality and regret that the path of the light wasn't more consistently from the bottom to the top of the scene.

> So blend the turrets and shadows there
> That all seems pendulous in air,
> While from a proud tower in the town
> Death looks gigantically down.

There, above all the fanes and domes and bowers, Death reigns. What an effect! *Pendulous . . . gigantically . . .* The diction is perfectly controlled here, these magniloquent words effectively pointed against lines of clear and simple Anglo-Saxon monosyllables. Death, imperious and all-presiding— but what he presides over is yet another surprise: it's *the dissolution of his own city*. The City in the Sea now slips and shudders . . .

> The waves have now a redder glow—
> The hours are breathing faint and low—
> And when, amid no earthly moans,
> Down, down that town shall settle hence,
> Hell, rising from a thousand thrones,
> Shall do it reverence.

This conclusion is more impressive than communicative. We sense a terror that we cannot explain. If the City in the Sea was the home of the shades of 'the good and the bad and the worst and the best,' who, then, is in Hell to do it reverence? It's worth remarking that for all we know the city is actually unpopulated, for we never see any of these best or

worst shades. Possibly I've been wrong in calling it a city of
the dead spirits; it may be the Earthly City at some apocalyptic moment when all who were alive 'Have gone to their
eternal rest' leaving behind them the 'Time-eaten towers'
that at first 'tremble not' but then, after Death has looked
'gigantically down,' sink into the sea.

Whatever the cryptic and aborted epic tale whose fore-
shortened terrors are evoked by the poem, we cannot miss
being gripped by the weirdly frozen aspect of 'The City in
the Sea.' At first the city is absolutely immobile in an en-
vironment which inverts our expectations of a natural
world; then, in the only action of the poem, the eerie light
climbs up from the sea to the highest tower, Death looks
down and the city slides beneath the waters. An apocalypse
—but what is the significance of its inexplicable terror?

Poe is describing, with his customary energy and inven-
tion, the most dramatic moment of all human perception:
the End of Everything. For some poets the most dramatic
moment is the union of the soul with nature, for others the
juncture of soul with soul in the physical union of love. For
others it is the image of their own death. For Poe it is the
death of the universe.

Why is the death of the universe Poe's most powerful
image? How can such a conception *be* a powerful image for
a poet, unless he be St. John revealing the Book of Revelation?

The answer leaps ahead like a vast electric charge splitting from this world to the next, as we will be told in *Eureka*
and in various preliminary sketches Poe has still to write between 'The City in the Sea' and his great apocalyptic treatise
in 1845. But how to make the end of everything a poetic
theme—that was Poe's problem. He kept on trying, tried
again (in 1845) in his poem 'Dream-Land':

> By a route obscure and lonely,
> Haunted by ill angels only,
> Where an Eidolon, named Night,
> On a black throne reigns upright,

> I have reached these lands but newly
> From an ultimate dim Thule—
> From a wild weird clime that lieth, sublime,
> Out of Space—out of Time.

This is the trip Poe's poetic persona is forever trying to take, 'Out of Space—out of Time,' denying the actual world— 'Bottomless vales and boundless floods . . . Mountains toppling evermore / Into seas without a shore,' as though we could even imagine a sea without a shore or a mountain that abused its own mountainhood by forever toppling. When we arrive by this impossible route at that inconceivable destination,

> There the traveller meets aghast
> Sheeted Memories of the Past—
> Shrouded forms that start and sigh
> As they pass the wanderer by—
> White-robed forms of friends long given,
> In agony, to the Earth—and Heaven.
>   .   .   .   .
> Never its mysteries are exposed
> To the weak human eye unclosed;
> So wills its King, who hath forbid
> The uplifting of the fringed lid;
> And thus the sad Soul that here passes
> Beholds it but through darkened glasses.

Although I have omitted such infelicities as Poe's rhyming 'still and chilly' 'With the snows of the lolling lily,' the poem still seems a Hallowe'en scare, or a Gothic parody. Until we think about it. For Poe isn't always in as full control of his language as he is of his vision. This of course is no excuse, a poet must be a poet clear through; but Poe sometimes (like Melville, like Hardy) seems trapped by a set of conventions inadequate to express the radical clarity of his vision. His diction is that of the Gothic spook story or ghost poem, his vision that of a man struggling to say what he has seen in a world so unlike ours that he has difficulty using the language of ours to describe it. What he is trying to say in 'Dream-Land' is that only in dreams can we follow that 'route ob-

scure and lonely,' which, though it leads us through terrors
(however banal), reunites us with the dead—who are in
Heaven. The phrase lifted from St. Paul who told us that
we now see through a glass darkly, does not allude to *his*
faith at all but rather to Poe's own conviction that after death
the soul will join the spirits in 'Eldorado' (not a happy phrase,
that). Poe does not propose their salvation, their redemption,
only their contentment in a realm we cannot view or know
until we join them. Once again the poem seems more portentous than communicative, and what communication it
achieves is more a matter of the mood than of the matter. I
spoke a moment ago of Poe's vision being clearer than his
language, but the fact is, what he so clearly saw was a vision
of something inexpressible. In poems. In his tales, this poet
to whom 'poetry has been not a purpose, but a passion' succeeded in creating what his poetry failed to create.

This is not to say that his poetry is all failure. He cannot
bring himself, while using the conventions of poetry—prin-
cipally the convention of Being A Poet—to speak of certain
truths at the very dead center of his own psychic life. He can
say things in tales like 'MS. Found in a Bottle,' 'The Purloined Letter,' 'Ligeia,' 'Narrative of Arthur Gordon Pym,'
and 'The Fall of the House of Usher' which none of his
poems found words, images, syntax to express. Yet none of
his tales speaks with the memorable haunting tone of his
cameo masterpiece, 'To Helen.'

No one who knows any poem of Poe's does not know this
one. I can't remember when I *didn't* know it. I recall being
made to memorize it in the eighth or ninth grade—in those
days poetry was properly taught by being learned by rote—but
I seem to remember that that was no problem, for I already
knew the poem. Long before buying *The Poems*, volume I
of the *Works*, before reading 'A Predicament' and starting
to twitch at night in response to Poe's spell. Long before I
went steady in high school (beginning with the Senior Class
trip to Washington) with a lovely girl named Helen. I always
knew 'To Helen' by heart.

> Helen, thy beauty is to me
>   Like those Nicéan barks of yore,
> That gently, o'er a perfumed sea,
>   The weary, way-worn wanderer bore
>   To his own native shore.
> On desperate seas long wont to roam,
>   Thy hyacinth hair, thy classic face,
> Thy Naiad airs have brought me home
>   To the glory that was Greece,
> And the grandeur that was Rome.
>
> Lo! in yon brilliant window-niche
>   How statue-like I see thee stand,
>   The agate lamp within thy hand!
> Ah, Psyche, from the regions which
>   Are Holy-Land!

See, I can't forbear from reciting it yet again. It seems inconceivable that in the first version of this poem, in 1831, Poe hadn't yet thought of the two lines everybody remembers, and had written instead,

> To the beauty of fair Greece,
> To the grandeur of old Rome.

Even Israfel nods at the lyre. He didn't change it 'To the glory that was Greece' until 1841, or 'And the grandeur that was Rome,' until 1845.

I've said that all of Poe's poems are narratives as well as songs. What about the tale told as the poet sings 'To Helen'? *Someone goes somewhere*, the Journey, the Quest: where are they?

Right in the poem. It's Helen who goes on the journey, it's the poet who is then left with the quest still to make— but the poem doubles back on itself since his recognition, in 'To Helen,' of the quest he had still to make is actually a form of his making it.

Helen in the first stanza is a living woman, a lovely woman, whose *beauty is to me* like . . . (I'll get back to what it's like; let's stay with her, with Helen, for the moment). In the second stanza, though, Helen is no longer an imaginable

woman in the room. Nor are we in present time. Indeed, the
very first simile has moved us with the swiftness of thought
from 1831, or 1845, or right now, back into a world of Nicéan
barks of yore. Which yore? The yore of Classical antiquity
so idealized by Keats's 'Ode on a Grecian Urn,' the antiquity
which Schliemann's excavations at Troy were making known
and accessible to imagination, known as a Golden Age of
repose, balance, beauty. A woman in Poe's poem is being
idealized as an image of Ideal Beauty, and so her hair is 'hyacinth,' her face 'classic,' her airs 'Naiad'; these qualities *have
brought me home*

> To the glory that was Greece,
> And the grandeur that was Rome.

Home, because the 'me' in the poem is in exile, dreaming
wistfully of the Nicéan barks which 'gently, o'er a perfumed
sea, / The weary, way-worn wanderer bore / To his own native
shore.' *Nicéan* must be Poe's spelling of Nikean, pertaining
to Nike, goddess of Victory—his wanderer may be Ulysses,
returning from his victorious campaign against Troy, weary,
wayworn, approaching Ithaca at last . . . Or is it Agamem-
non, son of Atreus, returning to Peloponnesus and disaster
from the same victory—in the war fought *because of Helen's
beauty?* For Edgarpoe's Helen is also Homer's Helen, the
Helen of the ages, Perfect Beauty. With 'Naiad airs.'

Helen is getting away from us, she has been turned, or
has turned herself in our imagination, from a human girl to
a Grecian Naiad with hyacinth hair. (It was years before I
figured out what *that* means. Not dyed purple, but coiffed
in tight curls, like a hyacinth bloom.)

Helen's apotheosis is completed in stanza three, where she
stands like a statue in a 'brilliant window-niche'—like the
statue of a saint or, better still, of the B.V.M., in a church,
a church which is interchangeably a temple to Helen-as-
Aphrodite, a temple like the Parthenon from which Lord
Elgin took the marbles celebrated by Keats. Whether in a
Temple to Aphrodite or a Cathédrale de Notre-Dame, Helen
is suddenly transformed yet again—with 'The agate lamp

within thy hand' she is now the goddess of Wisdom—not Athene merely, but the Spirit of Intellectual Beauty—

> Ah, Psyche, from the regions which
> Are Holy-Land!

Psyche! *Whose* soul would her statue-like image represent? Whose but the poet's, who alone has perceived her, perceived her dimly limned in the actual woman who is the occasion for the poem—the occasion for the vision which is the poem's subject—the woman so swiftly subsumed by Imagination into first the image of classical beauty, then the still more remote images of which classical beauty is only a nearer approximation than the living woman. From girl to Naiad to statue—to Psyche! The further we get from life, the closer to ideality: from life to antiquity, from antiquity to myth, from myth to art, from art to Intellectual Beauty, the ethereal spirit revealed at last. And with his vision of Psyche, the poet knows whence she has come: 'from the regions which / are Holy-Land.' Lucky the days, in 1831, 1843, and 1845, when that vision was vouchsafed to him, for then, then, he had briefly dwelt on Al Aaraaf.

W. H. Auden has said that 'Poe's best poems are not his most typical or original. "To Helen," which could have been written by Landor, and "The City in the Sea," which could have been written by Hood, are more successfully realized than a poem like "Ulalume," which could have been written by none but Poe.'

On the contrary, I would say that it's Poe's failures which could have been written by other (and lesser) poets. His successes, however much they *seem* to use the meters, forms, or themes of his contemporaries, are the poems indefinably stamped by the handmark of none but Edgarpoe. Hood's 'The Sea of Death' (I find it in Mr. Auden's and Norman Holmes Pearson's *Poets of the English Language*, vol. 4, *Blake to Poe*) is superficially like 'The City in the Sea'; but on inspection Hood's fragment proves a standard piece of graveyard poetry, notable only for its nautical venue. His sea filled with the dead, 'garmented in torpid light,' is a mood-piece, sad and faintly mysterious, but quite lacking in Poe's special light, which is lurid and rippling with energy, not torpor.

What made Auden think of Landor when he read 'To Helen'? Was it these lines from 'Ianthe'?—

> Past ruin'd Ilium Helen lives,
>   Alcestis rises from the shades;
> Verse calls them forth; 'tis verse that gives
>   Immortal youth to mortal maids . . .

Or perhaps the more familiar 'Rose Aylmer.' In 'To Helen,' and only in 'To Helen,' Poe seems to emulate Landor's characteristic qualities without using his themes. In 'To Helen' we find a Landor-like economy of means, the reliance upon classical imagery, the cameo whittling of the action down to the barest essentials and those essentials presented with a maximum of lyrical energy. Such Augustan Romanticism is not Poe's usual métier. Nothing could be further from the style he adopts for 'Ulalume,' or 'Lenore,' or 'The Raven.' I like to think that 'To Helen' is a poem that Landor might have wished to have written. None of his—much as I admire them— can equal its stunning compression and swift imaginative movement.

Curiously, however different in tone, diction, rhythm, and form are 'Ulalume' and the others I've just named from 'To Helen,' these longer poems of Poe's equally bear his handprint, for all share the one theme whose variations we've already found everywhere in Edgarpoe. Someone goes somewhere: a maiden dies, and her lover journeys in search of her spirit toward Dream-Land, or Paradise, or The City in the Sea, or 'To regions which / Are Holy-Land.' That's the masterplot in The Poems of Edgarpoe. It makes no matter whether the poem be a lyric, like 'To Helen,' or lyrical ballads, like 'Ulalume' and the rest. It's even the plot half-hidden in Part II of 'Al Aaraaf,' where Ianthe and Angelo fell, Poe told us,

> for Heaven to them no hope imparts
> Who hear not for the beating of their hearts.

But what kind of love is this, which Poe can express only when the beloved is dying or dead, a love to which passion is inimical?

Edgarpoe abhors passion. The love he seeks is incompatible with life. He imagines that it is the pure exercise in pure freedom of the pure imagination. He imagines—because it was true of his own life—that life itself, with its unassuageable physical passions, is a disease to be endured:

> The moaning and groaning,
>   The sighing and sobbing,
> Are quieted now,
>   With that horrible throbbing
> At heart:—ah, that horrible,
>   Horrible throbbing!
>
> The sickness—the nausea—
>   The pitiless pain—
> Have ceased, with the fever
>   That maddened my brain—
> With the fever called "Living"
>   That burned in my brain.
>
> ('For Annie,' lines 19–30)

The throbbing at heart is simply the remorseless muffled beating of our built-in pacemaker, our Time Machine. A heart-beat is the pitiless refrain of our exile from Ideality. Poe's poems are all wild and yet wilder efforts to escape from the fever of living either backwards or forwards in time, and to attain either by dream-vision or by the intensity of a lover's devotion to his departed Ideal, a momentary residence in that never-yet-experienced realm of Ideality which he calls Al Aaraaf, Paradise, Aidenn or whatever else.

His longest and most familiar poems either chart the fever or recount the escape of the beloved to a happier star, or tell of the bereaved lover's attempt—often baffled and incomplete—to rejoin her there. A poet with a tale to tell, alive and suffering in the first half of the nineteenth century, would, expectably, find at hand a very fitting form for his narrative. That form is the literary ballad.

A ballad, as everybody knows, is a narrative poem in regular stanzas, often with a refrain: a tale told in song, the song residually suggesting dance. How wise of Wordsworth and Coleridge, when they plotted the downfall of Augustan literary decorum, to imitate folk ballads, the archaic form of poetry most compatible with democratic sympathies. Wordsworth even thought he was imitating the speech of actual men. But Edgarpoe has no such demotic sentiments. If, like his contemporaries Longfellow and Whittier in this country, like Mangan and Davis and Ferguson in Ireland, or Coleridge and Wordsworth and Scott and Barnes in Britain, Poe writes literary ballads, he nonetheless remakes the ballad form into the servant of his own peculiar needs.

I propose that Edgar adapted the ballad convention in two ways. One set of his lyrical ballads—'Eldorado,' 'Annabel Lee,' and 'For Annie'—tell their tales in straightforward fashion, without refrains, the style approximating that of 'Israfel,' 'To One in Paradise,' and the songs in 'Al Aaraaf.' The narrative content in these poems deals with the putatively successful escape of the speaker from the 'horrible throbbing / At heart,' from 'the fever called living.' The other set of Edgarpoe's ballads includes 'Lenore,' 'Ulalume,' and 'The Raven': ballads wildly declaimed to a madder music, an insanely inescapable meter and the demented recurrences of far-fetched rhyme and interior rhyme. In these the speaker is desperately trying to burst out of the prison of his passions, but he cannot do so; he is trapped, and can only endure the thumping repetitions of a refrain like 'Nevermore.'

There's one poem which doesn't lend itself very well to my clear schematization. This is 'Bridal Ballad,' which has one of the most unfortunate rhymes in American poetry this side of Thomas Holley Chivers. The rhyme I mean comes toward the end of the third of five stanzas. The ballad-speaker is a lady who has just been re-married after being widowed; but alas, her new husband's 'voice seemed *his* who fell / In the battle down the dell, / And who is happy now.' Already we are supposed to feel a shudder that the bride is not as happy as her dead first husband is. But her new husband—

> . . . spoke to re-assure me,
>   And he kissed my pallid brow,
> While a reverie came o'er me,
> And I sighed to him before me
> (Thinking him dead D'Elormie),
>   'Oh, I am happy now!'

Edgar, how could you bruit a name like 'D'Elormie,' so patently a forced rhyme for 'o'er me' and 'before me'? I can see Edgar chewing his pencil, thinking of a name that would rhyme: Boremie, Coremie, Doremie, Foremie, Goremie . . . How could he invent so unlikely a name?

But that rhyme isn't all that's wrong with 'Bridal Ballad,' it's only a symptom of its graver flaw. Poe is trying to sing the sweet music of 'Israfel' in a situation requiring the hysterical ballad-cadenzas of 'The Raven' or 'Lenore.' The short lines, the insistent feminine rhymes, strain for a lilt at odds with the matter of the tale, a tale he tells more successfully in the prose of 'Ligeia.'

If I'm right about 'Bridal Ballad' then maybe there's something in my theory that Poe's ballads differ from each other because they attempt two separate variations on his masterplot. In the sweet ballads the speaker escapes his mortality. In 'Eldorado,' the knight sets out on his quest for that place, grows old without finding it, at last meets a 'pilgrim shadow' who directs him to press onward, 'Over the Mountains / Of the Moon, / Down the valley of the Shadow.' That's all; nothing is specified, not even the knight's name. It's nothing but the archetype, sung to a tune that suggests the quest may yet be accomplished. If we read 'For Annie' with only its plot in mind, we learn—as we have already learned—that the speaker has been delivered into the quietude of his death-sleep, freed at last from the torments of passion. He is now in good case because reunited in death with 'A dream of the truth / And the beauty of Annie.' In 'Annabel Lee,' the

quest is likewise successful although the speaker is still alive.
The intensity of his love for his bride 'in her sepulchre there
by the sea' is so great that he can sing triumphantly of their
'love that was more than a love,' a love coveted by the angels
who sent a cold wind 'killing and chilling my Annabel Lee.'
Now that she's been chilled and killed, he can go on wor-
shipping her. This must be so because their love was never a
gross passion but a Pure Ideality even when she was alive.
After all, she was only a child and he was a child in that
kingdom by the sea.

'Lenore,' on the other hand, is a ballad of a love thwarted
and a lover tormented. The first and third stanzas lament
her death—Richard Wilbur suggests that these lines are
spoken by 'either the family priest or one of the false friends
of the dead Lenore.' Whoever the speaker, he calls for conventional exequies—'Let the bell toll! . . . Come, let the
burial rite be read—the funeral song be sung!' and he up-
braids her dissenting lover: 'And, Guy de Vere, hast *thou*
no tear?—weep now or never more!' The second and fourth
stanzas are Guy de Vere's impassioned and contemptuous
reply, in which he attacks her wicked family ('Wretches! ye
loved her for her wealth, and ye hated her for her pride; / And
when she fell in feeble health, ye blessed her—that she died').
He refuses to join in their hypocritical rituals which would
but mock her soul 'from the damnéd Earth'; instead,

And I—tonight my heart is light—no dirge will I upraise,
But waft the angel on her flight with a Paean of old days.

Poe worked this poem over and over, publishing it first in
1831 as 'A Paean,' written in simple quatrains, with only
one speaker, the bereaved husband. This 'Paean' is so different from 'Lenore' (it does not even contain her name) that
it may be read as yet another of Poe's ballads; the dramatic
contrast achieved by dividing the tale between two speakers
first appears in the 1843 version, in short lines and sixteen-
line stanzas. The final version of 1844 made numerous
changes of diction and improved the poem further by regu-
larizing the meter into fourteeners. The diction is full of

operatic gesticulation—'Ah, broken is the golden bowl. . . .
See! on yon drear and rigid bier low lies thy love, Lenore. . . .
Peccavimus; yet rave not thus. . . . Avaunt! avaunt!' The
mise en scène, evidently contemporary in 'A Paean' has been
made vaguely medieval in 'Lenore,' and the conflicting views
argued and ranted by Guy de Vere and the friend or priest
—I think he *is* a priest who advises 'let a Sabbath Song / Go
up to God so solemnly the dead may feel no wrong!'—this
dialogue casts the priest as the villain in the piece, a convention familiar to readers of Gothic romances about wicked
prelates and evil monks. So 'Lenore' is a Gothic ballad in
the operatic mode, in which Guy de Vere upholds the ideality
of his pure devotion, while the priest is the spokesman of a
corrupt conventional Christian piety.

For years and years I thought 'Lenore' ridiculous; now,
having figured it out, have I proved too clever by half at the
expense of my own taste? I won't go so far as to say I *like*
the poem, but I find myself more tolerant of its excesses
than I ever thought possible. Now when I read 'Lenore' I
no longer think, Who can suspend disbelief in such incredible
language? No, I imagine the stage of the Met, murky in a
dull amber light, and a scene in an unwritten opera by Ber-
lioz.

Not even the stage of the Met can provide a reality, or
an artifice, sufficient for the mental staging of 'Ulalume.' This
ballad has to be taken on its own terms, or not at all. And
what are its own terms but that the reader or hearer surrender his own will, his own sense of how things are, how
poems move, how the language embodies a meaning—surrender all this to the hypnotic spell of 'Ulalume.' Here Edgarpoe has contrived a meter of mechanical precision and a diction of portentous obscurity. He tells his tale slowly, doubling
back with line after line of refrain-like redundancy, nearly
smothering the story-line in a concatenation of improbable
rhymes. Reading 'Ulalume' is like making a meal of marzi-
pan—there may be nourishment in it but the senses are dead-
ened by the taste, and the aftertaste gives one a pain in the
stomach.

For years, 'Ulalume' made me sick. I refused to surrender
my will, my rhythms, my hold on the reality of language, to
go along on the trip Edgarpoe's melancholy ballad-singer
describes. I have had on occasion—the occasion was the yearly
recurrence of Poe in my course in American Literature—to
flog myself through the poem again and yet again. And to
read all the exegetes and commentators. Of whom Richard
Wilbur is, as he is so often, the most helpful. And now, by
God, now at last I've got it! Look—

> The skies they were ashen and sober;
>   The leaves they were crispéd and sere—
>   The leaves they were withering and sere:
> It was night, in the lonesome October
>   Of my most immemorial year:
> It was hard by the dim lake of Auber,
>   In the misty mid region of Weir:—
> It was down by the dank tarn of Auber,
>   In the ghoul-haunted woodland of Weir.

Simple. What's he saying but that on a certain October night,
an unforgettable sad anniversary, he went for a walk in the
woods? But why is so slight a message delivered in such a
pompous, inflated, elephantine style? When Poe chants 'The
skies they were ashen and sober,' doesn't that periphrastic
they indicate his loss of control of the rhythm, the mark of
a frantic hack padding out the meter of his line? Ye gods, he
does it again in line 2, and yet again in line 3! And then,
introducing his 'dim lake of Auber' and his 'misty mid region
of Weir,' what does he do but *repeat* these lines! Not until
I took seriously the full title of the piece—'Ulalume—A Ballad'—did I recognize what he was up to. A ballad has incre-
mental repetition, tells its story *in song*. Poe's tale can't move
any faster than the music, the music is more important than
any of the words. Poe even scores his words for a particular
composer—for who is Auber but Daniel-François-Esprit
Auber, whose piece 'Le Lac des Fées' was in the popular
repertoire at the time (1847). Lewis Leary, who uncovered
this, also identified 'the misty mid regions of Weir' as al-

luding to the artist Robert Walter Weir of the Hudson River
School, a romantic landscape-painter. So I have to conclude
that Poe, setting his scene with the help of a faëry ballet and
a wispy painting, is not actually in the woods of Westchester
County at all, but is already in an ideal landscape imaginable
only to artists and bereaved lovers. At first convinced of madness in Poe's method, perhaps, I began to suspect, there was
also method in his madness.

> Here once, through an alley Titanic,
>   Of cypress, I roamed with my Soul—
>   Of cypress, with Psyche, my Soul.
> These were days when my heart was volcanic
>   As the scoriac rivers that roll—
>   As the lavas that restlessly roll
> Their sulphurous currents down Yaanek
>   In the ultimate climes of the Pole—
> That groan as they roll down Mount Yaanek
>   In the realms of the Boreal Pole.

Ten lolloping lines to say, 'I roamed with my Soul when my
heart was as turbulent as a volcano'—in fact, like Mount
covered Mount Erebus in the Antarctic, hence 'the ultimate
Yaanek, which Edward Davidson identifies as the recently dis-
climes of the Pole.' Well, all this sound and fury signifies
something, doesn't it?

The ballad continues as a debate between Self and Soul,
conducted in an allegorical nocturnal landscape. Self is swayed
by the heart, when

>   a miraculous crescent
>   Arose with a duplicate horn—
>   Astarte's bediamonded crescent
>   Distinct with its duplicate horn.

Which in the language of 'Ulalume' means the planet Venus,
the image of the Goddess of Love. 'And I said—"She is warmer
than Dian: / She rolls through an ether of sighs . . ."' Better
watch out, Self, for this Astarte may be warmer than Diana
but not as chaste: she's the figure of *passion*, so not to wonder
that your enthusiasm for her makes Psyche droop her wings.

Self 'pacified Psyche and kissed her / And tempted her out of
her gloom'; they take off in pursuit of Astarte, since Self
thinks she'll lead them 'To the Lethean peace in the skies'—
but they're brought up short

> By the door of a legended tomb:—
> And I said—"What is written, sweet sister,
> On the door of this legended tomb?"
> She replied: "Ulalume—Ulalume!—
> 'Tis the vault of thy lost Ulalume!"

Ulalume? There's a chiming euphony among the names
of Poe's lost loves: Ulalume, Eulalie, Helen, Lenore. Ulalume,
surely, is a nonce-word, and it has been suggested that it
means 'light of the dead,' for *Ule* is the Turkish word meaning 'dead,' as in 'Ule Deguisi,' which Poe misquoted in a
note to 'Al Aaraaf' as the Turkish name for the Dead Sea.
With these exotic names—Auber, Weir, Yaanek, Ulalume
—Poe is being at once exact and diaphonous, imputing the
meaning in the music, such as it is.

The rest of the tale goes on another two stanzas—Self's
heart 'it grew ashen and sober,' and Self recollects that tonight is the very date that he 'brought a dread burden down
here'—that is, he buried Ulalume a year ago, and now, on
this night of October (what can it be but the 31st, All Hal-
low's Eve, when the dead have a special influence upon the
living), he has *unwittingly revisited her tomb*. And Self and
Psyche conclude that the 'woodlandish ghouls,' that is, the
spirits of the dead who possess the dim woods of Auber on
this night, have tried to assuage their grief with 'the spectre
of . . . This sinfully scintillant planet.'

Self, Self, how could you be so unwitting? How wander
through such unforgettable landscape without knowing you'd
been there before? The fact that Self doesn't even know where
he is should tell us, this ballad-singer is mental. He has been
driven wild with grief, his heart is a seething volcano of scoriac rivers, and he wanders *in a trance*. Some have thought
that the Astarte image signifies that the singer's heart has
been drawn away from the path of Psyche—the unending

worship of his dead Ulalume—toward a new love, a more gross, less pure, heartfelt passion for a living woman, from which Psyche only with difficulty—and with the aid of the ghouls, or shades of the dead—redeems him.

That seems reasonable. But why, why, so many obfuscations in the telling? Why bury this kernel of meaning under such rivers of lava that roll?

Typical of Edgarpoe. His art conceals while it reveals, reveals while it conceals. Nothing is further from his intention than to sing a simple song, or use the language of clear and common speech. These meters, rhymes, redundancies, the portentous tone, the inflated diction, all, like the early references to musician and painter, put the actual experience at an aesthetic distance, impose upon it a new form, an expression completely different from that given to gross affairs like passions and hungers of the flesh, a language other than that in which this workaday world haggles over prices and orders breakfast. To explore his inward soulscape Edgarpoe had to take the vocables of this workaday dialect and from such unpromising stuff create moods and meanings ne'er attempted yet in prose or rhyme. Mallarmé understood his intention, but —I have asked it before and I ask it again—did Edgarpoe *really* 'donner un sens plus pur aux mots de la tribu'? Un sens *plus pur?* Aux mots *de la tribu?* Or did he obfuscate—not purify—the language of the human tribe, in order to disembody language from its gross husks of meaning. And what remained—what Edgarpoe wanted—was the rhythms of the songs sung by ghouls.

Ballads sung by ghouls and madmen. For the narrator of 'Ulalume' is in a scoriac frenzy, insane with grief and frustration. So is the ballad singer of 'The Raven,' although Poe very cleverly doesn't have him begin his ballad as though aware of the fact. But the ballad he sings tells us, shows us how it happened. In the course of his own ballad he traces the inexorable course of his condition, from his initial weakness and weariness, through his regretful grief at the death of Lenore, to a frenzied and masochistic persecution of his own soul. The plot of the ballad is, This is the way the nar-

rator went mad of grief for Lenore. (The narrator is doubtless
that same Guy de Vere whom we left at her bier in an earlier
ballad.) All this is told in stanzas which combine inexorable
metrical regularity with a rhyme and interior-rhyme scheme
of fiendish complication—everything not only ending with but
tending toward the one unbending, shiver-sending word in
the refrain: 'Nevermore!'

Edgarpoe at last wrote a poem based upon the repetition
of a single word, that word said o'er and o'er until its meaning becomes as nothing, or legion; the mesmeric spell of the
same repeated syllables overpowering the mind of his narrator, the sonorous chiming and sorrowful repetitions of 'Nevermore' sweeping away all propensity for independent thought.

Thus the mind of his narrator (Guy de Vere) and of his
reader—me—is paralyzed by all those Nevermores. They work
their spell all the more inexorably because spoken by no one,
spoken by a bird—the only bird (save the paroquet in 'Romance' who taught young Edgar his alphabet to say) with the
power of imitating human speech. The bird repeats its one-
word glossary of woe with an insane regularity, a regularity
which invites the still madder plausibility lent it by the narrator's *arranging his questions* not only so that they occupy
the regularly spaced interstices between the bird's cacophonous utterances, but arranging them so that the raven's single
word becomes a lingua franca of an oracular world, giving
the inevitable reply as though decreed by the fates to the in-
creasingly self-lacerating and desperate questions of its inter-
locutor.

Or so it seems, as long as we willingly sink into the intellectual stupor which Edgarpoe's pounding rhythms and clang-
ing rhymes are intended to produce in us. Just let your mind
fight back, just a little, against the maniacal regularity, the
hypnotic fanfare in which the same combinations of rhyme
recur with the inexorability of a Chinese water torture—just
resist the spell a little bit, and the whole contraption suddenly comes apart at the seams. You shake your ears and your
tongue gasps for a fresh breath. What an imposture. Are we
supposed, supinely, to admit the plausibility of a raven knock-

ing on the door of a lonely chamber on a stormy night, entering as the door is flung open, installing itself upon the bust of
Pallas, and forever croaking 'Nevermore'? Are we expected to
believe that the youth in his chamber actually would address
the errant bird as

"Prophet!" said I, "thing of evil!—prophet still, if bird
    or devil!—
Whether Tempter sent, or whether tempest tossed thee
    here ashore,
Desolate yet all undaunted, on this desert land enchanted—
On this home by Horror haunted—tell me truly, I implore—
Is there—*is* there balm in Gilead?—tell me—tell me, I
    implore!"

And we're not supposed to laugh when

                     Quoth the Raven, "Nevermore."

Now, I confess that one of the chief powers exercised upon
me by the poems of Edgarpoe is the power to make me wince.
As I once told an audience in France. I'm prone to wince
because—well, maybe not so much because of Poe as because
of my own taste in verse. Growing up, as I did, when the
New Criticism was shaking the periwigs from their Chairs
in the graduate schools and each new issue of the *Kenyon*
or *Sewanee* review exposed still another poem of Donne's or
Eliot's to the deft scalpel of a skilled explicator, I took it as
a matter of faith that the highest art in poetry is that which
heals dissociation of sensibility, the poem that thinks and
feels simultaneously. Being a child of the age, I didn't question the cognate apothegms (a) that poetry which thinks
at the expense of feeling is but versified prose; and (b) that
verse which feels without the analytical aid and enrichment
of the intellect is but slush or musical nonsense. How could
I fit the strophes of Edgarpoe into a sensibility so straitened
by training and circumstance?

Not only the foregoing, but also other, later accretions of
the Sensibility of the Age worked on me against the poems
of Poe. The idea that the language of poetry should not be a

special, artificial diction, but should partake of the demotic power of street-corner speech—this notion, enacted in an out-of-date way by Wordsworth and revived in cracker-barrel fashion by Frost and Williams, is rampant in our land. It is intrinsic with other muzzy notions about democracy, hatred of elitism in art as in politics, and a widespread need to accept—even to make imagination dine upon and digest—the very banality of the thing-ridden life which surrounds us. All of these impulses militate against one's finding plausible Edgarpoe's entire poetic enterprise. His desperate avoidance of ordinary life, of usual language, of the flexible rhythms of actual speech, all tend to make his verse seem either grotesquely incompetent or purposively artificial, mannered, and ridiculous.

So, although it was Eliot who helped to rescue Edgarpoe from the opprobrium of an age which in English-speaking countries considered his *œuvre* jejune, it was also Eliot who had earlier on urged Anglo-American taste away from any possibility of appreciating what Edgarpoe had wrought. History has many cunning passages. Turn the corner once again, and look—it's Edgarpoe himself who has so well instructed us in *explication de texte* that for years, for decades, we've used his own analytical method of reading poetry—against his poems. For what, after all, is Poe's famous essay, 'The Philosophy of Composition,' but a demonstration of how he wrote—and how we should read—'The Raven'? Unless, by an act of will (like that by means of which I wrote those appreciative paragraphs about 'The Raven' a page or so ago) we allow Poe's fantastication of language and the insistence of his meter to mesmerize our judgment, we will be likely to agree with Eliot's remark about 'The Philosophy of Composition':

> It is difficult for us to read that essay without reflecting, that if Poe plotted out his poem with such calculation, he might have taken a little more pains over it: the result hardly does credit to the method.

I propose to re-read 'The Philosophy of Composition' and to try to determine—once and for all!—whether Poe's professed method has merit, or whether the whole show is a put-on. We mustn't forget how much Edgar A. Poe liked to trip us up—us, his readers, the very ones on whose complicity with his designs his fame and immortality depend. Is Poe a mad dog, biting the hands that would clasp his hand? Or is his setting of intricate intellectual traps indispensable to the exercise of his genius, and those traps being baited for and then sprung upon *us* the unavoidable circumstances to which we must accommodate ourselves in order to savor the strange gifts and visions which Poe's genius dictates that he give us on no other terms? What, then, is the 'philosophy' which Poe secretes in his poetic compositions so that he may have the duplicitous pleasure of revealing it, so that he may revel in both the witless ignorance of those who cannot comprehend him and in injuring the sensibilities of those who can but find that they've been diddled by his mastering mind? Let me not conclude so prematurely: for perhaps in Edgarpoe's philosophy there *is* a verity about the poetic process— how the poet makes the poem, what the poem does to the reader, what the meaning of the poem means. That's what he says is there; let's see.

III

The Rationale of Verse

With 'The Raven,' Edgarpoe hit the jackpot. At first though there was a bad patch: he travelled to Philadelphia from New York to offer his great poem to the proprietor of *Graham's Magazine,* and was refused! A witness recorded years afterward that Graham and several others in his office gave Poe fifteen dollars 'as charity,' although they 'condemned the poem.' George R. Graham, take a bow. You goofed. But Graham knew Poe, had published his tales and reviews, in fact had hired him for a few years to help edit the magazine. So he knew how desperate was Edgar's need for money. Perhaps the reminiscence of Horace Wemyss Smyth is in fact accurate (though most of the eyewitness accounts of Poe cited in T. O. Mabbott's crazyquilt edition of the *Poems* seem improbable afterthoughts). Graham was a kind man, though as an editor he let 'The Raven' fly away.

Back in New York, Poe was soon richer by another fifteen dollars. 'The Raven' was bought for publication in *The American Review.* But editor George H. Colton, who ran it in his February number in 1845, seemed to have had doubts. He offered 'The Raven' with an apologia, perhaps composed by Poe (since it commends the poem for its intricate versification), but the signature to the poem is a pseudonym: '—— Quarles.' No matter, by then 'The Raven' had already appeared in the *Evening Mirror* on January 29th, for Edgarpoe was determined to be known as its author. Luckily this

paper's editor was Nathaniel Parker Willis, Poe's friend and
himself a minor poet of greater popularity than genius, yet an
honorable man. Mabbott, who turned up every stone along
Poe's path, doesn't say whether he got yet *another* fee from
the *Mirror*. But once the poem was out it was widely reprinted, imitated, and parodied. Poe Poe Poe Poe was now
a household name. Forevermore.

He was also a shrewd magazinist and knew how to con-
solidate his popular acclaim. So, a year later, proposing 'how
interesting a magazine paper might be written by any author'
who could reveal his own processes of composition, he naturally enough chose to do so with his own 'Raven' as the work
under analysis. Poe had the satisfaction of placing the essay
in the magazine which had first refused the poem: *Graham's*.
I won't go so far as to say that he *wrote* 'The Philosophy of
Composition' in order to make George R. Graham eat raven,
but that may well have been among his motives.

Of course he provides another motive:

> It is my design to render it manifest that no one point
> in its composition is referable either to accident or intui-
> tion—that the work proceeded, step by step, to its comple-
> tion with the precision and rigid consequence of a
> mathematical problem.

The rest of the essay, as everyone knows, carries out the proposed demonstration to the satisfaction, more or less, of, *inter
alia*, Baudelaire, Mallarmé, Verlaine, T. S. Eliot, and most
students as well as symbolist poets and explicators, except
for Yvor Winters and others whose viscera are numbed by
fear of The Intentional Fallacy.

But other fallacies than the Intentional may be intentional,
or unintentional. One of the things we must discover, or at
best decide, is whether Poe's 'Philosophy of Composition' is
in fact fallacious. Another is whether the poem and its philosophy of composition can possibly be as intentional as Poe
maintains. It is the *imagination* we are endeavoring to understand. I wish to discover, beyond cavil, whether this faculty is
indeed, as commonly supposed, an intuitive (and therefore

mysterious) process of associative 'thought' in which thought
may embody feeling and the mind leap inconsequently from
cause to consequence by invisible steps, or none, achieving
through metaphor, simile, and other such *enjambements* of
meaning a meaning toward which disciplined rational thinking might labor long but in vain; or whether 'imagination,' so-
called, is indeed, as Edgarpoe so stoutly maintains, itself a
species of such rational thinking, conducted, as he says, 'with
the precision and rigid consequence of a mathematical problem.'

And, assuming Edgarpoe's radical claim to be true, I must
next inquire why and how he came to make this discovery
so different from the traditional assumptions of mankind and
S. T. Coleridge.

When a philosopher—whether of composition or any other
human faculty—proposes a completely rational explanation
of a complex action but at the same time speaks in similes
and metaphors, I, being a controversialist and obstructor of
argument at heart, am inclined to analyse not the argument
but the metaphors. Poe, in getting his philosophical voyage
under way, alludes in his first four paragraphs to the premeditated solutions of detective stories (quoting a letter from
Dickens); and compares the composing of a poem to the
management of theatrical props and machinery: 'the wheels
and pinions—the tackle for scene-shifting—the stepladders
and demon-traps—the cock's feathers, the red paint and the
black patches, which, in ninety-nine cases out of the hundred, constitute the properties of the literary *histrio*.' Is Poe
then himself a 'literary histrio,' like 99 percent of his kind?
Or, as a genius, is he by definition himself the 1 percent who
have no truck with costume, make-up, tackle? Ah, but see the
metaphorical *environs* of the passage: detective solutions,
mathematical rigor. All points to the one inference: Imagination is a conscious and rational power which shifts scenes,
spins wheels and pinions, solves problems by a plan made
aforetimes.

This conclusion surprises me. It should surprise any of us
who has swotted out the meanings in Poe's poems. 'Sonnet—

To Science,' 'Al Aaraaf,' 'Dream-Land': are *these* glimpses of
sublunary transport the result of a linguistic game of chess?
I don't believe it! But surely Baudelaire, Eliot, and all that
lot can't have been *all* wrong in revering Poe as an aesthetician.
Maybe I haven't delved deeply enough into his philosophy.

So let's begin at the beginning. Which is to say, at the
end:

> It is only with the *dénouement* constantly in view that we
> can give a plot its indispensible air of consequence, or
> causation, by making incidents, and especially the tone at
> all points, tend to the development of the intention.

But this *dénouement* is predicated upon the *effect* it will have
upon the reader. Last things first. Therefore, Edgar argues,

> I prefer commencing with the consideration of an *effect*.
> Keeping originality *always* in view—for he is false to him-
> self who ventures to dispense with so obvious and so easily
> attainable a source of interest—I say to myself, in the first
> place, 'Of all the innumerable effects, or impressions, of
> which the heart, the intellect, or (more generally) the soul
> is susceptible, what one shall I, on the present occasion
> select.'

Exactly so. For just as the use of one word in a poem rules
out the use of any of its synonyms in that spot, so, in the very
conception of the poem itself, each step makes unavailable all
the alternative choices which that step causes to be rejected,
and therefore the choice of which effect to wring upon the
reader's susceptible soul is doubtless the most significant
choice in the entire process of poetic composition.

But before Edgar excogitates the steps of his process he
offers a demurrer; and so I enter it here:

> Let us dismiss as irrelevant to the poem, *per se*, the
> circumstance—or say the necessity—which, in the first place,
> gave rise to the intention of composing *a* poem that should
> suit at once the popular and the critical taste.

(Note the discrimination between circumstance and necessity; the former might imply the need to sell a verse to *Gra-*

ham's to pay the rent, the latter the impossibility of the Poet's mind suppressing what his soul must utter.) And so, having dismissed as irrelevant *per se* the impulse that led his mental hand to set the spring by which to catch the reader's soul, he then, logically enough, takes up the important question of the dimensions of the poetic trap. Having failed by his own lights to make a successful effect-producing poetic mechanism with 'Al Aaraaf,' with 'Politian,' or with 'Tamerlane,' Poe not surprisingly concludes,

> What we term a long poem is, in fact, merely a succession of brief ones—that is to say, of brief poetical effects. It is needless to demonstrate that a poem is such, only inasmuch as it intensely excites, by elevating the soul; and all intense excitements are, through a psychal necessity, brief.

Indeed, he avows that 'the extent of a poem may be made to bear mathematical relation to its merit . . . for it is clear that the brevity must be in direct ratio of the intensity of the intended effect.' By a mathematical process best known to himself, Poe arrives at the solution to his problem without having bothered the reader with the intervening equations. His desideratum is a poem short enough to be read at one sitting—but not too short; and aiming at 'that degree of excitement which I deemed not above the popular, while not below the critical, taste, I reached at once what I conceived the proper length for my intended poem—a length of about one hundred lines. It is, in fact, a hundred and eight.' How splendid! Only eight lines beyond the mark! Surely we can tolerate a mean error of eight percent in the mathematical precision of this process.

But I nearly overpassed an observation underemphasized by the syntax of these Poetics: Edgar would strike a level 'not above the popular, while not below the critical, taste. . . .' How circumspect an ambition, to please both the *hoi polloi* and the *cognoscenti*—exactly the double-deal, or compromise, which the editor of, or contributor to, a literary magazine *must* make in his need to please those so often

mutually exclusive constituencies, the public and the critics
of taste. In fact, as Michael Allen shows in his study, *Poe
and the British Magazine Tradition*, this was the predicament and the aim of the very journals on which Poe modelled
his style, from which he imitated his plot situations and
adapted his tone and framed his conceptions of how to edit
a journal in America. The horror tale in *Blackwood's*, so crucial to Edgar Poe's development, itself developed as an effort
to attract the sensation-loving vulgar readers into the same
tent as the loftier reviews and articles. And of this tenet
of pragmatic journalism Edgar Poe here makes a universal
law of aesthetics. How very like him.

Having determined length, he next considers subject.
'Beauty,' he says, 'is the sole legitimate province of the poem.'
And by beauty he means 'that intense and pure elevation of
soul—not of intellect, or of heart . . . which is experienced
in consequence of contemplating "the beautiful." '

It will be seen how forcefully Edgarpoe enacts into his
ars poetica the division of the sensibility assumed by the
facultative psychology which lingered on from the eighteenth
century. Here he develops the consequences of the distinction he had made at the end of his earliest poetic manifesto,
fifteen years before, the 'Letter to B——' prefacing his first
volume of *Poems* (1831):

> A poem, in my opinion, is opposed to work of science by
> having, for its *immediate* object, pleasure, not truth; to
> romance, by having for its object an *indefinite* instead of a
> *definite* pleasure, being a poem only so far as this object
> is attained. . . .

—sentiments which will be familiar to readers who have already read them elsewhere, viz.,

> A poem is that species of composition, which is opposed to
> works of science, by proposing for its *immediate* object
> pleasure, not truth;
>
> —*Biographia Literaria*, Ch. XIV

which comes *mighty close* to plagiarism on the part of that
original genius Edgarpoe. Less direct is his debt to the rest of
Coleridge's sentence—

> . . . [the poem] is discriminated by proposing to itself
> such delight from the *whole*, as is compatible with a dis-
> tinct gratification from each component *part*.

This becomes, for Poe, subsumed in his concentration upon
the effect of the whole, to which each attribute and element
of the poem's construction must be subordinate.

The philosophical breadth of Coleridge underlies Poe's
acute narrowness as the pyramid on the Great Seal of the
United States at its summit supports one assured and un-
blinking eye. Inheriting the faculty psychology, as did all of
the Romantic poet-philosophers of composition, Poe makes
more mutually exclusive the domains of the faculties, which
in their poetics other Romantics, like Shelley and Emerson,
were trying to bring together. Thus Shelley: 'The great instrument of moral good is the imagination, and poetry adminis-
ters to the effect by acting upon the cause.' The Neoplatonism of his 'Defence of Poetry' makes imagination the
perceptor of the universal harmony between the beautiful
and the good. Emerson, with a like philosophy, is driven in
wintry Concord to express it in a myth of his own devising:

> For the Universe has three children, born at one time,
> which reappear under different names in every system of
> thought, whether they be called cause, operation, and ef-
> fect; or, more poetically, Jove, Pluto, Neptune; or, theolog-
> ically, Father, the Spirit and the Son; but which we will
> call here the Knower, the Doer and the Sayer. These stand
> respectively for the love of truth, for the love of good, and
> for the love of beauty. These three are equal. Each is
> that which he is, essentially, so that he cannot be sur-
> mounted or analyzed, and each of these three has the power
> of the others latent in him and his own, patent.
>
> —'The Poet,' 1844

What Shelley and Emerson would join, Poe would rend
asunder. For as we know from his poems, Beauty is the prov-

ince of the soul, and hence of poetry; Truth, of the intellect; Passion, of the heart. And Passion is the enemy of Beauty, and Beauty is the only Truth, and poetry to be true to its truth must be pure, not impure. So having sliced into constituent parts the *gestalt* of the human psyche, Poe is free to make the most of the fragments he is left with: Beauty. Soul. Poetry.

And now come the syllogistic steps by which we are inexorably moved from the foregoing rigid exclusions toward a domain of absolute necessity still more rigidly maintained, still more exclusive in its concern. 'All experience,' says Edgarpoe, shows us that the *tone* of Beauty's 'highest manifestation' is 'one of *sadness.* . . . Beauty . . . in its supreme development, invariably excites the sensitive soul to tears.' Deny this, and you identify your own soul as insensitive. 'Melancholy,' we sensitive souls agree, 'is thus the most legitimate of all the poetical tones.'

So, let's see where we are. Poe's poem will address itself to the highest manifestation of poetry's supreme province, Beauty, rendered in a Melancholy Tone, and it will accomplish the excitation of the reader's sensitive soul in the space of a single sitting, i.e., within a hundred lines. And now, confesses the poet,

> I betook myself to ordinary induction, with the view of obtaining some artistic piquancy which might serve me as a key-note in the construction of the poem—some pivot upon which the whole structure might turn. . . . I did not fail to perceive immediately that no one had been so universally employed as the *refrain.* . . . I considered it, however, with regard to its susceptibility of improvement, and soon saw it to be in a primitive condition. . . . I resolved to diversify, and so heighten, the effect, by adhering, in general, to the monotone of sound, while I continually varied that of thought: that is to say, I determined to produce continuously novel effects, by the variation *of the application* of the *refrain*—the *refrain* itself remaining, for the most part, unvaried.

That's positively brilliant. See how Poe combines the charms of repetition with those of variation so as at once to enjoy the effects of both familiarity and surprise, soothing the *ear* with the repetition while surprising the *mind* by the *altered significance* of the similar sounds. The best refrain for this purpose, says Poe, is a single word. By logical analysis he shortly concludes that such a word 'must be sonorous and susceptible of protracted emphasis,' that it should possess 'the long *o* as the most sonorous vowel, in connection with *r* as the most producible consonant.' Although under no circumstances would I propose *r* as, of all things, 'the most producible consonant' (Mmm?), I would myself have leapt upon '*sonorous*' as the ideal refrain-word. But Poe makes a contrary claim: 'It would have been absolutely impossible to overlook the word "Nevermore." In fact, it was the very first which presented itself.'

But see into what a box one's mathematical precision can thrust one. Look what Edgar is stuck with: he must contrive a circumstance making plausible the continued repetition of the sonorous word, 'Nevermore,' *in a context of continually altered meaning*. How will he do this? His solution, as we all know, is absolutely inspired:

> I did not fail to perceive that this difficulty arose solely from the pre-assumption that the word was to be so continuously spoken by a *human* being. . . . Here, then immediately arose the idea of a *non*-reasoning creature capable of speech . . .

At first he thought of a parrot, but then, reminding himself of the Melancholy tone, the notion of a Raven supervened. And now—see how the solution of each problem leads inexorably to the next problem demanding a solution—now, having settled upon Beauty as subject, Melancholy as tone, 'Nevermore' as refrain, 100+ lines as length, and a raven as speaker—now, he must ask himself,

> 'Of all melancholy topics, what, according to the *universal* understanding of mankind, is the *most* melancholy?' Death was the obvious reply. 'And when,' I said, 'is this most melancholy of topics most poetical?' . . . the answer, here also, is obvious—'When it most closely allies itself to *Beauty*: the death, then, of a beautiful woman is, unques-

tionably, the most poetical topic in the world—and equally
is it beyond doubt that the lips best suited for such topic
are those of a bereaved lover.'

What a curious coincidence! This conclusion, so irresistibly
arrived at, points out, as the most poetical poems in the
world, the very writings—'Lenore,' 'Annabel Lee,' 'Ulalume,'
'For Annie'—of none other than Edgar Élan Poet. And now
all he has to do is set in motion, by a mechanically and
mathematically precise process, all those elements already
mentioned, to which is now added a bereaved lover.

At just this point in his precreative cogitations Edgarpoe
realized that he could contrive a progression of queries to
be posed by the lover to the raven, all of which require the
answer 'Nevermore.' Believing the bird to be merely repeating a lesson by rote, the lover, says Poe,

> experiences a phrenzied pleasure in so modeling his ques-
> tions as to receive from the *expected* 'Nevermore' the most
> delicious because most intolerable of sorrow . . .

Here then the poem may be said to have its beginning—
at the end, where all works of art should begin—and
Poe maintains he wrote the antepenultimate stanza first, so
that he might work backwards from his climax as well as set
out the metrical arrangement and rhyme scheme.

Like Edgar, I too believe that in our end is our beginning.
(I also believe, with Eliot, the reverse.) At issue here is, with
which end of 'The Raven' did Poe *really* begin? The beginning of the poem? The end of the poem? The beginning of
'The Philosophy of Composition,' which purports to describe the inception of the poem? Nevermore. I say Edgarpoe
began his poem at the very point which concludes his demonstration. Look, here is the clue:

> The raven addressed, answers with its customary word,
> 'Nevermore'—a word which finds immediate echo in the
> melancholy heart of the student, who, giving utterance
> aloud to certain thoughts suggested by the occasion, is again
> startled by the fowl's repetition of 'Nevermore.'

(The clue is 'a word which finds immediate echo in the melancholy heart of the student'—*an echo of what?*)

> The student now guesses the case, but is impelled . . . by the human thirst for self-torture, and in part by superstition, to propound such queries to the bird as may bring him, the lover, the most of the luxury of sorrow, through the anticipated answer 'Nevermore.'

The human thirst for self-torture . . . the luxury of sorrow! THESE are the themes of 'The Raven,' these, and not merely the poet's plot to excite the soul of a reader by the contemplation of Beauty. Even as he gives his game away, though, Edgarpoe still has his eye on the coiled springs and levers of his mechanism. The man is a daimonic master-mechanic of his watchmaker world:

> But in subjects so handled, however skillfully, or with however vivid an array of incident, there is always a certain hardness or nakedness, which repels the artistical eye. Two things are invariably required—first, some amount of complexity, or more properly, adaptation; and, secondly, some amount of suggestiveness—some under-current, however indefinite, of meaning. It is this latter, in especial, which imparts to a work of art so much of that *richness* . . . which we are too fond of confounding with the *ideal.*

And not until the last stanza, says Poe, does he give the reader cause 'to seek a moral in all that has previously been narrated.'

> It is not until the very last line of the very last stanza that the intention of making [the Raven] emblematical of *Mournful and Never-Ending Remembrance* is permitted distinctly to be seen.

Is it possible that Edgarpoe, for reasons of his own, has conducted his dissection and re-assembly of 'The Raven' backwards? That the circumstance, or necessity of the poem's composition made ineluctable the creation of an emblem of Mournful and Never-Ending Remembrance? That the necessity or circumstance from which the need for such an

emblem derived made unavoidable for the poet both the
luxury of sorrow and the attempt, reiterated throughout his
eighteen stanzas, to slake the human thirst for self-torture?
Is it possible that the mainspring of Poe's versified soul-
catcher is his own spiritual masochism, his unappeasable
pursuit of the phantom of a love eternally denied and forever mourned? The student, half-dreaming in a reverie over
an old book, is the lover of that will-o'-the-wisp figure, that
disembodied Mother, Muse, and unravish'd Mistress, who
presides over *all* the poetical productions, whether in verse
or prose, of Edgar Allan Poe.

A philosophy of composition indeed. An *ars poetica* for a
haunted sublunary mime of the unavoidable motions re-
hearsed by *his own* soul and imposed by his mind upon my
soul, your soul, our souls . . . The artist's unassuageable
need is to project upon the rest of mankind the terrors and
the losses, the sorrows and the insatiate longings of his own
soul. Even then, even then, he does not cease to suffer; but
his anguished days and self-tortured nights are made more
bearable—just a bit more bearable—by his satisfaction at the
successful exercise of skills upon the intractable materials—
the circumstances and necessities—provided by his own soul.

The heart it is, in Edgarpoe's divisive psychology, which
suffers, which feels the miserable passions of love-longing, of
loss, of sorrow, of grief never-ending. The soul it is which
rises above these passions, poor miserable human afflictions
that they are, by partaking itself and taking the reader toward a realm of pure being—or pure nonbeing—where passion is unknown. The odd thing is, though, that for Poe (because he is human) the way to escape from the toils of
passion is *through* passion. Through the human thirst for
self-torture, through the luxury of sorrow. In the absolute
depths of his misery there is a joy because what have those
passions stirred into action if not the soul?

But even Poe cannot dwell continually in self-torture or
luxuriate endlessly in never-ending sorrow. To do so would
be to surrender himself to the passivity latent within him,
at the cost of extinguishing, perhaps forever, the active

principle also latent within him. At the very moment that
he luxuriates in his precious sorrow and turns the screw of
self-torture tighter still, his active principle is reasserting itself, striving to control the uncontrollable obsessions which
haunt him. But control them how?

Control them in his verse. Control them by making of
these passions an intricate mechanism for the production
of the effects of passion in another person's soul—transferring
from the Self to the Other both the anguish of self-torture
and the sybaritic luxury of a sorrow passive and never-ending.
'The Philosophy of Composition' is Edgarpoe's analytical
description of how to do this—how to transfer from himself
to me, to you, those symptoms, those sufferings, those
haunted joys.

Yet it is a remarkable achievement *in candor*. It is the
first and perhaps still the fullest and the frankest self-
exposure of the artist in his workshop. If, and only if, poems
were indeed written completely on rational principles, how
else could a poem be plotted, composed, and assembled save
along the strategic lines detailed by Edgarpoe? As critics, as
analysts of literature, even, sometimes, as poets, we find it
a convenient fiction to assume that this is indeed the way
that poems are made. Every critical discussion, of whatever
kind, requires a full commitment to only a partial truth.

Poe knew this. Although he gives us no sources, he does
warn us, at the very end of his essay, to look more deeply
than his autopsy of 'The Raven' delved: look, he says, for
'some under-current, however indefinite, of meaning.' Even
as he revels in having so dextrously performed a complete
anatomy of his poem, he cannot stop his mouth from whis-
pering 'This wonderful dissection has merely skinned my
Raven, it hasn't exposed the vital organs or the soul.'

In everything written by Edgar Poe we must always seek
the Soul. 'Ah, Psyche, from the regions which / Are Holy
Land.'

Yet Poe could not *live* in those regions. At best, he could
dream there, while living here. And since his experience
of that 'psychal process' showed him how brief a span of time

is encompassed by transcendence—not more than it takes to
read a poem of 108 lines—he sought solace and strength in
the next-best thing, which is thinking.

Yes, the Mind in control of the passions which afflict the
Heart becomes the guiding pilot conducting Poe's tripartite
Self upward to the realms and regions properly the Soul's.
Therefore Poe's concentration upon himself as craftsman is
not mere vanity, or an aberrant infatuation with his own
verbal resources. No, he must attend to the use of the power
tools which shape his poetry, for it's the power as much as
the craft that he wants to be sure of wielding. The intellectual power. Even if to wield it he must pretend (or maybe
even actually convince himself) that the poem, the work of
art, is a wholly conscious construct. That way, the poet is
completely in charge of the manipulation of his own sufferings.

It would appear that one set of needs is served by Poe's
insistence upon the obligatorily ratiocinative method of his
composition, another by his obligatory subject and tone.
What is the relation between his claim that imagination is a
rational and orderly premeditated process and his need to
drape it in crepe at the bier of a beautiful woman? What is
the connection but that the straitjacket method enables the
poet to deal with his obsessive and inescapable subject by
compelling him to think about something else, something
other than the woe vibrating within him which to think of
would overcome him. So the method of his art enables the
madness of his matter to be spoken.

But surely this cannot account for the influence of Poe's
philosophy on the symbolist poets? Oh, but it can. Just as
Poe (or Yeats, or Swinburne) would put the intellect to sleep
with the regularity and insistence of their cadences, so as to
liberate the free association of the matter of the unconscious,
so too can those associative processes be encouraged when the
mind is so completely occupied with the management of
verse technique that it cannot interfere with that subliminal
allegory flowing beneath the manifest level of mental

activity. That is why, in a good poem, form is the tensor of theme.

Yet for Poe there must have been still another reason why he *had* to believe that imagination was controlled by thought. 'Thought', for Poe, is the activity by which man most closely resembles God. Ergo the most puissant man is he whose mental processes most closely resemble, in their operation if not in their scope, those of the deity. Such a 'thinker' is nowhere to be found in Poe's poems, where the protagonists are without exception suffering, passive beings. But if his theory of poetry denied him the creation of such a personage in verse, nothing need keep Poe from such exercise of 'thought' in his own criticism. He is indeed just such a 'thinker' in his 'Philosophy of Composition,' a master-creator working out the details of his preconceived plan, observing himself in the act of conceiving, choosing, shaping, succeeding. And, as Eliot has said, because of this self-awareness, Poe pointed the way to the symbolist poets, the way to their self-consciousness as artists: Makers, not merely Finders.

Poe's criticism of others, as well as his self-justifying scrutiny of his own practice, exhibits his mind at work, which is often the same thing as his mind at play. Like most of Poe's readers, I suppose, I didn't read his critical pieces until long after his tales had become familiars of my adolescence. Turning at last from the demented narrators of 'The Black Cat' and 'Berenice' to the character who, as a critic, assessed the work of his contemporaries in reviews by turns sympathetic, demanding, acidulous, or parodic, could I believe the creator of such convincing madmen to be himself possessed of an intellect of power and equability?

Although for decades Poe's reputation as a critic, like that as a poet and tale-teller, suffered from the evil character given him by Griswold, it's now generally acknowledged that he was the first critic in this country to insist that literary work be measured by literary standards alone. True, his own standards were not only high but a little odd: he couldn't keep himself from overpraising poetesses who wrote elegies to dead lovers, finding in the effusions of such nobodies as

Mrs. Amelia Welby and Elizabeth Oakes Smith the nearly articulated intimations of the theme which became the sole burden of his own verse, and its undoing. But when I read Poe's notes on poetry—not on contemporary poems (it was part of his hard luck to have to review mountains of balderdash; the 1830s and 1840s, before the American Renascence, were the dark ages of our poetry)—Poe on poetic principles makes a lot of good sense. In fact not until Ezra Pound's early essays, like 'A Few Don'ts for Imagists,' did anyone attend with such clarity and precision to the *craft* of verse. How eminently sensible is this advice, how useful to any young writer struggling to manage his material, the language—

> Perfection of rhyme is attainable only in the combination of the two elements, Equality and Unexpectedness. But as evil cannot exist without good, so unexpectedness must arise from expectedness. We do not contend for mere arbitrariness of rhyme. In the first place we must have equidistant or regularly recurring rhymes, to form the basis, expectedness, out of which arises the element, unexpectedness, by the introduction of rhymes, not arbitrarily, but with an eye to the greatest amount of unexpectedness . . .

and Poe goes on, in this entry in his *Marginalia*, to discuss the advantage of an interior rhyme that does not recur at regular multiples of the number of syllables within the line, to rhyme so regularized.

A later entry is just as applicable today as in 1849. Poe decries the practice of grammatical inversion in poetry:

> Such things, in general, serve only to betray the versifier's poverty of resource; and, when an inversion of this kind occurs, we may say to ourselves, 'Here the poet lacked the skill to make out his line without distorting the natural or colloquial order of the words.' Now and then, however, we must refer the error not to deficiency of skill, but to something far less defensible—to an idea that such things belong to the essence of poetry—that it needs them to distinguish it from prose. . . . The true artist will avail himself of no 'license' whatever . . . as regards verbal construction, the *more prosaic* a poetical style is, the better.

Would that some one of my teachers had said as much to me, and as well, when I was twenty. O to have been freed from poeticism before I could vote! Poe, Poe, why didn't I find your *Marginalia* then? But if I had, would I have read it, or heeded your advice?

Here are the reflections of a poet who has applied rigorous analysis to each of the component parts of his craft: he argues persuasively for unity of structure, natural order of language, and urges the advantages of unexpectedness in rhyme, of an organic adaptability of meter to mood. All of these technical points are, I think, universally valid. But Poe argues further that there is no such thing as a long poem, that poetry has only one proper object (Beauty), and that the expression of that object requires the poet's devotion to but a single subject (the death of a beautiful woman). I repeat myself, as Poe repeats himself—Poe, with his obsessional center of the circle of his soul, in which everything radiates from and returns to the awareness of that one haunted experience of vanished Beauty. 'Death is the mother of beauty,' said Wallace Stevens a century after Poe had struggled with such heroic energy to express the full consequences—emotional, intellectual, poetic—of the deprivation of love.

The other point at which our modern, enlightened, and liberated sensibility will likely find Poe out of joint is his insistence that the ultimate beauty at which he aims must be expressed by the inexpressible. Poe never stops praising *indefiniteness* as the handmaiden of beauty, whether in poetry, in music, or in thought. This seems foggy indeed, or did to me when I flexed the muscles of my mind after a couple of seasons' training in seminars and found that the indefinite poem was the ill-thought poem, the poem that didn't know what it was talking about, by the poet too lazy to put his Muse in a thinking cap before allowing his soul to be seduced by her blandishments. À bas l'indéfini! But Time on its condor wings has brought me to acknowledge that, quite apart from whether I *like* indefiniteness, Poe, at least, didn't seek it because too lazy to *think*. The Vates Poe figured *everything* out, claimed even to write by total premeditation (a

lie! a lie!), and consciously sought to produce *l'indéfini* because his theory proved that indefiniteness was as close as he,
or we, could come to experiencing the sublime!

Two questions. What is this sublime which can be experienced but not understood? And what is the use of thinking
if the highest experience a man can have is, by definition,
by its very nature, suprarational?

To answer the first I invoke the second.

We 'think,' or, as Poe preferred to call the process, we
'ratiocinate' in order to arrive at an approximation of the
suprarational which is Beauty, sublimity, or, to put it meta-
physically, the primal unity from which we come and
whence we shall return.

There's your naked archetype of existence. A formula as
devoid of feeling as an algebraic equation is bare of sensuous
appeal. That simile will do, for the archetypes Poe seeks are
very much indeed like algebraic equations representing 'existence,' 'life,' 'suffering,' 'beauty.'

Poe loved intellectual activity *pursued for its own sake.*
He insisted upon the identity of poetic meters with mathematical proportions. In fact his head betrayed his ear, so to
speak, through this insistence, for although his *Marginalia*
suggested a more flexible handling of rhythms, his use of
meter in his own poems, like his strictures in his criticisms
of others, proves to be mechanically regular. Poe takes over
the medieval and classical—ultimately the Pythagorean—notion of mathematical regularity as the proof and index to
the regular and harmonious structure of the universe. Thus
music, the sensuous experience nearest to mathematical proportions, is the most sublime and represents the condition at
which poetry, through its meters, rhymes, and putative indefiniteness of meaning, aims, or should aim.

Poe loved intellectual activity outside of poems too. Although no mathematician himself—he was after all an acolyte
of the Mistress of Words, not a thane of the Master of Numbers—he revelled in *the solution of problems,* especially
linguistic problems. Intellect exercised upon a field within
a circle. Like etymologies—the *Marginalia* annotates the der-

ivations of words in Hebrew, Greek, French, Spanish, Latin, Italian, English. The study of literary sources is another such puzzle to be solved. Poe becomes an adept at tracing the borrowings and thefts from one writer to another.

There's hardly a student of American Lit. who doesn't know of Poe's unfortunate persistence in charging the nationally respected and beloved Longfellow with plagiarism—from himself. This charge was no solitary freak in Edgarpoe's arsenal of darts and barbs. We, who have the benefit of nine thousand items in the annual bibliography of *PMLA* which trace the borrowings and influences and analogues between the masterpieces of X and the minorbits of Z, tend, in the nature of things, to overlook the extremely high priority placed by Poe, and by other poets and readers of his generation, upon *originality*. Now we know, after *The Road to Xanadu* and its hundreds of tributaries and imitations, that there is no such thing as absolute originality. Coleridge's own views on the creative process and its work as an amalgamator into new entities of separate experiences, whether lived or read, I have already mentioned. Poe knew Coleridge's theories as well as does any of us, but his own theories demanded an absolute autonomy of imagination. So that although Poe was in fact a very clever literary thief—for good reason did he title his greatest tale of detection 'The Purloined Letter'!—he went to great lengths to cover his tracks, and he went out of his way to demonstrate how derivative and unoriginal were his predecessors and rivals in picking one another's portmanteaux. (Not for nothing did Edgar introduce 'The Philosophy of Composition' by comparing the construction of a poem to the solution of a mystery tale.)

For many reasons Edgar revelled in showing up the plagiarisms of others while concealing his own heavy debts to E. T. A. Hoffmann, Tieck, the anonymous authors of tales in *Blackwood's*, and, in his poems, his liberal borrowings from Hood, Shelley, Moore, Byron, Milton.

He even proposed to write a work entitled *Chapters on American Cribbage*. His *Marginalia* is crammed with jottings for such a work. Nor does he confine his detection to the

exposure of American malefactors only. For instance, setting
out to show that Longfellow's 'Midnight Mass for the Dying
Year' is a tissue of imitations from Tennyson's 'Death of
the Old Year,' from Cordelia's death scene, and from
Comus, Poe continues his exposé by showing how Tasso stole
lines from Lucan and Sulpicius; Carey, translating Dante,
borrowed a line from Gray's 'Elegy'; Milton provided a
phrase for Pope; Blair stole a line from Campbell; Butler
from Young; Young from Goldsmith; Gray from Milton and
again from Butler; Pope from Dryden; Tickell from Boileau;
Ovid from Lucretius; and Freneau from Campbell. Again,
he discovers 'A Death-Bed' by Aldrich suspiciously to resemble a poem called 'The Death-Bed,' by Hood. For all
that, Poe admits, 'Keen sensibility of appreciation—that is to
say, the poetic *sentiment* (in distinction from the poetic
power) leads almost invariably to imitation. Thus all great
poets have been gross imitators.' This observation would,
ça va sans dire, exculpate Poe himself, who goes on to add,
'It is, however, a mere *non distributio medii* hence to infer
that all great imitators are poets.'

Think not that Poe can let rest the matter of plagiarism,
even after so many exposures, so voluminous a demonstration
of the range of his own reading and the acuity of his own
wit. With this as with all the other subjects that writ themselves large in his own sensibility, Poe seems obsessed, lacking
in proportion. We read further in *Marginalia* of paragraphs
lifted from an obscure essay by Channing by a still more
obscure and anonymous writer of a piece on Bonaparte in a
magazine. We learn that one Richard W. Dodson has stolen
a stanza from a Christmas poem by Mrs. Hemans, and that
a certain George Hill, in 1842, presents as his own a stanza
from a poem published in 1819 by Edward C. Pinckney of
Baltimore. Longfellow himself proves a source for 'One of
our truest poets,' Thomas Buchanan Read, which makes
Read 'but the echo of an echo,' sometimes echoing Lowell
as well. Best of all, perhaps, are the exposures of those authors
besides poor Longfellow who, like him, have plagiarised from
Poe himself: so much for Eugène Sue, accused of purloining

from the first French translation of 'The Murders in the Rue Morgue,' and a certain William W. Lord, who has come into my ken only as the accused imitator of a stanza from 'The Haunted Palace.'

These are the plagiarisms Poe recorded in *Marginalia*. In his reviews there are, *passim*, twice as many more examples.

Etymologies, plagiarisms: next among Poe's preoccupations is the solution of another species of mystery: SECRET WRITINGS. Poe becomes a self-proclaimed expert cryptographer.

There's something about creating or using a secret language which appeals to all mankind. To poets especially. And particularly to poets who know themselves the discoverers of secret knowledge, of truths as yet unrevealed to others. A poet can use a secret language to conceal such a truth. Even more exciting is the prospect that by his being the only man capable of cracking a code in which the truth he seeks is hidden, he may become the possessor of that truth.

I'll get around to the details of Poe's expertise when I brood upon 'The Gold Bug,' but anyone who has read his articles, 'A Few Words on Secret Writing' (*Graham's Magazine*, July–December 1841), will know more about codes and code-breaking than does even Legrand, the successful reader of the pirate's cypher. And he'll know that Poe issued an open challenge to all readers of *Graham's* that he could shortly break any code that they could make. He'll know, too, that Poe succeeded in doing so. (Imagine what that stunt must have done for the circulation of *Graham's*, of which Poe was an editor!)

What is there about a secret writing which so appeals to us? Think of it. If you were a general in Napoleon's army, victorious in Egypt, and a sergeant came to your tent bearing on a cart a large stone upon which were chipped, in clear French calligraphy, the record of one particular day's stock prices on the bourse, what would you do with that stone or that sergeant? But suppose, now, that this same sergeant came to you in your same tent, bearing a large stone on which, in careful calligraphy, are three separate long inscriptions, not a syllable of any being legible to you or to your

staff. Three secret languages! What does this suggest but the
key to three vanished civilizations, the unlocking of untold
unknowns! Here are varieties of human experience which it
will take the linguists and archaeological scholars of half a
dozen nations twenty years to decipher! And when they have
at last transcribed the Rosetta Stone and found that what
it says in hieroglyphs is a translation of what it says in
demotic Egyptian and Greek, they will then have a price-list
of stocks on the Coptic Bourse.

For the poet, even more than for the linguist, historian,
occupational jargon-maker, a secret code of writing in an unknown language is a simulacrum of the relationship between
ordinary human experience and the ultimate significance
which lies, unread, behind that experience. Therefore Poe
the cryptographer is enjoying himself as he does a dry run
on each code submitted by a gentleman reader of *Graham's
Magazine*, a dry run for his *real* effort at code-cracking, the
solution to the mystery of the universe.

Poe's poems were efforts to crack that Ultimate Secret
Code. So were all his other writings, even his spoofs, his paro-
dies and send-ups. But the most concerted and obvious, indeed in a lot of ways the most enjoyable and most successful
of such efforts are the stories he called 'Tales of Ratiocination.' In these the hero is a detective.

Even before I read that story about the clock tower I had
found, on the shelf inside the door to the local candy store,
a Classic Comic Book devoted to a topic whose lurid title
appealed to my pre-adolescent—or maybe already adolescent,
I was in some ways precocious—curiosity. It was a comic-strip
redo of 'The Murders in the Rue Morgue.' I had found a dim
copy of the first detective story. Later I read the original,
which is so superior that I'll say no more about that comic
book. But Monsieur Dupin has been a familiar of my mind
for all these many years, the details of his seemingly inscrutable thought-processes staying fresh in my memory long after I had forgotten the ingenious solutions to other puzzling
mysteries worked out by the horde of his imitators—Philo
Vance, Lord Peter Whimsey, Father Brown, even Sherlock

Holmes. Like Monsieur Dupin, all of these later detectives seemed to 'think' in streaks of genius-like intuition, they all pursued arcane hobbies, read strange books on unusual subjects, lived in a life style of enviable and eccentric individuality, and most were attended by a rather dimwit companion who saved them the embarrassment of having to tell the tales of their own glorious performances. However glorious were those, the intellectual antics of Monsieur Dupin outshone them all.

IV

Disentanglements

I met Monsieur C. Auguste Dupin when, given a clue to his
whereabouts by the garbled account in Classic Comics, I
took down from the shelf of the school library—in a long
vaulted chamber beneath the mansard roof—a copy of Poe's
Complete Tales. It must have been this book, rather than
the anthology containing 'Paul's Case,' 'Hands,' and 'Silent
Snow, Secret Snow,' in which I first read 'A Predicament.'
Since then I've bought the volume—a Modern Library Giant
—and I see that it is copyright 1938, the very year when I,
in high school, began to be troubled by a dream about a clock
with murderous hands . . . But I was on my way to an 'obscure library in the Rue Montmartre, where the accident of
our both being in search of the same very rare and very remarkable volume, brought us into closer communion. We
saw each other again and again.'

It is of Monsieur Dupin I speak, for he and I met in a
library, the rare and obscure volume we sought being the one
I've just mentioned. And indeed did we see each other again
and again. Poe tells his ratiocinative tale in such a way that
the tale's author is its narrator and becomes indistinguishable
from its reader. Dupin is exactly as remarkable to you and
to me as he appears to his companion who tells us about his
extraordinary intellectual propensities:

> As the strong man exults in his physical ability, delighting
> in such exercises as call his muscles into action, so glories
> the analyst in that moral activity which *disentangles*.

So Poe's narrator begins. This is the first of several general propositions about the nature of intellect, introduced in a philosophical vein with no seeming narrative interest or connection to any visible plot. Now, Poe was very careful about the construction of his tales, *particularly* his tales of ratiocination and mystery. Commenting, in *Graham's*, November 1846, on a novel called *Mysteries of Paris* by Eugène Sue, Poe remarks with disdain that while 'the incidents are *consequential* from the premises . . . the premises themselves are laughably incredible.' Further, a work like Sue's exhibits 'the total want of the *ars celare artem*. In effect the writer is always saying to the reader, "Now—in one moment—you shall see what you shall see. I am about to produce upon you a remarkable impression. Prepare to have your imagination, or your pity, greatly excited." The wires are not only not concealed, but displayed as things to be admired, equally with the puppets they set in motion.' This, *à propos* an author whom Poe salutes as having plagiarised (in another place) from the first French translation of his own 'Murders in the Rue Morgue.' The *romancier* should have learned from that masterpiece that the premises of a mystery tale must be unassailable, and that the mechanism on which the plot turns ought to be as nearly invisible as can be managed. He should have learned, too, had he read Poe's review of Hawthorne, that the short tale is preferable to the novel, because, as is true of poems, 'the unity of effect is a point of the greatest importance,' and

> this unity cannot be thoroughly preserved in productions whose perusal cannot be completed at one sitting. . . . Without unity of impression, the deepest effects cannot be brought about. . . .
> A skilful literary artist has constructed a tale. If wise, he has not fashioned his thoughts to accommodate his incidents; but having conceived, with deliberate care, a certain unique or single *effect* to be wrought out, he then invents such incidents—he then combines such events as may best aid him in establishing this preconceived effect.

Exactly the process Poe proposed for writing 'The Raven': all is premeditated, all tends toward the single effect—the excitation of the reader's soul—and all is completely in the control of the omniscient creator.

If his very initial sentence tend not to the outbringing of this effect, then he has failed in his first step. In the whole composition there should be no word written, of which the tendency, direct or indirect, is not to the one pre-established design.

Well then, Poe's sentence about the similarity between the 'analyst' and the strong man must therefore tend to 'the outbringing of this effect,' even though detached from any glint of either a character or a plot. I guess I'll have to *parse* it.

Poe is equating analytical *intellect* with physical *strength* and at the same time calling its exercise a *moral activity*. He is saying that the analyst *glories* in his intellectual action, and that action is one which *disentangles*. In short, such a man has that unusual mind which can free the ends of the rope of life from among the twisted knots of human events. We are being introduced to the mind of Dupin before we have as yet met him in the library or become a familiar of his 'time-eaten and grotesque mansion . . . tottering to its fall in a retired and desolate portion of the Faubourg St. Germain.' It is meet that we be told of the quality of his intellect before seeing his face or sitting opposite his *fauteuil* to smoke a pipe in his presence, because 'The Murders in the Rue Morgue' tends to this single effect—the demonstration of the extraordinary intellect of Monsieur Dupin. Poe's narrator continues to speak of such an intellect as a rare type among mankind:

He derives pleasure from even the most trivial occupations bringing his talent into play. He is fond of enigmas, of conundrums, hieroglyphics; exhibiting in his solutions of each a degree of *acumen* which appears to the ordinary apprehension praeternatural. His results, brought about by the very soul and essence of method, have, in truth, the whole air of intuition.

Aha, a lover of puzzles and conundrums. We can sense who
else besides Dupin possesses an intellect so analytical, a
method so seemingly intuitive. 'Analyst' Poe uses in the sense
of a mathematical analyst, but its latterday use in psychiatry
certainly comes to mind. Nor is this accretion of the word
amiss in thinking of Poe and the kind of intellect he values
so highly, the mind which *disentangles.* Just now, however,
he is about to construct a series of events for Dupin to disentangle which will produce the effect upon us Poe has predetermined shall excite our sensibility. For, as he says in the
Hawthorne review, 'During the hour of perusal the soul of
the reader is at the writer's control.' This control is just as
much a strength in which Poe the writer glories as is the dis-
entanglement of human actions the glory of an intellect like
Dupin's.

Who has not thrilled to the bizarre mystery, the terrifying
violence, the motiveless malignancy of what happened that
day in 18— in the Quartier St. Roch in the fourth-storey
apartment of Madame L'Espanaye and her daughter Ca-
mille? If queried by the busybody U.S. Census, or by the
analysts of popular thought in Princeton, would there be any
high school graduate in these States who has not read, or
has forgotten, how the two women were savagely hacked,
stabbed, murdered, the younger one's body forced up the
chimney, with nary a clue to the murderer's identity? How
Monsieur Dupin, attracted to the case by accounts in the
newspaper—and the accusation brought against a certain Le
Bon, who had once done Dupin a good turn—brought to bear
upon the grotesque events his analytical intellect, and shortly
proved, beyond a doubt, the identity of the murderer, an
orang outang brought ashore by a seaman returned from
Malta?

Damn, I've given it all away. The plot, I mean—given away
the wires and the puppets, as did the bungler Sue. But since
for Poe the marionettes and wires are merely mechanisms,
what I've so clumsily and prematurely divulged doesn't much
matter anyway. Because the center of the tale, the effect at
which all this machinery of horror and bepuzzlement is

aimed, is not *Who is guilty?* but *How will Dupin infer his guilt?* And in preparation for this effect, near the beginning—before Dupin read about the murder in the press—Poe had both exhibited and *analysed* the mental operations of M. Dupin. It's a trivial example of that 'very soul and essence of method' which yet has about it 'the whole air of intuition.'

Dupin is a *mind-reader*. He tells Narrator exactly what Narrator is thinking, although they had been walking down the street in silence. Telepathy? Supernatural power? We are not to doubt that Dupin might call upon these, were he to need them; but he needs them not. For he is endowed with analytical intellect and can intuit that Narrator, thinking about the inappropriate casting of the short-statured actor Chantilly in the role of Crébillon's Xerxes, had concluded that he 'would do better for *Théâtre des Variétés.*' Incredible! How can Dupin pull *that* out of the thin air?

Simple. His mind merely retraced the probable chain of associations likely to occur to Narrator after his being jostled by a fruiterer a quarter-hour before. 'The larger links in the chain run thus—Chantilly, Orion, Dr. Nichols, Epicurus, Stereotomy, the street stones, the fruiterer.' No need now to retrace what these key words, or *code words*, suggest; suffice it to say that one thought led waywardly into another, and by simply attending the associative linkages of each with each, Dupin was able to make the unstated leap from *fruiterer* to *Chantilly*, and, taking advantage of his knowing which attack on the actor his friend had read that morning, he could then propose the *exact words* likely to be in his companion's mind.

The point of the episode—it takes several pages—is, Dupin's mind *works by association*. His *method* is a finer thing, a seemingly more supersensual mechanism, than the ordinary processes of rational reckoning. It partakes of the *irrational*, and is therefore the highest kind of ratiocination, since it is not the captive of its own premises. What Dupin is so adept at looks to me very much like what 'analysts' in our own day call the *preconscious mind*. Dupin can summon and surrender to the associative linkages of preconscious

thought, that wonderworking network of similes which the
rest of us have papered o'er with the sickly cast of conscious,
rational thinking. Therefore he is that much more sophisti-
cated than we, in his conundrum-disentangling, because he
is just so much closer to the origins of our being. His mind,
working by metaphoric analogies, combines poetic intuition
with mathematical exactitude.

Dupin alone is able to disentangle the conflicting testimony of the ten witnesses (none of whom had *seen* a thing),
and thus absolves his friend Le Bon, who admitted to the
court that 'on the day in question, about noon, he had accompanied Madame L'Espinaye to her residence with the
4000 francs' and then, allegedly, left the old lady alone with
the money.

It might occur even to a reader like you or me that if one
were to rob an old woman and a young girl of 4000 francs
it mightn't be *necessary* to hack and scratch their bodies in
maniacal fury and stuff one of them head-downwards up the
chimney. Further, as Dupin perused the testimony of the
witnesses—they were rather auditors, since they reported what
they'd heard, not what they'd seen—he found a singular dis-
crepancy. Everyone within earshot reported a horrid commotion. The gendarme thought the shrieks were in Spanish. The
neighboring silversmith took the words for Italian. A passing
Dutch tourist was certain the shrieks were in French, as was
an English tailor, though the latter thought it might have
been German. A Spaniard took the tongue spoken to be English. An Italian thought the uproar was in Russian. So it
proved to be a language problem. A secret language, a code
by which the world was informed of some creature's guilt,
but none who heard the proclamation possessed the secret
code-breaker by which to identify either the language or its
speaker.

This linguistic confusion, plus other circumstances—the
murderer must have escaped through a high window, etc.—
leads Dupin to reconsider the evidence. He ponders the
nature of the crime. 'In the manner of thrusting the corpse

up the chimney, you will admit that there was something *excessively outré. . . .'*

If now, in addition to all these things, you have properly reflected upon the odd disorder of the chamber, we have gone so far as to combine the ideas of an agility astounding, a strength superhuman, a ferocity brutal, a butchery without motive, a *grotesquerie* in horror absolutely alien from humanity, and a voice foreign in tone to the ears of men of many nations, and devoid of all distinct or intelligible syllabification. What result, then, has ensued? What impression have I made upon your fancy?

Dupin asks his companion, me, or you, just before producing his result. Dupin, who knows himself to be a man of genius and me to be merely a man, for he appeals to my *fancy* only, not to that superior quality he well knows I do not possess, an analytic intellect like his own. ('It will be found, in fact,' says Narrator just before introducing Dupin, 'that the ingenious are always fanciful, and the *truly* imaginative never otherwise than analytic.')

Before I could gather my wits to reply to his question, Narrator thrust *his* reply before my eyes:

I felt a creeping of the flesh as Dupin asked me the question. 'A madman,' I said, 'has done this deed—some raving maniac, escaped from a neighboring *Maison de Santé.'*

My very thoughts. But Dupin has further evidence—a tuft of hair taken 'from the rigidly clutched fingers of Madame L'Espanaye'—not human hair; and the finger-marks on the victim's throat were too huge, too widely spaced, for any *human* hand.

I don't blame myself for not having noticed the size of the finger-marks, or the thickness of the hair. Who wouldn't think the deed done by a madman, done, in the first instance by a *man*, then by a man who was mad? In not being snared by *that* premise Dupin demonstrates his superiority to the merely ingenious. He alone dared analyze away the very premise of all argument—human agency, requiring both opportunity and motive. An ape requires no motive, since stuffing ladies into chimneys is consonant with its own nature.

Besides, I read about the Rue Morgue after having already made Poe's acquaintance elsewhere—'A Predicament,' 'Berenice,' 'The Fall of the House of Usher.' And the crime which Dupin is able to recognize as committed by *no human agent* did not appal me all *that* much; horrible though it was, it didn't seem worse in kind than Roderick Usher's putting his sister living in the tomb. Or more horrible than the finale of 'Berenice,' where the lunatic lover and dentist digs up the body of his cousin Berenice, wasted by her disease, and *tears out the teeth* from her jaws, bringing home in a small box the thirty-two ivory treasures—and the realization that Berenice—like Madeline Usher!—had been buried alive. These horrifying crimes had been done by *men*—by madmen, true, but not by *apes*. Yet Dupin is certain that murders so horrible as those in the Rue Morgue must have been committed by a beast—as though a human murderer (he'd *have* to be insane) became an orang outang, a primal beast without intellect, without responsibility, without *language*, in the commission of his compulsive crime.

Even for an ape, a Caliban, the crime is an obsessional act. And in fact it is the same act, the same as in the tales of horror, the same as in the poems of transcendent beauty. For what is the 'subject' of the 'The Murders in the Rue Morgue' but, as in 'Lenore,' 'Ulalume,' 'Annabel Lee,' and 'The Raven,' *the death of a beautiful woman*—the very subject which Poe's aesthetic defines as the one most fitting for poetry because of its ideality and melancholy? What the poems render with pathos, longing, the music of despair and a dreamy vagueness, is dramatized in the tale with circumstantial horror and terrifying precision.

What! You seriously propose that the brutal murder, the savage dismemberment, the grotesque stuffing of the lovely Mlle L'Espinaye up the chimney with her head torn off is the same subject as in those ethereal poems? Well yes I do. The *theme* is essentially the same; it is the *tone* which is different. Poe's versions of this theme alternate in tone between the indistinct melancholy of the poems and the terrible, the grotesque, the bizarre in the tales. Both tones manage to excite a strangeness, an ecstasy, in the reader. Terror is an ecstatic state for Poe, as is grief.

In 'The Poe Mystery Case' (*New York Review of Books*, 13 July 1967), Richard Wilbur proposed a somewhat different understanding of Dupin's adventure. Wilbur relates 'The Rue Morgue' to a number of Poe's other tales 'in which a woman's love or honor is the ground of contention between two men, one of them lofty-minded and the other base or brutish. The woman, in such cases, symbolizes Psyche, or redemptive Beauty, while . . . the rivals stand for the spiritual and corrupt principles of a single nature.' Having observed that the name 'Adolphe Le Bon' is 'a variation' upon 'Auguste Dupin,' and, further, that like Dupin the sailor who owned the murderous ape and Mme L'Espinaye all lived '*au troisième*' floors of their respective buildings, Wilbur concludes,

> The imaginative consequence of this is that . . . the three secluded ménages of the story are telescoped into one, the three buildings becoming a single structure which signifies the reintegrated and harmonized consciousness of Dupin. Allegorically, the action of the story has been a soul's fathoming and ordering of itself, its 'apprehension' of that base or evil force within it (the orangutan) which would destroy the redemptive principle embodied in Mme L'Espinaye and her daughter. . . . Dupin, in 'The Murders in the Rue Morgue,' uses his genius to detect and restrain the brute in himself, thus exorcising the fiend.

This is indeed to take the tale 'allegorically,' perhaps too much so. One can't help but be tempted to discover in Poe's tales the kind of reintegrative unification which his theories of art expound as though to nullify the divisiveness of his theories of psychology. Yet, although Le Bon and the brute are doubtless aspects of Dupin's character (how otherwise could he respond to the one or understand the irrational passion of the other?), to make this triplication of his character the spring of the story seems to me to wind that spring

on a different key from the one which actually turns the dy-
namically interlocked actions of the tale. We run the risk,
in reading fictions as though they were poems, of making the
images more significant than the actions they are designed to
dramatize. Wilbur's suggestion is a shadowy undertone, an
implication, but not, I think, a primary meaning of 'The
Murders in the Rue Morgue.'

It's not that Dupin is never involved in the sort of duplicate identities Wilbur proposes here. Exactly such duplication is the primary meaning of 'The Purloined Letter,'
where that theme is so clearly the dynamic principle of the
plot that I can't help concluding that, had Poe intended it
to be the theme also of 'The Rue Morgue,' he would have
organized that tale the better to illustrate it.

Its real subject is neither Dupin's resolution of his trip-
licate identity, nor the death of the Mmes L'Espinaye; it is
the workings of the mind of Dupin. The young lady's dismemberment is the occasion for the ecstatic operation of the
detective's intuitive ratiocination. In the poems, too, the
lady's death is not so much the subject as the occasion, the
subject being the revelation of the narrator's emotion. In
the one case an ecstasy of ratiocination, the passion of an
intuitive intelligence comprehending truth in a world of violent action; in the other, an ecstasy of grief, the passion of
a suffering sensibility to pursue its own bereavement to the
point of self-destruction. Both the fantasy of absolute power
and the fantasy of total loss lead to an ecstatic excitation of
the soul. The only condition, for Poe, approaching that of
terror and of grief in the stimulation of ecstasy is *the ratiocinative control of the mind aware of the operation of its
own powers.*

Such reasoning, for Poe, is not only man's highest power,
it is his most characteristic human act. In his *Marginalia*
he wrote,

> The theorizers of Government, who pretend always to
> 'begin with the beginning, commence with Man in what
> they call his *natural* state—the savage. What right have they
> to suppose this his natural state? Man's chief idiosyncrasy

being reason, it follows that his savage condition—his condition of action *without* reason—is his *un*natural state. The more he reasons, the nearer he approaches the position to which this chief idiosyncrasy irresistably impels him; and not until he attains this position with exactitude—not until his reason has exhausted itself for his improvement—not until he has stepped upon the highest pinnacle of civilization—will his *natural* state be ultimately reached, or thoroughly determined.

Yet a few months earlier, in 1844, Poe had written to James Russell Lowell,

I really perceive that vanity about which most men merely prate—the vanity of human or temporal life. I live continually in a reverie of the future. I have no faith in human perfectibility. I think that human exertion will have no appreciable effect upon humanity. Man is now only more active—not more happy—nor more wise—than he was 6000 years ago. . . .

and went on to startle the proper Bostonian by avowing that 'The unparticled matter, permeating & impelling all things, is God. Its activity is the thought of God—which creates. Man, and other thinking beings, are individualizations of the unparticled matter.' How *this* heresy connects with the 'thinking' of Dupin will take the activity of much unparticled grey matter of my own. But what I started to say, before Poe broke in with his truth about the thought of God, is that Man Thinking represents Man in his natural state, although Poe is aware that Man is not yet in that state, nor is he making any appreciable progress toward its attainment.

Although Mankind is active without being either happy or wise, an individual man—a genius—may fulfil his true, natural state and think as God thinks, create as God creates. Dupin the detective is such a genius; and of all of Poe's imitators in the detective tale, I guess only Chesterton really understood what Poe was doing. For in *The Man Who Was Thursday*, the adept in a ring of secret agents, joining the anarchist circle as a double operative really working for the police (whose head he has never seen), discovers that the chief detective is really the chief anarchist—is both God and the Devil, since the Devil works in the service of God. A plot whose hidden, Byzantine workings would have delighted Poe, and would take a Dupin to disentangle.

Monsieur Dupin is one of Poe's finest creations, his most believable portrait of the Man of Thought. Poe set himself to study the type of genius—of course by phrenology and every other method of self-scrutiny available to him, to analyse, with Dupin-like subtlety and fervor, that genius whose image gazed back at him from his looking glass. Dupin is not the only guise that image wore, but certainly Dupin is its most attractive. To create Dupin, however, Poe had to invent his bland and dim narrator. He had written two other tales of detection and analysis without that intermediary, and they somehow fail to engage us as does 'The Murders in the Rue Morgue.' In 'Maelzel's Chess Player' we see Poe's analytical mind at work, figuring out the mystery and exposing the seemingly mechanical chess-player as in fact a hoax, a false computer containing a human being secreted within it. But there's no real suspense in the sketch, nor does the reader feel engaged by the analysis, since he knows that the author knew the answer all along.

The other detective tale is 'Thou Art the Man,' a much more interesting sort of failure in this line. This is one of Poe's rare excursions into backwoods humor of the kind he praised in Longstreet's *Georgia Scenes*. Poe here works a vein properly belonging to Mark Twain: the satire of the rural county town, the overdrawn Dickensian caricature of its denizens, the drama of a courtroom confrontation, and an ingenious solution to a murder which has the cleverness of a plot of Tom Sawyer's. But here again the narrator is himself the detective, with the result that he manages to make a mystery for the reader out of a problem to which he has known the solution all along.

But by introducing an intermediary as narrator who seems as mystified as is the reader by the intricacies of the plot,

Poe freed his plot from the appearance of imposition. This he explains in a letter to a friendly critic, the Southern writer Philip Pendleton Cooke (9 August, 1846):

> You are right about the hair-splitting of my French friend: —that is all done for effect. These tales of ratiocination owe most of their popularity to being something in a new key. I do not mean to say they are not ingenious—but people think them more ingenious than they are—on account of their method and *air* of method. In the 'Murders in the Rue Morgue,' for instance, where is the ingenuity of un-ravelling a web which you (the author) have woven for the express purpose of unravelling? The reader is made to con-found the ingenuity of the suppositious Dupin with that of the writer of the story.

So the credit redounds to the writer, but not at the expense of the credibility of his tale.

There's something appropriate in the fact that Poe became the first of his own imitators, the first hack writer to be un-done by reducing a work of genius to a formula. Of course it's true that at this time—1842—Edgar Allan Poe was a starveling scrivener who pushed his pen with frenetic speed to fill issue after issue of ill-paying magazines with his tales, poems, reviews, cribs, comments, and sheer hackwork, among which were interspersed, at the same miserable rate of recompense, his masterpieces. Having scored a great success with Dupin in 'The Rue Morgue' he next undertook to use his detective's genius to solve an actual crime which the police were in the midst of trying to disentangle. Again the crime is the mysterious murder of a girl, a certain Mary Rogers, a cigar-seller, on Staten Island, New York. Poe's laborious story slightly disguises the facts of this case and calls it 'The Mys-tery of Marie Rogêt, a Sequel to the "Murders in the Rue Morgue." ' John Walsh has written an entire book showing how many difficulties Poe got himself ensnared in as he tried to keep ahead of the police and to make the 'facts,' as re-ported in the press, amenable to the intuitions of Dupin. This story, which he had to rework and revise, has about it a dogged pursuit of a point far beyond the gratification of the reader. It seems to me to be as fixated as those tedious works which cross-examine the depositions from the Texas Book Depository to prove some conspiratorial theory of President Kennedy's assassination, in despite of the Warren Commission report. Poe's Dupin's narrator was much better occupied, as he says at the start of this unfortunate sally into the world of fact, when, having solved the tragedy of the Rue Morgue, he and Dupin 'gave the Future to the winds, and slumbered tranquilly in the Present, weaving the dull world around us into dreams.' For Dupin is essentially a creature of dreams, not of facts; the crimes he solves are best solved when committed for the purpose of his disentangling them, not when they are the actual deeds of others. Dupin's essence is to be the counter-principle to the Imp of the Perverse, and whose imp should he best counter but his own?

His duality was implicit from the first, implicit even in the mind of his none-too-bright companion. Admiring Dupin's 'rich ideality,' in 'The Rue Morgue' he noted also that the detective, when preoccupied, had a manner 'frigid and abstract; while his eyes were vacant in expression. . . .' In short, Dupin when devoted to the exercise of his analytical faculty becomes a man possessed, a man set apart from the ordinary concerns of life. 'Observing him in these moods,' says Narrator, 'I often dwelt meditatively upon the old philosophy of the Bi-Part Soul, and amused myself with the fancy of a double Dupin—the creative and the resolvent.' What more clue do we need to suggest that Dupin can create and commit whatever crime he can solve?

This in fact is just about what happens in his next adventure, 'The Purloined Letter.' At the time I first read this story I had just seen the original movie of 'The Thirty-Nine Steps.' Nineteen thirty-eight was a big year for me, I seem to have made all sorts of discoveries—plumbed my soul with nightmare horrors, exalted it with ratiocinative solutions to hard problems, discovered the lure of espionage with its dangerous rebellion against the state and its reliance upon secret writings, conspiracy, secret crime. 'The Purloined Letter' is a boy's tale *par excellence*—all the characters are men, as boys dream of men. There are Dupin, his faithful companion, the Prefect of the Parisian Police, and the culprit who has purloined the incriminating letter from the apartment of a royal lady (described by the Prefect only as 'a certain personage'). Curiously, in this tale the identity of the culprit—which was the mystery to be solved in 'The Murders in the Rue Morgue'—is known from the start. The letter was obviously stolen by the Minister D——, who has been blackmailing the royal lady with it ever since, and by means of its possession has in effect seized control of the government. The problem is, to recover the purloined letter. But where can it be?

These characters are a boy's dreams of men because they interact only one-dimensionally, that being in the dimension of the intellect. Dimly, in the shadows of the far background, are intimations, not to be much noticed by boys, that these men, Dupin, G. the Prefect, the Minister D——, have other strands in their lives than the commission or solution of intricate problems. For example, in this tale of a purloined letter we are never told *what the letter says*. The blackmailed lady must have been *guilty* of some indiscretion, perhaps even some crime. What the hold on her is which D—— possesses is nowhere divulged.

What ensues is a three-sided battle of wits between the Minister D——, the Prefect of Police, and Monsieur Dupin. D—— knows that the Prefect knows that he has purloined the letter, and so he has hidden it in such a fashion that none of the stratagems for search-and-destroy followed by the police with persistence and exactitude will discover the location of the document. D——, however, does not know that Dupin is also seeking to recover the purloined letter. Dupin, for his part, takes a faintly contemptuous tone toward his professional rival, the Prefect, knowing that a man of D——'s propensities will easily outwit a bureaucrat whose methods, although proficient and thoroughgoing, are so limited from the start. So, although much of the tale is given to a de-

scription of those methods of the Prefect, the real contest is
that between the unscrupulous genius of D— and the resolvent genius of Dupin.

It is clear that this plot puts into *imaginative* operation
the plot taken from life in 'The Mystery of Marie Rogêt,'
at least so much of that story as showed the superiority of
Dupin's intuitional detective work to the rational methodology of the metropolitan police force. Now, freed from the
tyranny of facts which had hobbled him in 'Marie Rogêt,'
Poe contrives an all but perfect plot. It goes beyond the demonstration of Dupin's superiority to the Prefect to embrace
a much more interesting and significant theme: the identity
of his mental operations—those of genius—with the workings
of the mind of his real adversary, the criminal.

This tale, of course, sets the pattern that all 'private eye'
stories have followed since. The detective is shrewder and
smarter than the cops, is therefore above and outside the law
as the crooks are outside and beneath it. Poe's foresight into
the limitations of the police made the writing of 'private eye'
tales easy for a thousand of his successors.

Police work, like all civil service, is by nature a bureaucracy,
an arm and extension of the social establishment—indeed,
the arm delegated to protect the life and private property
rights of the rest of the establishment. In every bureaucracy
success is achieved through the practice of bureaucratic virtues: at their lower levels these include coming to work
punctually, showing deference to one's superiors, and the
like. The higher bureaucratic virtues, not to be fleered at,
include dedication to one's duty and the application of an
approved method to its performance. G., the Prefect of Police, is a first-rate bureaucrat, the finest flower which the
system that produced him can produce. That even his talents
are unavailing to recover the purloined letter Poe intends as
an indictment not merely of the man but of the system: the
bureaucracy. And not merely the civil service, but the entire
establishment—society—of which that bureaucracy is a formal
expression. An indictment because the system operates by

method and intention *to exclude from its calculations any place for intellectual distinction, for genius.*

The Prefect is nothing if not diligent. Knowing that D—— has the letter, the *policier* has had the suspect waylaid by footpads (detectives in disguise) who searched his person. Meanwhile, using his ring of master-keys, 'for three months a night has not passed during the greater part of which I have not been engaged, personally, in ransacking the D—— Hotel. . . . I fancy that I have investigated every nook and corner of the premises in which it is possible that the paper can be concealed.'

'Suppose you detail,' suggested Dupin's confidant, 'the particulars of your search.'

'Why, the fact is, we took our time, and we searched *everywhere.* I have had long experience in these affairs. I took the entire building, room by room; devoting the nights of a whole week to each. We examined, first, the furniture of each apartment. We opened every possible drawer; and I presume you know that, to a properly trained police-agent, such a thing as a *secret* drawer is impossible. . . . Then we have accurate rules. The fiftieth part of a line could not escape us. After the cabinets we took the chairs. The cushions we probed with the fine long needles you have seen me employ. From the tables we removed the tops. . . .'

—because the letter may have been rolled up and secreted in a hollow leg. And so forth, for several pages.

The narrator has not, it would seem, been alert to a slightly rivalrous repartee between G. and Dupin which immediately precedes this inventory of police methodicalness. Commenting on the Prefect's cleverness in arranging for his agents to waylay the minister as though they were thieves, in order to frisk him, Dupin had said,

'You might have spared yourself this trouble. D——, I presume, is not altogether a fool, and, if not, must have anticipated these waylayings, as a matter of course.'

'Not *altogether* a fool,' said G., 'but then he is a poet, which I take to be only one remove from a fool.'

'True,' said Dupin, after a long and thoughtful whiff from his meerschaum, 'although I have been guilty of certain doggerel myself.'

Neither his friend nor the Prefect picks up this clue that in Dupin's opinion a composer of poems may be far from a fool, in fact his verse may be the warrant of his creative imagination.

The rest of the tale—Dupin's involvement and resolution— is readily told. Dupin himself tells his friend how he does it, comparing the workings of his own mind, and that of his adversary, D—, to various schoolboy games, the winning of which, his friend acknowledges, depends upon 'an identification of the reasoner's intellect with that of his opponent.' As for the elaborate methodology of the police, Dupin remarks, 'A certain set of highly ingenious resources are, with the Prefect, a sort of Procrustean bed, to which he forcibly adapts his designs. But he perpetually errs by being too deep or too shallow for the matter in hand.' The example of the schoolboy guessing in which hand his friend holds a marble is given as though to make crystal-clear to his friend the principles of reasoning on which such a case may be solved. But it is also given to show that the Prefect is a less able reasoner than many a boy in school. The Procrustean bed of the Prefect and his cohorts is their 'non-measurement of the intellect with which they are engaged.'

Dupin's resolvent intellect solves the mystery by side-stepping the self-imprisoning assumptions on which the Prefect based his entire *modus operandi*. That assumption was, most proximately, that D— had *concealed* the letter, as an ordinary man surely would have done. But, adds Dupin, 'the remote source of his defeat is the supposition that the Minister is a fool, because he has acquired renown as a poet. All fools are poets; this the Prefect *feels*; and he is merely guilty of a *non distributio medii* in thence inferring that all poets are fools.'

And where was the letter hidden? Have you forgotten? It wasn't hidden at all, it was left in broad unconcealment,

dangling under the Prefect's nose during each of the ninety
nights that he ransacked the Minister's apartment. A letter,
in those days, was addressed on the reverse of the sheet containing the message; the sheet was folded into quarters and
the edges sealed with wax. The Minister, knowing the Prefect
would assume him so foolish as to hide the letter away, merely
reversed the fold of the letter, re-addressed it to the Minister
himself in a 'diminutive and feminine' hand, and re-sealed it
with the large, black seal of the D— family, while the small
red seal of the original sender was hidden inside the fold.
There it was, thrust 'almost contemptuously' in a pasteboard
card-rack which hung from a brass knob in the middle of the
Minister's mantelpiece. Dupin, knowing D— 'as both a
mathematician and a poet . . . knew him as a courtier too,
and as a bold *intriguant*,' knew also that such a man 'must
have foreseen the secret investigations of his premises.' His
frequent absences (which the Prefect regarded as fortuitous)
were doubtless '*ruses*, to afford an opportunity for thorough
search,' and thus to help the police swiftly conclude that the
letter was not on the premises.

Monsieur Dupin, identifying his mental processes with
those of the Minister D—, retraced his thought *exactly*
and, entering his apartment on a pretext, recovered the purloined letter. It takes one poet-mathematician to untie the
plot which another has contrived. Dupin has earned the
check for fifty thousand francs which is his reward.

There is of course a diverting twist to the story's end, just
as in 'The Rue Morgue' Dupin did not stop when he had
deduced the *identity* of the murderer but contrived a newspaper advertisement which made the owner of the guilty
ape come forward to identify himself. Now it's not sufficient merely to *recover* the letter. Monsieur Dupin foresees
the preferability of letting Minister D— induce his own
downfall. Should D— suppose that he still possesses the
letter, he will continue to act, in his ministerial capacity, as
though he still has the power over the royal lady which possession of the letter confers. Let him, then, continue on this
course, while Dupin, knowing that D— will not re-examine

the letter, substitutes for the purloined letter a facsimile he has prepared for this purpose! Thus at one stroke the purloined letter is recovered and the culprit brings about his own downfall. Only incidentally are we likely to notice that Dupin, in purloining the purloined letter and in leaving its facsimile in plain view, has *exactly duplicated* the crime he has set out to resolve.

The resolvent intellect of Monsieur Dupin had been quite fully anticipated in Poe's first detection tale, 'The Gold Bug.' This is one of those American stories which, like 'The Legend of Sleepy Hollow,' 'Rip Van Winkle,' 'The Jumping Frog of Calaveras County,' and, for those who have read them, 'The Grey Champion' and 'The May-Pole of Merry Mount,' seem always to have existed, fully formed, in one's mind. Who can remember first reading these tales? They are so instinct with our own experiences that we seem never not to have known them. 'The Gold Bug' is, as far as I know, Poe's only effort to use an existing folk legend in his own fiction; and if one compares Poe's use of the traditions about the hidden treasure of Captain Kidd to what Irving made of the same materials in 'The Money-Diggers,' it's plain enough that what for Irving was the center of the plot became for Poe only the suggestion of a *mise en scène*, of a *modus operandi*.

Poe took over the motif of the search for the pirate's buried gold, and he situated that search in an actual landscape—how rarely Poe's landscapes are actual places!—in this case, the South Carolina coast near Fort Moultrie. Poe was stationed at the army base there when, having left the bed and board of his tetchy adoptive father—rather I should say his non-adoptive unfather, John Allan—he enlisted as a common soldier and served thirteen months at that post. This land- and sea-scape, with its crags, forests, islands and beaches, he fully explored when off duty, and he must have loved the rugged terrain, perhaps even longed for its grandeur while living in terrible poverty in one city after another—Richmond,

Philadelphia, Baltimore, New York. For this is the country-
side he recreates in 'The Gold Bug.'

An American legend, an American scene. Having the conviction that I have never *not known* the story of 'The Gold
Bug,' I ask myself what else in this tale has so strongly
branded its intricately simple story upon the deeper cellules
of my memory? It has that irresistible attraction Poe later
embodied in the Dupin tales, the solution of a problem
which intrigues the reader or the rememberer. It introduces
him to a memorable character, one whose intellectual powers
are formidably exercised to disentangle the mystery. This personage is here called Legrand, and, as though to foreshadow
Dupin, he too lives apart from the bustle of many men. He
too 'had once been wealthy, but a series of misfortunes had
reduced him to want.' Now a recluse, living (like Thoreau)
in a hut he had built himself, it was there on Sullivan's Island that the narrator made his acquaintance. 'I found him
well educated, with unusual powers of mind, but infected
with misanthropy, and subject to perverse moods of alternate
enthusiasm and melancholy. He had with him many books,
but rarely employed them.' This man of intellect, by the
world scorned, is thought by his relatives to be mentally un-
balanced. They have persuaded a manumitted slave, Jupiter,
to stay with Legrand 'with a view to the supervision and
guardianship' of the ruined millionaire.

And now the plot, with that beautiful economy in which
every sentence contributes to the desired effect, begins to
accumulate its relevant details. One of Legrand's unusual intellectual pastimes is the collection of natural specimens, and
when the narrator calls on him he finds Legrand revelling
in his latest find, a golden beetle. Here begins that dandiacal
distinctiveness of mind which sets off the master ratiocinator
from the *hoi polloi*. His interest may be in natural sciences,
or in foreign languages, or in cryptographic problems, or in
mathematical puzzles, or *any* such variety of arcana requiring
both special information and unusual intellectual propensities: Poe's version of the genius of the age.

A Romantic genius. He has all the powers of a man of

the Renaissance like Michelangelo or Leonardo, all the capacities of a man of the Enlightenment like Dr. Johnson or
Thomas Jefferson, save that in no way does he show any interest toward man in society. *Au contraire*, he pursues his
excellences in isolation. He cares not a whistle for the knowledge that benefits mankind, as did Franklin, but devotes all
his leisure hours—and they are many—to the knowledge that
interests himself. His sole occupation, in the event, is to
understand the universe, not for the utility such understanding might confer upon his country or his race, but because
his curiosity will not be assuaged until he himself has mas-
tered the secrets written into the world by the Author of its
so far uncracked code. By analogy with the feat Dupin will
later perform at Poe's behest in disentangling the plot of
Minister D——, we can infer that if the detective, or to be
more generic, the genius, can crack the code of that Author,
he has made himself coequal with the perpetrator of the
code.

We learn how Legrand makes a sketch of the new specimen on a scrap of rough paper he finds in his pocket, and
how the narrator, momentarily diverted by Legrand's frisky
dog, lets his hand holding the paper slip off his lap and near
the fire. When he looks at the sketch he mistakes it for a
death's head. Legrand is annoyed at his misconstruing a clear
sketch, then, examining the paper more closely, locks it up
in a case and seems very abstracted. A month later the narrator is visited by Jupiter, who delivers a letter urging him
to come to Legrand at once. Jupiter by now is convinced that
Legrand has lost his wits.

The narrator proves to be a physician, and he too rapidly
associates himself with Jupiter's opinion. Legrand seems to
mistake the gold bug for real gold, he has sent Jupiter on a
fool's errand to buy spades and a pickaxe, and he leads his
servant and his doctor on a mad expedition into the wilder-
ness, where, at a certain spot, he commands the Negro to
climb a tree.

   By this time what little doubt I might have entertained
of my poor friend's insanity was put finally at rest. I had

no alternative but to consider him stricken with lunacy, and I became seriously anxious about getting him home.

Ah, I've done it again. Like Sue I've prematurely revealed the strings and joints of the plot, enough so that any reader who has never read 'The Gold Bug'—is there such a person?—can infer that there was method in the madness of Legrand, that the paper on which he sketched the gold bug contained a secret writing, the disentangling of which led the misanthropic philosopher to the recovery of hidden treasure. Not so Poe, of course; with superb pacing his narrator proceeds. I've always thought the really masterful touch in the tale's telling was the digging of the hole in the wrong place when Jupiter, directed by Legrand to drop the gold bug on its string through the left eye of the skull nailed to the tree, proves to have mistaken its right eyehole for its left one. Legrand, having drawn a line from the trunk to the resulting spot, then paced off fifty feet extending it, directs the futile digging. He reveals his acuity by thinking to cross-examine the old Negro about his lefts and rights. Then up the tree again for Jupiter, down the correct eyehole for the gold bug, fifty feet beyond in a slightly different direction for Legrand, and backs bent to shovels for all three until—they find the treasure!

Dupin, too, had reaped a reward for his pains in the matter of the purloined letter—fifty thousand francs. But that's a paltry sum compared to the contents of the oblong wooden chest (shaped like a coffin) to which Legrand was led by his deciphering of a letter left by Captain Kidd. There it was, after they had unearthed two skeletons from the hole, a starved and penniless boy's dream of the opulence of heaven, conferred upon the genius his own mind has imagined who alone among two centuries of treasure-hunters has found the secreted treasures purloined from the Spanish Main:

. . . we spent the whole day, and the greater part of the next night, in a scrutiny of its contents. . . . Every thing had been heaped promiscuously. . . . In coin there was rather more than four hundred and fifty thousand dollars—

estimating the value of the pieces, as accurately as we could, by the tables of the period. There was not a particle of silver. All was gold of antique date and of great variety. . . . There were several very large and heavy coins, so worn that we could make nothing of their inscriptions. There was no American money.

I savor those last two details—*real* riches antedate anything struck by this moneygrubbing nation of merchant materialists, and the most valuable coins comprise a mystery within the mystery, being so old and worn there isn't even a secret writing on their face for Legrand to translate. The narrator goes on to catalogue the jewels, finger rings, censers, 'a prodigious golden punch-bowl, ornamented with richly chased vine-leaves and Bacchanalian figures,' and the like. The total value they estimated 'at a million and a half of dollars,' a figure later proved to be 'greatly undervalued.'

Now they are rich beyond their wildest dreams, though 'The Gold Bug' is but a tale half-told. The remaining pages of course allow Legrand to reveal to the doctor how he pulled it off. It seems as though the wayward perusal of volumes in his desultory readings in chemistry, history, psychology, and etymology had been prefigurations of an unrevealed design. The same seems true of a series of events, accidents, really, which to anyone but a Legrand would have passed unnoticed. For instance, the doctor's discovery of the death's head on a paper that had borne none. Legrand's analytic mind reconstructed the event, and he intuited that it was the exposure of the paper to the heat of the fire which brought out the figure hitherto unseen. Knowing that zaffre (cobalt oxide) makes an invisible ink rendered legible by heat, Legrand re-examines the paper. Where did he get it? He found a corner of it protruding from the sand when he had first seized the gold bug, near the wreck of an old longboat. It isn't actually paper, it's a sort of papyrus, nearly indestructible. Who would leave something written on papyrus near a beached rowboat? He applies heat again, and sees what he takes to be a goat's head—no, the head of a *kid*. A

visual pun! Now he knows what he has found; all that remains is to read the letter.

The letter of course is written in hieroglyphic code—curiously, the pirate anticipated the very symbols to be found
in a nineteenth-century print shop. Seeing the letter's message, the doctor is dismayed. But Legrand assures him, 'It
may well be doubted whether human ingenuity can construct
an enigma of the kind which human ingenuity may not, by
proper application, resolve. . . . In all cases of secret writing—the first question regards the *language* of the cipher.'
The language proves to be English, and by counting the repetition of characters Legrand, who happens to know the relative
frequency of all the letters in the alphabet in a characteristic
utterance in English, can thus crack the code.

Of course the message isn't a simple one. When reduced
to English it's *still* in code: 'A good glass in the bishop's
hostel in the devil's seat . . . etc.' The decipherment of *this*
code requires Legrand's intuitive application to place names
in the locality, his intuitive realization, on finding a cliff on
the property of the Bessop family known as Bessop's castle,
that somewhere on its face he'd find the devil's seat: in the
event, an odd, chair-like rock formation—from which a tele-
scopic view at the specified angle reveals, in a cleft between
the branches of a certain tree, a white speck: a skull. The
rest of the message tells how to triangulate the treasure spot
by dropping a bullet through the left eye socket of this skull
and pacing off at the correct angle from the tree. Brilliant!

I'm intrigued by the whole thing, the plot, the cipher
within the cipher, the treasure within the treasure, the richest
treasure of all being the intellect which cracked the intricacies
of the code. I'm intrigued, too, that whereas Dupin is always
presented as intelligence incarnate, Legrand is given to the
reader in such a way that we are likely to agree with the doctor and old Jup in thinking him quite mad. Yet he ends up
richer than Croesus.

'But your grandiloquence, and your conduct in swinging
the beetle—how excessively odd! I was sure you were mad.

And why did you insist upon letting fall the bug, instead of a bullet, from the skull?'

'Why, to be frank, I felt somewhat annoyed by your evident suspicions touching my sanity, and so resolved to punish you quietly, in my own way, by a little bit of sober mystification. . . .'

All that remains to be solved is the identity of those two skeletons. 'It is dreadful to believe in such atrocity as my suggestion would imply,' says Legrand. He opines that Kidd must have had the assistance of two accomplices in hiding the treasure. 'But this labor concluded, he may have thought it expedient to remove all participants in his secret. Perhaps a couple of blows with a mattock were sufficient, while his coadjutors were busy in the pit; perhaps it required a dozen —who shall tell?'

It's evident that Legrand is able to resolve Kidd's mystery, and therefore he is also capable of having perpetrated it. Either kind of genius, the creative or the resolvent, is so unlike the common run of men that to such a person as the doctor (whose intellect resembles that of the Prefect as much as it does Dupin's companion), Legrand seems insane. Perhaps the line between the sane and the insane is not an easy one to discriminate, when the world, which thinks itself not mad, is unable to distinguish the great sanity in the reasoning powers of a Legrand. Suppose, just suppose, for a moment, that Legrand, being like Kidd in his intellectual equipment, were also like Kidd in his moral equipment. He, too, has two coadjutors busy in the pit, the only human beings besides himself who know the location of Kidd's treasure. He stands above them on the rim of the pit, a mattock in *his* hand . . . By how thin a thread hang the lives of Doctor and old Jup; the thinness of that thread may mark the distinction between the greatest sanity and a madness so horrible that Dupin associates its consequences with the nature of a beast incapable of language.

Or is the cipher within the solution of these crimes that the fabrications of genius may fall out equally to be resolvent, benefitting the innocent and the injured, or creative,

resulting in horrible crimes? Or is it that genius wears everywhere two complementary faces, and the disentangling intellect of the detective is but the mirror-image of the mon-
strously amoral genius whose nature requires that he commit
piracy, purloining, murder?

Poe has had so many imitators in the detective line that
theories have been offered to explain the appeal of this genre
of story. The most persuasive, I think, is W. H. Auden's,
in 'The Guilty Vicarage.' There Auden proposes that the
private eye is, or should be, motivated to restore a fallen
world to its prelapsarian innocence by solving the crime
which represents the sin of Cain, and thus making possible
the restoration of order under justice. But this is not the case
with Poe's detectives. Legrand is just as greedy for treasure
as was Captain Kidd. Dupin solves the murders in the Rue
Morgue to save a falsely accused suspect—not because Dupin
so values truth and justice, but because that particular fellow
(Le Bon) had once done him a good turn he can now repay.
Most telling of all is the motive for Dupin's involvement in
'The Purloined Letter.' He lets his companion suppose it
is a desire for the reward of fifty thousand francs. But at the
end he reveals it is the opportunity to avenge himself upon
the Minister, D——, who had once done him 'an evil turn,
which I told him, quite good-humoredly, that I should remember.' The last lines of that tale are those which Dupin
himself had written, *inside the letter he substituted* for the
letter which D—— had purloined. Knowing that the minister
will not look at it until, having continued to blackmail the
queen, he will overreach himself and bring about his own
downfall, Dupin relishes the thought that D—— will then
read, in his enemy Dupin's hand,

'—Un dessein si funeste,
S'il n'est digne d'Atrée, est digne de Thyeste.'

—a quotation from Crébillon, the same author of whom the
narrator was thinking when Dupin, at the beginning of 'Rue
Morgue,' read his mind. (How apt, that Dupin should quote
Crébillon, who, after rivalling Voltaire with his early trage-

dies, fell on evil days, the victim of slanders circulated against
him at court, and retired to a garret with his dogs, cats, and
ravens, until, after a seclusion of two decades, he was elected
to the Académie Française and given a pension by Mme
Pompadour. Dupin would *intuitively* think of this tragedian
who lived to triumph over his enemies. Le poète manqué sera
vainqueur.)

The great detective has conceived his revenge in the spirit
of Thyestes, who in revenge for having seduced Atreus' wife,
was fed a meal of his own murdered sons. Whatever the 'evil
turn' of D——'s which Dupin 'good-humoredly' promised
never to forget, this is the fantasy of horror which wound the
springs of the master-detective's ratiocination. His 'ideality,'
his 'disentangling' are consonant with a planned revenge compared to which that of Montresor, who walled Fortunato
alive in the wine cave, is crude and self-defeating. Poe had
prefaced 'The Cask of Amontillado' with an apothegm of
Montresor's about revenge: 'I must not only punish, but punish with impunity. A wrong is unredressed when retribution
overtakes its redresser. It is equally unredressed when the
avenger fails to make himself felt as such to him who has
done the wrong.' And, in his *Marginalia*, years later, Poe had
mused,

> What can be more soothing, at once to a man's Pride
> and to his Conscience, than the conviction that, in taking
> vengeance on his enemies for injustice done him, he is
> simply to do them *justice* in return?

The letter—the secret letter—which Dupin leaves for D——
meets all these conditions for a perfect revenge. What remains a secret is the exact injury done him by D——.

There is a wild consistency running through all this. Monsieur Dupin, I venture, would not have bothered with the
Prefect's mystery had not he recognized that its solution
would prove a *peculiarly appropriate* manner of avenging
himself upon D——, who is, in every conceivable respect, his
mirror-image, his unscrupulous double. Now, the nature of
D——'s offense, the theft of a letter incriminating the royal

lady (doubtless the queen), must have been what so appealed to Dupin. To repay D——'s injury to himself, Dupin will undo D——'s injury to the queen and entrap him into political self-destruction—doubtless his beheading—to boot. So D——'s offense against Dupin is somehow analogous to his black-mailing the queen. But we are never told the contents of the purloined letter. What, however, could it be but a love-letter received by her from a suitor not her husband? And how else could Dupin's revenge be so perfect were not the author of the facsimile letter also the author of the letter first pur-loined?

You can see from this how dangerous is one's exposure to the ratiocinations of genius. Who wouldn't be Dupin, were only his own bulging temples to prove, by phrenological analysis, sufficiently ample to contain the like propensities of mind? By the time I have come to accept the propositions I've just advanced, that Dupin is the queen's suitor, I can't forbear to venture further into the entanglement of motives I have with such ratiocinative impunity unravelled: D——'s injury to Dupin involved either, or both, a purloining and the affections of a highborn lady. D—— had stolen from Dupin the love, which was rightfully his, of a lady of noblest birth. When D—— later purloins from the queen a letter in which (putatively) Dupin declares his heart, the injury is doubly compounded and Dupin proceeds with both genius and justice to construct his perfect revenge.

How am I doing as an 'analyst'? Too near the bone? Too much the psychoanalyst at the expense of the perhaps more necessary skills shown by Dupin in linguistics and the gather-ing of evidence, or by Legrand in chemical analysis and cryptography? Maybe you have a better solution than mine, in which 'Dupin' is a pseudonym the genius detective has taken, his real name being one that begins with the same initial, and may be that represented in his friend's narration as 'D——.'

Granted? Then—ah, then—exactly *what* is the significance of the letter which Dupin has left for his namesake whose injury against him was an attempt to bar him from the affections of the queen? The Minister, D——, being 'that *monstrum horrendum,* an unprincipled man of genius,' Dupin has left him a quotation from Crébillon's *Atrée,* inviting him to partake of a casserole containing his own son. And if D—— is who I think he is, then *it is Dupin who is in the dish.* The perfect revenge against a father is to deprive him of his fatherhood, a revenge made still more sweet to the injured son by being made more horrible for the father who is imagined as a cannibal devouring his own posterity. And that posterity is the son who perpetrates the plot. Such are the images of hopeless love and savory horror and suicide which wind the mainspring of 'The Purloined Letter.'

In his essay on Poe in Perry Miller's *Major Writers of America,* Richard Wilbur has resolved these problems of identity in a different way: 'Poe invites the reader to play detective himself, and to discover that the Minister D—— is the worldly, unprincipled "brother" or double of Auguste Dupin,' and 'the queen whom Dupin liberates from the Minister's power . . . is that sense of beauty which must not be the captive of our lower natures.' This reading, like all of Wilbur's, is at once consistent with Poe's images, is related to his other works, and is directed toward the elucidation therefrom of Poe's aesthetic. I do not doubt that Wilbur's reading is a true one—that D—— is a double of Dupin's and the queen a figure of inviolate beauty, whatever else they may be—but I would think that such an aesthetic, which is as implicit in Poe's stories of deeply felt terror as in his detective tales and poems, is itself as much a result as it is a cause. If it is a cause for the tales to exhibit their characters in the disguised and ambiguous relationships we have met and have yet to meet, it may result in its turn from still deeper instinctual conflicts than the desire, however passionately held, to create an inviolate figure or realm of beauty untouched by physical passion or bodily decay. The intricate ambiguities in Poe's work are compelled by his inescapable need to master his own unspeakable secrets.

This masterpiece of ratiocination, 'The Purloined Letter,' like so much else among Poe's poems and tales, is a disguised love story in which the images are images of images, their involutions the results of subliminal processes—like Dupin's intellection—of remembering back. Back before the beginnings of consciousness, to those analogies which, when once laid bare, even in cryptograms and in disguise, dramatize what they conceal, the primal truths and anguish of our being.

V

Voyages

GOING DOWN

Axiom: The *happy* characters in Poe are those who use their heads; the tormented, those who lose their minds.

Query: Who besides Monsieur Dupin and Legrand are the satisfied users of their ratiocinative powers?

These powers, if you concur with my ratiocinative analysis of Poe's ratiocinators, include the poetical, the intuitive, and the mathematical. The first is exercised by Poe himself, in his own person, as the author of his poems, tales, and critiques. The intuitive power of mind, insofar as it can be distinguished from the creative power, is that resolvent faculty by which his detectives disentangle human motives and decode the secret writings made by human agents. But the mathematical faculty—insofar as it is separable from the two powers aforesaid—takes as its province the operation of the physical properties of the universe, the natural, material world. So those heroes, or characters, or narrators of Poe's who enjoy the exercise of their mathematical ratiocinative powers are those who venture to pit their minds against the secret mysteries of nature.

The odd thing is, though, that they don't often set out to do this on purpose. Nor are they, at first glimpse, particularly fitted by training or station to grapple with the greatest secrets of the creation. They may be *des hommes moyens sensuels*, ordinary fellows in the midst of a humdrum life, taking an unexceptionable voyage, say, from Java, or perhaps,

as in 'A Descent into the Maelstrom,' setting out on the daily
run in their fishing-smack. Only then are they overtaken by
sudden and unexampled catastrophes, as though the laws
of Nature, heeding some hidden behest, cause the very elements to rear up in violent manifestations inimical to the
existence of man and his works. In such a case how does a
man survive? How does he comprehend his situation? What
can he learn from his catastrophic adventures?

'I have brought you here,' says the old Norse fisherman
who tells his tale—as did the Ancient Mariner—to one he
stoppeth on his way, as they reach the pinnacle of a lofty
crag overlooking the sea, 'so that you might have the best
possible view of the scene of that event I mentioned'—he
means the dreaded Maelstrom—'and to tell you the whole
story with the spot just under your eye.'

So while we watch the sea below (we of course are looking
through the eyes of the beholder on the crag) we witness the
tidal maelstrom—

> Here the vast bed of the waters, seamed and scarred into a
> thousand conflicting channels, burst suddenly into phren-
> sied convulsions—heaving, boiling, hissing—gyrating in gi-
> gantic and innumerable vortices. . . . In a few minutes
> more, . . . the general surface grew somewhat more
> smooth, and the whirlpools, one by one, disappeared, while
> prodigious streaks of foam . . . spreading out to a great
> distance, and entering into combination, took unto them-
> selves the gyratory motion of the subsided vortices, and
> seemed to form the germ of another more vast. Suddenly
> —very suddenly—this assumed a distinct and definite exist-
> ence, in a circle of more than a mile in diameter. . . .

I quote this vivid description, not out of an interest in maelstroms but because the *pattern* here described proves to be
Poe's singular and recurrent image for all natural processes,
for the nature of Nature, the subliminal current in which
our lives are unwitting participants. This is the resolution
of a thousand phrensied convulsions into a single concentric
circle:

> The edge of the whirl was represented by a broad belt
> of gleaming spray; but no particle of this slipped into the

mouth of the terrific funnel, whose interior, as far as the eye could fathom it, was a smooth, shining, and jet-black wall of water, inclined to the horizon at an angle of some forty-five degrees, speeding dizzily round and round with a swaying and sweltering motion, and sending forth to the winds an appalling voice, half shriek, half roar, such as not even the mighty cataract of Niagara ever lifts up in its agony to Heaven.

Yet, as we are fascinatedly drawn toward the vertiginous lure of this funnel in the sea, we become aware that it is not only Nature enacting the pattern of its own ulterior motive —the incorporation of a thousand convolutions into the unity of a single vortex. It is also exactly that lure toward self-annihilation, that fall into the precipice, toward which the Imp of the Perverse within propels us. The energies of the created world are in this image fused with the energies of the psyche, both being subject to the same laws.

Although in 'The Imp of the Perverse' Poe had avowed that 'To indulge, for a moment, in any attempt at *thought*, is to be inevitably lost,' the Norse seaman has evidently not been lost. For he has survived, and is telling us his all but unbelievable tale, now, atop the crag, as we peer down into the abyss from which he has miraculously escaped. And his escape is due solely to his having exercised the ratiocinative faculty when in the relentless grip of a catastrophe.

He tells how it was his custom to fish with his brothers in the dangerous grounds near the waters where the maelstrom formed, they always depending upon their skill in seamanship to negotiate the homeward passage in safety. But on one certain day, although his watch assured him that the tide was safe, they found their craft irresistibly drawn toward the rushing waters, in 'the sickening sweep of the descent.' His watch had run down, and now the brothers are rushing toward a destruction the view of which is as magniloquently beautiful, as instinct with grandeur, as would be a glimpse of omnipotence itself:

The boat appeared to be hanging, as if by magic, midway down, upon the interior surface of a funnel cast in circumference, prodigious in depth, and whose perfectly

smooth sides might have been mistaken for ebony, but for
the bewildering rapidity with which they spun around,
and for the gleaming and ghastly radiance they shot forth.
. . . The rays of the moon seemed to search the very bottom of the profound gulf; but still I could make out nothing distinctly on account of a thick mist in which everything
was there enveloped, and over which there hung a magnificent rainbow, like that narrow and tottering bridge
which Musselmen say is the only pathway between Time
and Eternity.

And that is where we are, suspended between Time and
Eternity, caught in this paroxysm of the natural forces of
the seas. I think of myself as being in that boat, spinning
with ever wilder motion in an ever-narrowing circle, and I
ask myself—the part of me that is typing this page in the
solid security of a room lined with books in a farmhouse
beside the placid tides of Penobscot Bay asks that part of
me which is vertiginously plummeting down, down, down—
What would I have noticed, thought, remembered, of my
terrifying predicament? And I turn again to the page, to Poe's
page, and notice the extraordinary observational and nota-
tional powers of his simple Norseman, who has seen and recalled *everything* that happened to him, and whose command
of the language of his recollection (Norse? English?) is in
fact superb. What swelling periods, what billowing syntax,
what clear resolutions of his sentences. A style of complete
and reasonable perspicuity, a style we do not even notice
as style, so complete is the identification of its structure and
its language with those of the phenomena it is employed to
describe, to recreate.

This simple fisherman has a head on those sturdy shoulders. A head he knew enough to use. Although, as I've mentioned, the Imp of the Perverse is impervious to thought,
inimical to thought, undeterred by thought, what does
Norseman do as his smack whirls around in the maelstrom
but—

I now began to watch, with a strange interest, the numerous things that floated in our company. I *must* have been

delirious, for I even sought *amusement* in speculating upon
the relative velocities of their several descents toward the
foam below.

And, noticing that a Dutch merchant ship plunged downward more swiftly than a pine tree, and making numerous
other comparisons of the kind, and recollecting his observations of the bulk, the weight, the buoyancy, and the condition (whether shattered or whole) of various bits of debris
cast up on shore by the afterwaves of the maelstrom, he came
to three general conclusions, conclusions made possible by
his Dupin-like intuitive ratiocination, applied with mathematical precision to the observation of physical phenomena:

> The first was, that as a general rule, the larger the bodies
> were, the more rapid their descent—the second, that, be-
> tween two masses of equal extent, the one spherical, the
> other *of any other shape*, the superiority in speed of descent
> was with the sphere—the third, that, between two masses of
> equal size, the one cylindrical, and the other of any other
> shape, the cylinder was absorbed the more slowly.

How's that for level-headed intuitive ratiocination? Imagine this Norse fisherman, figuring away about velocities,
masses, rates of descent, cylinders and spheres! Full marks
in Intermediate Physics, a subject in which I was always at
sea. No, I'd have gone down, down, with the boat, with the
brother, never to be cast up—as is the Norseman, who leaps
overboard clutching a *cylindrical cask*—upon the surface of
the sea, to be rescued by a boatload of his mates. 'They
knew me no more than they would have known a traveler
from the spirit-land. My hair, which had been raven black
the day before, was as white as you see it now.'

What strikes me about this fisherman, so much more intuitive and mathematical and fortunate than I—is how much
amusement, how much joy, he exacted from both his swift
calculations and from the telling of his tale. He is in fact the
ratiocinative principle incarnate, and to that fact of his being he both owes his continued life and derives his pleasure
in the exercise of his nature.

But the man to whom such terrifying adventures befall
may *not* be able to save himself, as does the Norseman, by
that freedom from fear given by the power of disengagement
from disaster which the instantaneous computations of an
intuitive intellect confers upon the suffering body. There
may even be predicaments a man may find himself in which
do not lend themselves to ratiocinative analysis.

Turn the page, and here's such a one. A chap has taken
ship from Java, an ordinary ship but a rather curious fellow.
Not a simple soul, like the fisherman, but an odd duck,
similar in fact to the reclusive, misanthropic detectives we
have already met and to the haunted lovers we have yet to
meet in Poe's Arabesques:

> Of my country and my family I have little to say. Ill
> usage and length of years have driven me from the one and
> estranged me from the other. Hereditary wealth afforded
> me an education of no common order, and a contemplative
> turn of mind enabled me to methodise the stories which
> early study diligently garnered up. . . .

This familiar fellow is about to write the 'MS. Found in a
Bottle.' He goes on, in this first paragraph, to assure us of
'the aridity of my genius, a deficiency of imagination has been
imputed to me as a crime.'

> Upon the whole, no person could be less liable than my-
> self to be led away from the severe precincts of truth by
> the *ignes fatui* of superstition. I have thought proper to
> premise thus much, lest the incredible tale I have to tell
> should be considered the raving of a crude imagination,
> than the positive experience of a mind to which the rever-
> ies of fancy have been a dead letter and a nullity.

Edgar, Edgar, you protest too much. But Poe has learned
well the need, in a fantastic adventure tale, of a credible witness—learned well from *Gulliver's Travels* and *Robinson
Crusoe* the indispensability, to the fabulist, of a downright,
commonsensical narrator. If we cannot fault him when he
says, 'Our ship was a beautiful ship of about four hundred
tons, copper-fastened, and built at Bombay of Malabar teak,'

why would we be likely to doubt his word a page later when he notices that 'The air now became intolerably hot, and was loaded with spiral exhalations similar to those arising from heated iron'? We have suddenly stepped from the matter-of-fact discourse about the cargo and the ship's itinerary into the wonderworld of 'The Ancient Mariner.' The ship is overtaken, smitten, and stunned by a storm, a tidal wave, and the narrator plus one old Swede are the only survivors of the demasted and waterlogged hulk.

This narrator, who thinks himself devoid of imagination, proves the truth of an apothegm Wallace Stevens a century later would inscribe in his own marginalia, which he, after Erasmus, called 'Adagia': 'In the presence of extraordinary actuality, consciousness takes the place of imagination.' Poe's narrator turns nothing that happens to him into metaphor, he seems simply to record the actual. He is a scrupulously accurate *noticer*, and if the terrifying energy of the destructive elements hurtles him onward in wild career, his account of the fact becomes infused with that dire and threatening energy itself. Now for five days and nights 'the hulk flew at a rate defying comprehension. . . . Eternal night continued to envelop us. . . . All around were horror, and thick gloom, and a black sweltering desert of ebony . . . . having made farther to southward than any previous navigators . . . . I could not help feeling the utter hopelessness of hope itself.'

We are in what will become a familiar predicament for Poe's explorers. We have ventured farther from the world, farther from recorded experience, than anyone hitherto has gone. What happens to us now has never before been the lot of man, at least of none who has survived to tell the tale:

> We were at the bottom of one of these abysses, when a quick scream from my companion broke fearfully upon the night. 'See! see!' cried he, shrieking in my ears, 'Almighty God! see! see!' As he spoke I became aware of a dull sullen glare of red light which streamed down the sides of the vast chasm where we lay, and threw a fitful brilliancy upon our deck. Casting my eyes upwards, I beheld a spectacle which froze the current of my blood. At a terrific height

directly above us, and upon the very verge of the precipitous descent, hovered a gigantic ship of perhaps four thousand tons . . . what mainly inspired us with horror and
astonishment, was that she bore up under a press of sail in
the very teeth of that supernatural sea, and of that un-
governable hurricane.

This ghostly ship bears right down upon the hulk, and the
force of the collision throws the narrator into the rigging of
the huge vessel. He falls to the deck unnoticed by her crew,
'and soon found an opportunity of secreting myself in the
hold.'
Why does he secrete himself in her hold?

Why I did so I can hardly tell. An indefinite sense of awe,
which at first sight of the navigators of the ship had taken
hold of my mind, was perhaps the principle of my con-
cealment.

One of these awe-inspiring navigators passes by the concealed
narrator, who sees on his face the evidence of great age, hears
him mutter 'some words of a language I could not understand.' His aspect 'was a wild mixture of the peevishness of
second childhood, and the solemn dignity of a God.'
Although Narrator does not know it, he has passed the
nadir of horror. His transference from a sinking ship 'of about
four hundred tons, copper-fastened, and built at Bombay
of Malabar teak' to 'a gigantic ship of perhaps four thousand
tons,' built and fastened and bound Heaven alone knows
where or how, signifies a *change of state*. Narrator has passed
out of our life, and now that he has seen one of his
new navigators up close, 'A feeling, for which I have no name,
has taken possession of my soul—a sensation which will admit
of no analysis, to which the lessons of bygone times are
inadequate.'
We are now beyond the reach of ratiocination, for all
analysis is based necessarily upon the laws and experiences
of the known life. Now that an awareness of his unex-

ampled destiny overtakes Narrator, he ventures into the captain's cabin—he is *invisible* to the crew!—and he

> took thence the materials with which I write, and have written. I shall from time to time continue this journal. It is true that I may not find an opportunity of transmitting it to the world, but I will not fail to make the endeavor. At the last moment I will enclose the MS. in a bottle, and cast it within the sea.

Well now, where are you, Narrator? Who are these aged Godlike creatures in their second childhoods, who guide their ship toward God knows where, and pass you by as though you were not there?

The rest of the tale endeavors to make the answers to such questions opaque. For opacity is as close to definitiveness as we, with our five senses, our limited powers of conceptualization, our meagre wordhoard of language, can come in such a realm. We cannot be certain whether that realm is one of being, or of becoming, or of unbeing or unbecoming. Poe tries to achieve the clarity of opacity by having his narrator jot disjointedly into his journal such observations as this one:

> While musing upon the singularity of my fate, I unwittingly daubed with a tar-brush the edges of a neatly-folded studding-sail which lay near me on a barrel. The studding-sail is now bent upon the ship, and the thoughtless touches of the brush are spread out into the word DISCOVERY.

Ah, Poe, here is your true 'Philosophy of Composition'! In *this* wise, not by your exposition of predestination fore-ordained, as in 'The Raven,' does the imagination cross the bourne between this life of sufferings and the realm of revelations toward which it is the nature of the soul to yearn! Or so it is when the soul has already arrived, or is well on its way, there. Then, and only then, will the random daubings of a wayward hand unfurl into the decoded word, *Discovery*. But what has been discovered?

Take it, Narrator: 'We are surely doomed to hover continually upon the brink of eternity, without taking a final plunge into the abyss. . . . It is evident that we are hurrying

onward to some exciting knowledge—some never-to-be-
imparted secret, whose attainment is destruction.'

And strange as is everything his eye beholds, strange and
'imbued with the spirit of Eld,' the crew gliding 'like the
ghosts of buried centuries,' yet 'there will occasionally flash
across my mind a sensation of familiar things . . . an un-
accountable memory of old foreign chronicles and ages long
ago.' Amid all these unfathomable recollections as of a former
existence, Narrator recalls an apothegm by which an old
Dutch seaman gave witness to his own veracity: 'It is as sure
as there is a sea where the ship itself will grow in bulk like
the living body of the seaman.'

I have nearly catalogued the curiosa of this MS., am
nearly done. I've yet to give the description of the captain of
the ship, and him we must inspect if we're to know whose
ship this is, and what her itinerary:

> . . . a feeling of irrepressible reverence and awe mingled
> with the sensation of wonder with which I regarded him.
> In stature, he is nearly my own height; that is, about five
> feet eight inches. He is of a well-knit and compact frame
> of body, neither robust, nor remarkably otherwise . . .

—that actually was Edgar Allan Poe's height. It is also my
own stature exactly—

> . . . But it is the singularity of the expression which reigns
> upon the face—it is the intense, the wonderful, the thrilling
> evidence of old age so utter, so extreme, which excites
> within my spirit a sense—a sentiment ineffable. . . . His
> grey hairs are records of the past, and his greyer eyes are
> sybils of the future. The cabin floor was thickly strewn
> with strange, iron-clasped folios, and mouldering instru-
> ments of science, and obsolete long-forgotten charts. . . .
> He pored, with a fiery, unquiet eye, over a paper which I
> took to be a commission, and which, at all events, bore
> the signature of a monarch. He murmured to himself . . .
> some low peevish syllables of a foreign tongue; and al-
> though the speaker was close at my elbow, his voice seemed
> to reach my ears from the distance of a mile.

And now, quickly, before the ship spins on her immutable course between the crags of ice, let me tell what I have found. For I have daubed, nearly at random, these words and syllables upon the foregoing pages, and now they furl, they swell and billow with the word DISCOVERY—

I can tell you, if you do not already know, who is the captain; what ship is under his command; to which monarch he is subject; the secret writing upon his commission—

What ship is this, in perpetual existence on a rushing torrential sea, bearing her crew 'like the ghosts of buried centuries'? A ship that we are to believe, if we believe a word of this report, grows in bulk like the body of a living seaman. A ship like Poe's 'Dream-Land'—'Out of Space, Out of Time.' A ship hovering over the vast abyss of eternity.

Eternity: the perpetual continuation of the past, in which the present is scarcely visible, and the captain's eyes are sybils of the future.

A map of this voyage will show her course, heaving on titanic winds and waves in southernmost seas, avoiding all archipelagoes, until, at the end, the end of the voyage and of the tale,

Oh, horror upon horror!—the ice opens suddenly to the right, and to the left, and we are whirling dizzily, in immense concentric circles, round and round the borders of a gigantic amphitheatre, the summit of whose walls is lost in the darkness and the distance. But little time will be left me to ponder upon my destiny! The circle rapidly grows small—we are plunging madly within the grasp of the whirlpool—and amid a roaring, and bellowing, and thundering of ocean and tempest, the ship is quivering—oh God! and—going down!

Down without a trace, save the bottle, cast overboard, in which this MS. was preserved.

Well, I'm calmer now about my discoveries. I see I took care not to make them very specific, and so my hints may not entrap me. But I'll come clean and say: the voyage toward 'exciting knowledge,' that 'never-to-be-imparted secret, whose attainment is destruction,' is the journey of the 'soul' remembering back, back, back, to its very beginnings. Back through the vortex of birth. The ship, 'her' bulk swelling like a living body in whose hold he secretes himself—what is 'she' but an image of the mother's womb, wherein dwelt those other images of a past almost remembered, the spooky captain and his spirit-crew? For indeed the womb is the well-fount of our unconsciousness before we emerge into the pains of consciousness, and in the womb we are imbued with that instinctual knowledge of our own past, our own beginnings, the state of unity toward which we ever after yearn. But to attain that state after being banished from it by our birth—this is to court, to seek, to embrace destruction. The life in which we seek that unity is by its nature incompatible with the unity we seek, and to gain the one we must forfeit the other, either way. Life without unity, unity without *our* life.

This is Edgar Allan Poe's revision of the books of Genesis and Revelation.

This is a revealed knowledge to which neither mathematics nor science can lead us. The instruments of science lie unattended on the captain's floor. The captain—who is he, who is so terribly aged, yet has the same height and stature as Poe and I? The captain whose hairs are the records of the past, whose eyes the sybils of the future. And with those second-seeing eyes he broods upon a commission, signed by a monarch.

If, in the allegory which I discover here, the ship—among its other meanings—represents a remembrance of prenatal life, who would likely be the captain of that vessel? Who, looking like me, the unseen observer-participant-narrator, but the figure of my onlie begettor, the father? He, too, partakes of Eld, for are we not descended from the men who are descended from the beginnings of time? And do we not contain within ourselves the history, and the future, of our race?

And what of that monarchical seal upon his patent? To the bidding of which monarch would he be subject, on this voyage in eternity, but the monarch of all?

Yes, I call this tale Poe's allegory, though I know full well

Poe's contemptuous dismissal of the allegory he found in Hawthorne's moral-burdened *Twice-Told Tales:*

> In defense of allegory, (however, or for whatever object employed,) there is scarcely one respectable word to be said. Its best appeals are made to the fancy—that is to say, to our sense of adaptation, not of matters proper, but of matters improper for the purpose, of the real with the unreal; . . . The deepest emotion aroused within us by the happiest allegory, *as* allegory, is a very, very imperfectly satisfied sense of the writer's ingenuity in overcoming a difficulty we should have preferred his not having attempted to overcome. . . . One thing is clear, that if allegory ever establishes a fact, it is by dint of overturning a fiction.

That's rather good, isn't it? Not to be surprised that he next calls *The Pilgrim's Progress* 'a ludicrously over-rated book'! It might take a C. S. Lewis to restore allegory to our good opinion, if Poe's demolition of the mode seems convincing. But, as a matter of fact, it is Edgar himself who restores allegory—*when properly executed*—to its deserving place in our affections.

> Where the suggested meaning runs through the obvious one in a *very* profound under-current so as never to interfere with the upper one without our own volition, so as never to show itself unless *called* to the surface, there only, for the proper uses of fictitious narrative, is it available at all.

So there is allegory and allegory. There is the intrusive inversion of a fact by a fiction, in which a chap whose name may well be Edgar Drambuie has to be called Christian because the author insists that we acknowledge him as Everyman in search of salvation. Not so good. How can the author of such a fable achieve the *unity of effect* at which the true fabulist aims? But there's also the subliminal kind of allegory—as Poe, using the then-available critical vocabulary, had to call what we would describe as symbolism. A set of *correspondences* (as Baudelaire, the symbolist, acknowledged them to be), which are ever-present in the story but as a *'very* profound under-current,' coming to the surface only when called up by the reader.

O.K.? From this I take my commission, sealed by a monarch, to call up the under-currents in the tales of Poe. *This* is the secret writing which his cryptographic imagination is forever interweaving with his reports of believable or fabulous adventures. We follow the course of the voyage, its proximate end—destruction, or survival and return. We read the MS. in a bottle we have picked up from the upper current of the sea, where it has washed ashore on our beach. We give our credence, or fealty, to the verbatim report of the humdrums and the wonders that Poe's voyagers have witnessed. Only below the surface, beneath the currents of the oceans, in the central veins and arteries beneath our own skins, do these submerged analogies flow and pulse into our awareness. Then, by our own ratiocinative processes, we intuitively put together the correspondences with the meanings to which they correspond.

When I was in graduate school they used to call this feat 'the New Criticism.' But it is at least as old as the tales and poems, the plays and novels upon which it was exercised. For who imagines that the poets are really, as Socrates thought them to be, so smitten by madness that they know not what they write?

And yet, and yet . . . for Poe it was a necessity that the Truth he tried to discover be embodied, rather than stated, in his tales and poems. Embodied as that under-current which never interferes with the manifest level of the narrative. So that even at its most proximate revelation, the final meaning of his fables remains shrouded in the perplexing ambiguities of the metaphors by which it is made perceptible. It is as though Poe himself cannot bear to rip away those ambiguities and baldly state his themes, in the artistically cruder form of an allegory. Why cannot Poe bear to say out what is on his mind?

Easy for me to complain, or for you to demand, 'See here, Poe, none of your impositions and ambiguities, understand?'

But that's no way to treat a Sooth-Sayer. Like the Cumaean Sybil, Poe brings us truths he cannot, truths we *could not*, bear to hear, and so speaks in prophetic riddles, in secret writings which seem to have an interest, a different interest altogether, of their own. We are caught up in the adventure, the plot, and spin around and around the maelstrom or wander about the spectral ship, rigid with empathetic fright or wide-eyed with the contagion of the observer's wonder. We all but forget the unstated theme, the theme which works *its will on us* while we are attending to other things, like the speed of objects rotating in the whirlpool or the strange attributes of the ship and crew. This is Poe's way, this is a poet's way, of making a revelation a revelation.

Also, and not merely incidentally, this way protects him. Protects him from that most primitive of tabus, saying the Unsayable. The ancient Israelites, I have been somewhere told, denied themselves the pleasure we so cavalierly indulge of taking the Lord's name—not merely in vain, but at all. They feared to pronounce the forbidden syllables, and even in their writings spelt the sacred name without vowels, so that it would remain forever unsayable: YHVH. Jumping Jehosophat! Poe doesn't scruple to call God God, but there are more sacred revelations still which he dare not say out loud. The terror in Poe's tales is a real terror. The exhilaration in the telling is his way of surmounting his fear, the complex interrelationship of images in the tales his way of busying his mind, his ratiocinative power fusing together into a new unity the parts of the secret that obsesses him. Thus he cannot, need not, say directly what is his terror, for in its indirect expression he has assuaged the fear.

The fear of what? You dumdum, I asked myself, after reading these tales of going down a dozen times over, the fear of what? That too unfurled upon the swelling sail of my ratiocinative powers, surging across Poe's tempestuous seas. The fear, the guilty fear, of re-entering his mother's womb.

Obvious. But not at first to me. From which I sadly infer my resemblance, after all, to the Prefect of Police. To live at the emotional pitch of Edgar Poe, with all your nerves throbbing out loud, this is too painful. I can't bear it. I protect my nerves, protect my sobersided sensibilities, from such hard home truths by a lifetime's training in various bureaucracies, Prefectlike, the methodical application of techniques designed for the systematic missing of the point. That way I keep busy, and need not tear my guts out every time I stop, and think.

Of course I speak of myself as a representative of the mass of men. 'I'=the reading public.

And yet, had I, myself, like the Prefect, gone into police bureaucracy, I'd not be quite like *him*. For like Dupin—, like Minister D——, —I have something of a name as a poet.

The vice that redeems, by bringing home the soul to the truths it is its nature to know. And turns that painful knowledge into the pleasure of Art.

SENT UP

> 'All voyages to the moon, an ever-recurring human phantasy, always, in their deepest sense, represent a yearning to return to the mother.'
>   —Marie Bonaparte, *The Life and Works of Edgar Allan Poe, A Psycho-Analytic Interpretation*

If Princess Bonaparte (yes, she was a real princess) is right —and she studied with Freud himself—then what have I been listening to on my shortwave radio this summer, as accolades crackle across the oceans from the B.B.C., Radio Moscow (grudgingly), Radio France, Radio Denmark, the Australian Broadcasting Company, etc., displacing even reports of the lull in Viet Nam, the religious riots in Ulster, the war between El Salvador and Honduras? What have I been hearing but mankind's yearning to return to its mother. For no other motive can so strongly act on nations so diverse, peoples so rivalrous, to unite them in their fascinated, their mesmerized following of the thrust of the phallic rocket, the detachment of the little spermship, the slow and calculated opening thereof and the cautious emergence therefrom of Astronaut

Neil Armstrong, in the protective encasement of his pressure
suit. We can, we must, conclude that this yearning for the
totality of the moon's maternal embrace was the hidden un-
dercurrent which shaped the policies of the administrations
of three presidents—Kennedy, Johnson, Nixon; was the interior motive (masked by the manifest profit rationalization)
of the military-industrial complex; was and is the chief desire
of those thousands of artisans in the space and electronics
industries, the wiring and welding shops, the public relations
and crowd control minions of NASA. A nation of mother's
boys.

How apt, to be gawking and harking to the hoopla about
our Conquest of the Moon (the astronauts, as I type this,
are just emerging from the womb of their clinical isolation
trailer, after a three-week incubation—they're being reborn
with tickertape parades in three places: New York, Chicago,
Los Angeles!)—how apt, that the nation's public life is
fixated by these goings-on, just when I got around to reading
Edgar Poe's 'The Unparalleled Adventures of One Hans
Pfaall.'

Hans Pfaall flew to the moon, in a balloon of his own design and manufacture, in 1835, anticipating by one hundred and thirty-four years what it took the United States
Government—its science, R & D, military, that whole gang
—to bring off at last.

Edgar Poe had an exploring mind.

In 'A Descent into the Maelstrom' and 'MS. Found in a
Bottle' he explored the ocean and its depths; in the *Narrative
of Arthur Gordon Pym* (to which I'll come) he explores its
extent as well. In these tales he simply took hold of a popular
genre of the day, the explorer's narrative, and made what
was often in life nearly legendary into a fable pregnant with
the meanings his own needs dictated. In 'Hans Pfaall' and
another sketch, 'The Balloon Hoax,' Poe explored the
heavens. These explorations of space are his so-called science
fictions, the genre he invented and bequeathed to a host of
later, more successful writers, from Jules Verne to Ray
Bradbury.

He also explores time. 'Mellonta Tauta' is a letter from
the future to the present, telling us what our world—that
is, Poe's world of 1848—looks like a thousand years hence.
Poe can imagine backwards as well as forwards in time, and
in 'Some Words with a Mummy' he causes a worthy Egyptian to arise from his long slumber and tell an assemblage of
present-day savants what their world looks like compared to
the standards of his own time, several thousand years ago.

The explorations of space and time all have these features
in common: Their protagonists have left our dull workaday
existence for a journey elsewhere. They have journeyed toward a revelation—and they bring back knowledge thereof.
Bring back or send it. For often they stay where they are, or
can't get back to our life; and what we learn of their new
existence comes by way of an epistle.

A letter bearing great news. As in 'MS. Found in a Bottle.'

Or 'The Unparalleled Adventures of One Hans Pfaall.'

The account of Hans's balloon trip to the moon is Poe's
sequel to an earlier send-up of his that caused a lot of
notoriety and thus delighted the author. In 1831 he had the
fortuitous notion of writing a suppositious journal kept by a
couple of aeronauts who inflate a balloon in Wales, intending to land in Paris, but are blown by an unexpected tempest
out over the Atlantic. Deciding to ride their ill wind, they
have the good fortune to arrive, only three days later, on
Sullivan's Island, South Carolina, putting down, I suppose,
within eyeshot of the spot where Legrand would soon dig up
the treasure and the bones. This tale, written with great circumstantiality in a breathless prose that convincingly suggests the intoxicated enthusiasm of amateur aeronauts succeeding in their conquest of space, was actually taken
seriously by the New York *Sun*, and for the day or so between
receipt of the 'report' and a reply, by post, to the paper's
request for confirming details from South Carolina, the
Balloon Hoax was the talk of the town.

I think this day may have been the happiest day of Poe's
career.

Hoaxiepoe. That's one of the mirror-images of Horror-Haunted Edgar. The one that laughs—immoderately.

Hoaxiepoe later wrote up another spoof, 'Hans Pfaall.' Not even the ninnies of the New York press and public could mistake this send-up for a sober truth, though, for its style of humor is a steal from Irving's *Knickerbocker History of New York*.

And the epigraph to the tale is a stanza from 'Tom O'Bedlam's Song'—

> With a heart of furious fancies,
>   Whereof I am commander,
> With a burning spear *and a horse of air*
> To the wilderness I wander.

Hans Pfaall is the very soul of methodicalness, a mender of bellows who, by reading treatises on aeronautics purchased in Rotterdam bookstalls, teaches himself what it would take the U.S.A. industrial complex so long to learn. But for Poe, as we know, genius and madness are coeval stars in the firmament. So it is meet that Pfaall's adventure be prefaced by the song of a madman. Just as it is meet that Hoaxiepoe write a send-up to tell us something serious.

The jocularity of the *Knickerbocker History* style inflicts on us such felicities as the name of the burgomaster of Rotterdam, Superbus Von Underduk, and the locations of Hans Pfaall's house in Sauerkraut Alley. Poe's jovial writings seem to us nowadays unseasonably labored, but perhaps they really struck *his* contemporaries as funny. Anyhow, this one begins with the arrival in Rotterdam of 'a balloon manufactured entirely of dirty newspapers' (an allusion, mayhap, to 'The Balloon Hoax'?), shaped like 'a huge fool's-cap turned upside down.' In its gondola is 'a very singular somebody,' two feet tall—a moonman who drops at the feet of the burgomaster 'a huge letter sealed with red sealing-wax' and flies off. The letter is Hans Pfaall's account of himself, phrased as an appeal for pardon for his offense—killing (in the explosion which launched his balloon) three creditors who had been hounding him to death.

Now I don't doubt that Hans Pfaall's hidden motive in
his moon-flight is, as the princess says, 'to return to the
mother.' But let's put mother aside for now. I'm intrigued
by other yearnings of Hans Pfaall's.

For instance, he seems a caricature foreshadowing a later,
greater wanderer, when he says,

> I soon grew poor as a rat, and, having a wife and children
> to provide for, my burdens at length became intolerable,
> and I spent hour after hour in reflecting upon the most
> convenient method of putting an end to my life.

And a little later,

> In this state of mind, wishing to live, yet wearied with life,
> the treatise at the stall of the bookseller, backed by the
> opportune discovery of my cousin of Nantz, opened a re-
> source to my imagination. I then finally made up my mind.
> I determined to depart, yet live—to leave the world, yet con-
> tinue to exist—in short, to drop enigmas, I resolved, let
> what would ensue, to force a passage, if I could, *to the
> moon.*

Well, once again I've prematurely revealed Poe's plot so
that the climax of his send-up is a let-down. But how very
like Ishmael's departure from this world! And there's no
Dutch vaudeville in this part of the telling. In fact there's
none at all in the body of Pfaall's letter, the tone of which
alternates between a tremendously detailed recapitulation
of his means of procedure (which, like the detective stories,
has 'the *air* of method'), and 'much of madness in the calm
survey which I began to take of my situation.' For despite
Hans's careful calculations and his ingenious improvisations,
his adventure is from the beginning one that teeters on the
rims of jeopardy, as when

> The balloon at first collapsed, then furiously expanded,
> then whirled round and round with sickening velocity, and
> finally, reeling and staggering like a drunken man, hurled
> me over the rim of the car, and left me dangling, at a ter-
> rific height, with my head downward, and my face outward,
> by a piece of slender cord about three feet in length, which

hung accidentally through a crevice . . . and in which, as
I fell, my left foot became most providentially entangled.
. . . I gasped convulsively for breath . . . I felt my eyes
starting from their sockets—a horrible nausea overwhelmed
me—and at length I lost all consciousness in a swoon.

But not to worry, the date is the first of April, and Hans,
recovering consciousness, begins to use that fool's head of
his. 'If I felt any emotion at all, it was a kind of chuckling
satisfaction at the cleverness I was about to display in ex-
tricating myself from this dilemma.' Never mind, now, how
he does it, it's the dilemma that enchants me. For I've been
in that dilemma before—my eyes falling out of their sockets
as my face was pressed against the clock in 'A Predicament';
my head dangling downward from a terrific height as I
whirled round and round with sickening velocity in the
whirlpool of the maelstrom; and as for gasping 'convulsively for breath,' well, I've read 'The Fall of the House of
Usher'—why did Roderick Usher inter his sister living in the
tomb? Roderick, why did you bury Madeline alive?

So, under the Dutch costumes in 'Hans Pfaall' the sensibilities of Hoaxiepoe vibrate to the same terrors as do the
tales of Horror-Haunted Edgar.

Poe Poe Poe Poe Poe—you always get what you aim at,
your *unity of effect*.

Well, Hans Pfaall—Mme Bonaparte notes that his name
may allude to '*pfahl*,' the German word for *stake*, i.e.,
phallus. It may. It's also pronounced 'fall,' in opposition to
his effort, to rise. But then, that's what a phall-us is always
trying to do. As Dr. Williams advised Paterson, 'Keep your
pecker up.'

The rest of the story tells how he did it—got to the moon,
that is. I kept thinking of Hans Pfaall's journal as I listened
to our bold astronauts communicate with Houston via UHF
radio. What a rhetoric they used to report their state: 'That
you, Houston? All systems Go.' Odd that a self-taught
bellows-mender of Rotterdam should be able to report *his*
progress in a style so much more supple, so little burdened
with jargon, so instinct with the exhilarating rhythms of the

experiences described. For all that, Poe's Pfaall is nothing if not exact and seeming-scientific in his descriptions, citing authorities, measuring velocities and bulks, observing the earth, the moon, the meteorites from different apogees each day. He has built a balloon inflated by the action of a certain gas upon a certain metal-like substance; he has outfitted its wicker gondola with all the necessary apparatus; he has brought with him a cat, whose ease of breathing will guide his own (to his surprise she proves pregnant and gives birth en route through the heavens). All this and more.

All this and more the burgomaster and the Royal Astronomers of Rotterdam find on the document thrown down to them. The pardon requested, of course, would be of little use to Hans Pfaall, since he has remained on the moon.

> To the truth of this observation the burgomaster assented, and the matter was therefore at an end. Not so, however, rumors and speculations. The letter, having been published, gave rise to a variety of gossip and opinion. Some of the over-wise even made themselves ridiculous by decrying the whole business as nothing better than a hoax. But hoax, with these sort of people, is, I believe, a general term for all matters above their comprehension.

Hoaxiepoe, you've tipped your hand. When *you* wish to reveal a matter above *our* comprehension—you know very well how limited, how intolerant, how unimaginative is our comprehension—you trick out your truth as hoax. A hoax within a hoax. Because the joke is, it's no joke at all.

Very funny.

And where should we think Hans Pfaall has arisen to, what planet is that where he will 'leave the world, yet continue to exist,' but Tycho Brahe's star, Al Aaraaf? That's moon enough, the only moon where such things can be.

That's the truth inscribed on the unwritten letter brought back from the common moon by her later visitants, Messrs. Armstong, Aldrin and Collins. On *that* moon there's nobody, nothing, nothing but a beautiful desolation which still stares upon us with its single eye, like the spirit of a distant mother regarding her errant, yearning children far below.

COUNTERCLOCKWISE

Another of Poe's French *analystes*, M. Jean-Paul Weber, following the psychoanalytic clues suggested by Mme Bonaparte, has proved that the chief theme in Poe's work is his struggle against time. There it is: the pendulum sweeping over the pit, the savage 'Scimitar of Time,' as Poe subtitled 'A Predicament,' the ticktock telling of the expository heart. And more: In 'MS. Found in a Bottle,' M. Weber discovers that 'The gigantic ship (the minute hand) glides rapidly upon the waters.' And more: 'The intimate and uncanny relationship between the house and the Ushers parallels that which exists between the clock and the hands that "dwell" within it and are wholly governed by its mechanisms.' So the hour hand inters the minute hand living in its tomb!

Bullfeathers.

You can wind a clock just so tight. It will tell the time, the time of day. But not the time of eternity. *That's* the time that Edgarpoe is trying to tell, and the dials and hands of this world are useless in his quest. The ratiocinative mind, so deliriously employed by Hans Pfaall to right the balloon, so redemptorily indulged by the Norse seaman to save himself from the maelstrom, that ratiocinative power is wound on the mainsprings of our daily clock. It won't tell us the time on Al Aaraaf or the moon.

And so it is that although Poe's voyagers may spend all their time ratiocinating like mad, the knowledge they send back to us in their letters cast on the sea is not the knowledge they ratiocinated to learn. It came to them while they were ratiocinating, came from a nonratiocinative order of experience. It is revelation.

The Norse fisherman was too simple to know what he knew. The tale he stopped the traveller to tell is of his *escape*. His escape from what the nameless voyager *into* the maelstrom found, and left in the bottle: 'some never-to-be-imparted secret, whose attainment is destruction.' Hans Pfaall sent back to Rotterdam the account of how he got to the moon, but not a word of what he found there. His inventive mind got him there—that was its role; a higher intuition takes over once ratiocination has gained ascent into the heavens.

The final destination for Poe's discoveries is that bourne beyond the City in the Sea, 'Out of Space, out of Time.' That secret knowledge toward which the soul on its phantom dreamship rushes ever onward is a knowledge beyond the cognition of our world, our clock-ridden world, where Time, with its condor wings, hovers over us, its dark shadow intervening between the soul and the pure light of that pure revelation.

How can we cross the border into that undiscovered country?

Poe's tales of temporal exploration make free with the *air* of scientific method, although in fact both his oceanography and his aerospace theories are quite inaccurate. No matter that; he persuades us while we read to suspend disbelief in the absurdity of both the action and the theory supposed to justify it. This is Poe's own form of ratiocinative mastery, mastery of his characters' fates, mastery of the spaces they explore, mastery of the souls of his readers.

To conquer TIME he uses 'science' too.

For who conquers time but the ghosts, the spirits who live—well anyway they *exist*—free from the finite decrepitude of the human body?

Scientific ghost tales.

The Romantic period specialized in ghostly tales, spectral poems, haunted dreams, all the spooky and fear-inspiring means of exploring the inner life of the individual which, like a wraith fulfilling some ancestral curse, rears up in defiance of those general laws of nature by which the heirs of Augustan rationalism tried to explain human behavior. So we get such spooks as 'Christabel,' 'The Terribly Strange Bed,' the weird goings-on in the tales of Tieck and E. T. A.

Hoffmann,–not to mention the Gothic Romance itself, *The Castle of Otranto, Frankenstein, The Monk.*

But Poe is too intense to write a novel. He writes instead a few brief sketches. Although now nearly forgotten, these were what first attracted Baudelaire to Poe–the French poet's first translation of Poe's work was a rendering of 'Mesmeric Revelations,' a tale a Swedenborgian journal welcomed as a genuine report of a scientific experiment.

Ah, those innocents. So great was *their* need to believe anything which purported to prove the existence of the soul that they were taken in by Hoaxiepoe. Like the editors and readers of the New York *Sun* in the matter of the balloon-crossing of the Atlantic. But, admits Poe, 'The story is a pure fiction from beginning to end.'

A pure fiction, telling one of Edgar's most solemn truths, but cast as a send-up. Because readers like us would call a hoax whatever we cannot understand, remember? So Poe steals our thunder by making it a hoax to begin with. As ever, a hoax that both is and is not a hoax.

'Mesmeric Revelations' being the *most* solemn of Poe's counterclockwise explorations of the undiscovered country, I make it wait until I've re-read two sketches through which we have to pass along the way: 'A Tale of the Ragged Mountains' and 'The Facts in the Case of Monsieur Valdemar.'

In 'A Tale of the Ragged Mountains' we have quite a strange protagonist–Mr. Bedloe, a cadaverous young man attended by his solicitous physician, Dr. Templeton. Bedloe likes to take walks in the Ragged Mountains near Charlottesville, walks as long as his ravaged physique will permit. Ravaged by disease–phthisis (*all* of the chief characters in these three stories are ravaged by phthisis, or congestion of the lungs)–and ravaged as well by *his strong addiction to morphine.*

Like the Norse fisherman, like the traveller setting out from Java, like Hans Pfaall, Bedloe is about to take a trip.

A drug trip. For it matters not *how* the explorer gets himself launched out of our world, whether by ship, balloon, or drug trance. A further route is by hypnosis, as in 'Mesmeric Revelations' and 'Monsieur Valdemar.' Once the soul is set free from the cruel limits of our space-time world, it soars or whirls in exhilarating jeopardy around the rims of another order of existence.

Bedloe, the drug-taker, returns from one of his walks in the mountains and tells his friends of an extraordinary sight. He describes, with great detail and seeming accuracy, a battle in an opulent Oriental city, a hairbreadth escape by one of the participants, a charge by the rabble armed with poisoned darts,—he is himself wounded by one of these, he reels, he *dies*.

Dr. Templeton produces a portrait, evidently of Bedloe, but in the attire of a British officer of fifty years earlier. The subject of the portrait had been present, with Dr. Templeton, at the insurrection in Benares in 1780. The officer, named Oldeb, was killed in precisely the manner that Bedloe, in his vision, saw happening to himself. Dr. Templeton, having met the younger Bedloe at Saratoga (also the site of a revolution), and noticing his uncanny resemblance to his dead friend, attached himself to the invalid as his personal physician. We may suspect that Templeton is something of a sorcerer—perhaps, like Hawthorne's Chillingworth, one of those doctors educated in German mysticism and magic—for within a week of Bedloe's vision the poor fellow dies. The newspaper obituary reports the cause of his death as his being bled by a *poisonous leech* accidentally applied by his physician, Dr. Templeton. The narrator notices at the end of the tale what we have already seen, that Bedloe is the reverse spelling of Oldeb, give or take an *e*.

This adventure into transubstantiation of souls is not a very thoroughgoing exploration of the subject or of the terrain of timelessness. It simply establishes, as though facts, that the trance induced by drugs can free the soul from this world to a realization of its true nature, and that nature is eternal, for the soul persists through time, circumstance, and changes of the body.

With 'The Facts in the Case of M. Valdemar' we penetrate more deeply into this bourne of mysteries.

> It is now rendered necessary that I give the *facts*—as far as I comprehend them myself. They are, succinctly, these:
> My attention, for the last three years, had been repeatedly drawn to the subject of Mesmerism . . .

The experiment undertaken in this account is not merely the putting of a subject under the direction of the mesmerist's will. The experimenter early on proposes the course of his research:

> No person had as yet been mesmerized *in articulo mortis*. It remained to be seen, first, whether, in such condition, there existed in the patient any susceptibility to the magnetic influence; secondly, whether, if any existed, it was impaired or increased by the condition; thirdly, to what extent, or for how long a period, the encroachments of Death might be arrested by the process.

Luckily for him—luckily for me, since by now I was really hooked—the Mesmerist has a good friend, one M. Valdemar, his longtime subject, who suffers from 'a confirmed phthisis' and who agrees to be the subject of this very inquiry. A letter arrives from Valdemar saying that his physicians have no hope of his survival beyond the morrow. Will the Mesmerist (called 'My dear P——'), come at once!

Now I know, as I then did not, that this whole rigadoon is a pure send-up. How I was taken in by the matter-of-fact tone, the tone of Swift and Defoe:

> Mr. L——l was so kind as to accede to my desire that he would take notes of all that occurred; and it is from his memoranda that what I now have to relate is, for the most part, either condensed or copied *verbatim*.

Well, to get to the point, P—— mesmerizes the dying Valdemar, who is barely able—yet able—to speak.

There was no longer the faintest sign of vitality in
M. Valdemar, and concluding him to be dead, we were
consigning him to the charge of the nurses, when a strong
vibratory motion was observable in the tongue. This continued for perhaps a minute. At the expiration of this period, there issued from the distended and motionless jaws
a voice . . . harsh, and broken and hollow; but the hideous
whole is indescribable. . . . the voice seemed to reach
our ears—at least mine—from a vast distance, or from some
deep cavern within the earth. In the second place, it im-
pressed me . . . as gelatinous or glutinous matters impress
the sense of touch.

This voice now says, 'I *have been* sleeping—and now—now—
I *am dead.*' And for *seven months* P—— keeps this voice, the
voice of the soul of M. Valdemar, in its state of suspended
animation!

Where have I heard of such a voice before, a voice that
seemed to be speaking across vast distances? Isn't that the
very voice of the captain of the gigantic ship which rushed
onward toward some secret knowledge which it would be
annihilation to possess? So the captain, too, was a spirit, one
of the undead whose intellect yet functioned although separated from its perishable, corporeal body. And hadn't the
fisherman, hauled up from the maelstrom by his mates white-
headed and aghast, looked as though he had just returned
from 'spirit-land'? Then in those voyages, too, the explorer
had, all unwitting, crossed the forbidden bourne between the
living and the unliving, and returned from the spirit world!

And now I start awake into the knowledge of why Poe is
forever trying to mesmerize himself—by the repetition of a
word until it loses all meaning; by the contemplation of a
candle flame; by losing himself in the design on the margin
of a book—remember 'Berenice'? Poe is trying to mesmerize
himself to be both P—— and Valdemar, so that he may himself enter that unknown existence of the spirit freed from
the body.

But what of M. Valdemar? His name strikes me as rather odd, for *I've* never known anyone called Valdemar. But I've known Poe for a long time as a champion cryptographer, composer and decoder of secret writings, and etymological scout. Surely the polyglot Poe would want us to *feel*, if not knowingly to see, that his name suggests *valley-of-the-sea*. And where else in Poe's work have we encountered valleys in the sea? Certainly in the maelstrom, in the funnel down which the author disappears while his MS. floats safely in its bottle. And in that early poem, 'Dream-Land,' with its

> Bottomless vales and boundless floods.

Here, in an 'ultimate dim Thule,' reached 'By a route obscure and lonely,' dwell 'the Ghouls . . . Sheeted Memories of the Past . . . White-robed forms of friends long given / In agony, to the Earth—and Heaven.' All this, anticipated by the subject's name.

The facts are these: after seven months he makes known his desperate desire, 'For God's sake!—quick!—quick!—put me to sleep—or, quick!—waken me!—quick!—*I say to you that I am dead!*' And then, as the subject hovers between the quick and the dead,

> As I rapidly made the mesmeric passes, amid ejaculations of 'dead! dead!' absolutely *bursting* from the tongue and not from the lips of the sufferer, his whole frame at once—within the space of a single minute, or less, shrunk—crumbled—absolutely *rotted* away beneath my hands. Upon the bed, before that whole company, there lay a nearly liquid mass of loathsome—of detestable putrescence.

Ugh. Yyeccch!

Poe's 'facts' are not for the queasy. Edgarpoe is not, decidedly not, the Samuel Smiles of American Literature.

A great tale by a great author?

In what sort of taste?

But what sort of taste is that which turns in horrified disgust from the acknowledgment of the expendability of our corporeal form? Isn't Poe being perfectly serious, within the

frame of his send-up (as usual), serious about the existence
of the soul? For if the body was held from decomposition
for seven months by the passes of a Mesmerist, what then
was speaking if not the soul?

The soul, of which we get more news in 'Mesmeric Revelations.'

The Mesmerist, P., begins, 'Whatever doubt may still envelop the *rationale* of mesmerism, its startling *facts* are now
almost universally admitted. . . .' P. has another subject,
again a chap on the brink of death, once more an acute sufferer from phthisis. The poor fellow's name is Vankirk.
Hoaxiepoe, I'm on to you now: your subject is *a son of the
church.* (A Dutch son of the Scottish church, i.e., a Presby-
terian of an old New York family.)

Now this Vankirk is a special sort of subject—he *wants*
to be mesmerized because he doubts, with his conscious
mind, the existence of the soul's immortality. But, he explains to the ever-willing P., 'the mesmeric exaltation enables me to perceive a train of ratiocination which, in my
abnormal existence, convinces, but which, in full accordance
with the mesmeric phenomena, does not extend, except
through its *effect,* into my normal condition.' So, Vankirk
wishes first to be mesmerized, and then, under the spell, to
be asked a catechism.

This is swiftly accomplished, and now I'll have to run
through some of the questions and their answers. For although once again Hoaxiepoe has got us into one of his put-
ons, what he says in it is absolutely and unequivocally *serious.*
He's in *dead earnest.* This is a true revelation, for Poe, in
his own person. It is in fact at the very center of the maelstrom of his mind, it's what his art is designed to discover
and his tales to embody.

P. Is not God immaterial?

V. There is no immateriality; it is a mere word. That
which is not matter, is not at all—unless qualities are
things.

P. Is God, then, material?

V. No. [This reply startled me very much.]

P. What, then, is he?

V. [After a long pause, and mutteringly.] I see—but it is a thing difficult to tell. [Another long pause.] He is not spirit, for he exists. Nor is he matter, *as you understand it*. But there are *gradations* of matter of which man knows nothing; the grosser impelling the finer, the finer pervading the grosser. The atmosphere, for example, impels the electric principle, while the electric principle permeates the atmosphere. These gradations of matter increase in rarity or fineness, until we arrive at a matter *unparticled*—without particles—indivisible—*one*; and here the law of impulsion and permeation is modified. The ultimate or unparticled matter not only permeates all things, but impels all things; and thus *is* all things within itself. This matter is God. What men attempt to embody in the word 'thought,' is this matter in motion.

Whew!

He's a deep one, Vankirk.

P., the skillful mesmerist, has conducted his subject clear out of the realm of ordinary thought, even beyond the realm of such extraordinary ratiocination as Dupin's. He is now in the spirit world toward which Poe's other voyagers rushed by ghostly ship or careening balloon—a peaceful passage, yet he has gone further than any of them. He has unlocked the cabinet in which the nature of Nature was hidden behind the painted screen of appearances. Even to describe what he sees there, he has to have the glossary of a metaphysician. Luckily for us, his words are equal to his vision.

The catechism continues:

P. You say that divested of the body man will be God?

V. [After much hesitation.] I could not have said this!

P. [Referring to my notes.] You *did* say that 'divested of corporate investiture man were God.'

V. And this is true. Man thus divested *would be* God—would be unindividualized. But he can never be thus divested—at least never *will be*—else we must imagine an action of God returning upon itself—a purposeless and futile action. Man is a creature. Creatures are thoughts of God. It is the nature of thought to be irrevocable.

P. I do not comprehend. You say that man will never put off the body?

V. I say that he will never be bodiless.

P. Explain.

V. There are two bodies—the rudimental and the complete, corresponding with the two conditions of the worm and the butterfly. What we call 'death,' is but the painful metamorphosis. Our present incarnation is progressive, preparatory, temporary. Our future is perfected, ultimate, immortal. The ultimate life is the full design.

P. But of the worm's metamorphosis we are palpably cognizant.

V. We, certainly—but not the worm.

Enough, enough! My brain is spinning!

But, if you're a real Poe buff, you have to sort this out.

Because it explains a lot of things. It's the secret code-breaker to the whole *œuvre*.

Don't think that it was *easy* for Vankirk to discover it, just because he endures no vertiginous whirlpools. He has learned, as he says just before he ceases to speak, that 'The pain of the primitive life of Earth, is the sole basis of the bliss of the ultimate life of Heaven.' A few sentences more, and then, as his voice grows more feeble, a change—an alarming change—overtakes his appearance. P. awakes him at once, and as he awakens, he dies. 'His brow was of the coldness of ice. . . . Had the sleep-waker, indeed, during the latter portion of his discourse, been addressing me from out the region of the shadows?'

Finis.

Yes, Vankirk has crossed into that other kingdom, and, thanks to the ministrations of mesmerical science, he was not obliged to launch a letter but could speak his revelation. And die, into whatever happiness was prepared for him by his sufferings in this primitive life of ours.

So he's given P.—and you and me—the code-cracker. Already we know toward where it is that his fellow-voyagers were hurrying. And we are learning, gradually learning, what is that knowledge never-to-be-revealed whose attainment is destruction.

And we know about God. God is the ultimate unparticled matter which impels all things.

That's God? What kind of a God is that?

No wonder Griswold went to maniacal pains to present Poe posthumously to the world as the Antichrist! A God made of physical energy, of unparticled matter!

And although not even the dourest dominie in the Dutch Reformed Church (such as, say Herman Melville's mamma's pastor) could better the antihumanist sentiment of the dying—or the dead—Vankirk's aperçu, '*The pain of the primitive life of Earth is the sole basis of the bliss of the ultimate life of Heaven*,' where in *this* philosophy is there the consolation of our possible redemption through the sacrifice of Our Lord? No Christ, no redeemer, no redemption. Only the assurance that *the more we suffer* on earth, the happier our bliss in Heaven. But what a Heaven! A Heaven of unparticled matter, of disembodied thought which infuses molecules as electric impulses flow through the atmosphere!

Who needs it?

Who'd be enheartened, consoled, redeemed, or guided toward the better conduct of a better life, by such a brain-cracking knot of materialistic theories!

Not a word anywhere, not a niche or a chink in the edifice, for *ethics*. This is a metaphysics all physics.

It has nothing to do with mankind, only with energy, and ghouls.

'The latest form of infidelity.' (Andrews Norton, after hearing that pious though unconventional Christian, R. W. Emerson, in the chapel of the Harvard Divinity School the year Poe died. Lucky for New England that its thinkers and leaders didn't read or heed this Southern archangel of an antichurch!)

But, if 'Mesmeric Revelations' cracks the code of Poe's *œuvre*, what, then, is the connection between its disclosures and the crimes committed by the Imp of the Perverse; or their solutions by Monsieur Dupin; or the explorations of

the farthest seas by Arthur Gordon Pym; or the murder of
the black cat or the benevolent old man? What use is this
universe of unparticled propensities when we contemplate the
repossession by the spirit of Ligeia of the body of Lady
Rowena Trevanion of Tremaine, or think about Roderick
Usher, interring his sister living in her tomb?

Edgar Poe, as we have seen, insists upon the absolute necessity of unity of effect, yet Edgar Poe, as we have seen, insists upon the absolute independence from each other of such
human perceptions as Beauty, Truth, and Morality. Edgar
Poe, with his faculty psychology, splits man—splits himself—
apart into mutually exclusive functions, yet insists upon the
essentiality of their unification. His sanest sage is therefore
all but indistinguishable from a madman, his direst maniac
a covert genius. Man, man, man, that suffering conglomera-
tion of irreconcilable passions, in whom, mysteriously, resides
a soul, a unifying principle which partakes its nature from the
nature of the universe itself. *The universe extrinsic to man*,
the universe of physical forces which operate in the eternal
rhythm of their own processes—processes which the often
disordered rhythms of *our* small lives faultily participate in,
processes which our experiences reflect but do not determine.

This is a universe in which history, I mean human history,
is irrelevant to truth. I remember Poe's curious letter to
James Russell Lowell, the one in which he said that mankind could grow neither more happy nor more wise than it
was six thousand years ago, and then wandered off into a
seemingly inconsequent speculation about forces and energies. . . . What could Russell Lowell have made of that!

The fact is, Poe's insistence upon unity is really obsessional, and although in each single poem or tale (I mean
his ratiocinative stories and Arabesques) he does achieve a
unity of effect, when we consider his work as a whole, his
œuvre, we can't help but be struck by the *particularity of its
parts*. Oh yes, we can link together the images in one tale
with those in another or with those in a poem or poems, and
connect the ideas in the imaginative writings with the theories in the criticism—just what I've been doing all along here

—but it's damned near impossible to bolt the whole shebang together into *one unitary whole*. Just like this book I'm
writing about Poe, what a hell of a time I'm having holding
it together when it keeps wanting to go off on tangents and
become a treatise on detectives and secret writings; or on
science fictions and explorations of the mind in terms of
nineteenth-century theories of psychology reinterpreted by
twentieth; or—other temptations which lie ahead on my path
—a study of the Gothic imagination in Poe, or in his German
sources, or in his English antecedents; or yet another study
of the Coleridgean poetics as reduced by Edgarpoe—this
temptation I think I did avoid; or, a discussion of Poe's satires
of society (about which I will have to say *something*, later
on). Or heaven knows what else. For Edgar Allan Poe was
always about to explode into the pieces of his divided, anguished self. His efforts at unification are arbitrary, willed,
obsessional, incomplete. His consoling philosophical solution
to his sufferings is to conceive of the universe as an impulsion-
machine, the nature of whose inherent motions his own mind
could trace, and imitate.

BEYOND APOCALYPSE

Beyond mesmeric revelation—beyond the beyond—is it possible to push onward, past the farthest bounds of being? In
his heroic attempt to discover the immortality of the soul
Vankirk perished into the immortality his soul had discovered. Human protagonists can do no more. For the still farther explorations which Poe, as navigator of the Universe,
had to make, he must imagine protagonists who are no longer
human.

How can there be unity of effect in the reports of conversations among the shades? Poe's sketches in this weird genre
aren't even cast as tales, they are 'Conversations,' 'Colloquies,'
'Parables.' As in the Bible. But of course Poe's parables are
not, like the Biblical stories, moral allegories. They are simply
demonstrations of truth beyond the power of mortal ratiocination, even of intuition, to uncover.

In 'The Conversation of Eiros and Charmion,' the characters so named have taken those names on the dissolution of their earthly existences. They converse, these disembodied shades, in 'Aidenn,' where they will suffer no longer.

> Oh, God!—pity me, Charmion!—I am overburdened with the majesty of all things!—of the unknown now known—of the speculative Future merged in the august and certain Present.

Eiros goes on to outline, for Charmion's benefit, the final catastrophe in which the earth itself was consumed, in a fiery apocalypse when a great comet cast its mantle of flame across the orbit of our world.

By 1839 (the year Poe wrote up this dream of murdering the world), four years after Halley's comet had passed by, America was running a high fever, with apocalyptic visions a common symptom of the nation's mass delirium. It was, for most, a religious delirium, as Millerites and sectarians of every sort of the Gospel of the Burning Bush assembled on hilltops to await the coming Day of Judgment. Matthew Wigglesworth's grim legacy from Puritan times! Even so sane and sensible a genius as Nathaniel Hawthorne couldn't help but notice the phrensy that gripped his fellow citizens, and in 'Earth's Holocaust' he wrote an ironical send-up of their apocalyptic lust for destruction.

But of course there's no moral, no conventional Christian redemption, in Poe's lust for redemption. What is redeemed, we learn in Eiros and Charmion's conversation, is the soul which survives apocalypse quite independently of any good or evil, any piety or impiety, it committed while *in corpore situo*. The soul survives, as Vankirk discovered, because when in the body it suffered; and *what* survives is a disembodied capacity for ratiocination. Soul=pure Mind.

For pure mind to be exercised without the intervention of the impurity of bodily suffering, Poe must extinguish the entire world. He must consume it in fire, then forget it. Then and only then, as the logicians say, can pure mind exercise its pure capacity for pure thought. And *that* is the bliss of Heaven guaranteed us by the intensity of our earthly woes.

'The Colloquy of Monos and Una' is yet another discourse among these happy ghouls. At a later date than the conversation of Eiros and Charmion, if it's possible to speak of dates after the annihilation of the material world, these latterday saints discover that they have been 'born again'!

Edgar, Edgar, is there no end to your imprudence! How can you take over lock, stock, and barrel the terms of the very Christian belief that you otherwise completely ignore! As Allen Tate has said, Poe wrote as though Christianity had never been invented. Yet he uses its imagery of apocalypse and regeneration. For his own ends, of course.

> For myself [says Monos], the Earth's records had taught me to look for widest ruin as the price of highest civilization. . . . for the infected world at large I could anticipate no regeneration save in death. That man, as a race, should not become extinct, I saw that he must be *'born again.'* And now it was, fairest and dearest, that we wrapped our spirits, daily, in dreams.

And now, in the knowledge that he had died 'in the Earth's dotage,' Monos describes again the process of his dying, the hyperexcitation of his senses, his awareness, his eerie awareness that

> from the wreck and the chaos of the usual senses, there appears to have arisen within me a sixth, all perfect. In its exercise I found a wild delight—yet a delight still physical, inasmuch as the understanding in it had no part. . . . No muscle quivered; no nerve thrilled; no artery throbbed. But there seemed to have sprung up in the brain, *that* of which no words could convey to the merely human intelligence even an indistinct conception. Let me term it a mental pendulous pulsation. It was the moral equivalent of man's abstract idea of *Time.* . . . this sixth sense, upspringing from the ashes of the rest, was the first obvious and certain step of the intemporal soul upon the threshold of the temporal Eternity.

Dr. Johnson had opined, 'Sir, if a man has experienced the inexpressible he is under no obligation to attempt to express it,' or words to that effect. But Poe takes the attempt as his own challenge. 'The moral equivalent of man's abstract idea of *Time*'! What under heaven does *that* mean? Yet it means what it *means*, it *is* a conception incomprehensible to the merely human. When we are dead and as happy as Monos and Una, and as unified within the beings of our disembodied intelligence, we'll understand it, as they do.

Whoa! Am I being perhaps a little supine, accepting all this guff? Do I really go along with these lunatic consolations of a desperately unhappy man? Do I in my heart accept his nihilism as a metaphysics, do I—as I seem to—take these wild and jejune reductions of everything which culture has achieved to a single materialistic idea, do I take all this malarkey as Poe does? As a religion?

Don't be impatient. We must have a full and fair exposition before we pass judgment. I've nearly done with Poe's Diet of Worms. When we've digested his banquet of metaphysical speculation, we bring into play those nearly atrophied organs of criticism and judgment.

One more sketch to go. Poe calls it 'The Power of Words.'

Another colloquy, or dialogue, this time between two bodiless spectres named Agathos (the Good) and Oinos (get it? WINE-BIBBER: another way to take the trip!).

And what are they nattering about but the creative propensities of the Divine intelligence. Agathos is the soothsayer, the dead one, instructing Oinos, the adept, in these mysteries:

> To a being of infinite understanding—one to whom the *perfection* of the algebraic analysis lay unfolded—there could be no difficulty in tracing every impulse given the air—and the ether through the air—to the remotest consequences at any even infinitely remote epoch of time. It is indeed demonstrable that every such impulse *given the air*, must, *in the end*, impress every individual thing that exists *within the universe*;—and the being of infinite un-

derstanding—the being whom we have imagined might trace the remote undulations of the impulse . . . back from the throne of the Godhead.

So then, every action, every impulse launched upon the air reverberates forever in widening circles of ever-lessening energy, like the rings sent outward by a stone cast in a pool. The principle holds whether for the creation of a comet or *the speaking of a word.* A word, once spoken, reverberates forever, its impulses lapping upon the furthest shores of space and time. For, so these angels conclude, 'all motion, of whatever nature, creates'; and 'the source of all motion is thought —and the source of all thought is—God.'

From God, then comes '*the physical power of words.*' And Agathos droops his wings as he hovers over a 'fair star,' for, he cries, concluding his dialogue on 'The Power of Words,'

This wild star—it is now three centuries since, with clasped hands, and with streaming eyes, at the feet of my beloved—I spoke it—with a few passionate sentences—into birth. Its brilliant flowers *are* the dearest of all unfulfilled dreams, and its raging volcanoes *are* the passions of the most turbulent and unhallowed of hearts.

And where are we now, but back where we began—on the fairest star, Al Aaraaf. The rationale of the power of words has led Edgarpoe through the mazes of his own ratiocination in a vast circle right back to the very theory which killed his verse!

His prosaics are exactly like his poetics. In the rationale for both tale and poem he operates, he would like us to think, simultaneously and in unison, in two directions which in fact contradict each other. Technique and theme. When it comes to how to write a poem or how to tell a story, Poe is a great technician, a contriver of efficient contraptions for the excitation of the reader's sensibilities. Unity of effect, uses of rhyme and refrain, economy of plot, all that. He draws on his own observation of his own experience, with the *savoir faire* of a writer who can tell his own meteors from his duds.

But Edgarpoe is the child, the orphaned child, of the Machine Age to Come, and a citizen, an unwilling citizen, of a nation of tinkerers and bicycle-shop mechanics. His rules for Art are a How-to-Do-It kit for the home electrician, who need but follow Poe's manual—and add the dash of his own genius—to emulate the work of the master.

So far so good. But when Poe prescribes the themes to be expressed, as he does the means for expressing them, he does not cease to be the mechanician of literature. His analytical propensities, *reinforcing certain obsessional repetitions and avoidances of experiences* which Poe professes are beyond analysis, lead him to insist upon two nearly impossible subjects as the ideal matter for his Art. Poetry *must be* about the death of a beautiful woman, expressed as indefinitely (and therefore as spiritually) as possible. Tales should exhibit the autonomous power of words which the ratiocinative intellect best expresses *when freed* from the dross material of our earthly life.

And where does that leave us? Where does it leave Poe, but with a beautiful *method* for expressing nearly *nothing*. E.g., look at those last words of Agathos. What a flaming cloud of clichés, his description of the star. Who could care? Who is touched by his thought? Poe's theory commands us to be over-whelmed by the ever-reverberating tide of the power of his words, but his words, expressing what no one has seen or touched (though to be sure perhaps a few of us have tried to imagine), his words have no power at all.

A brilliant method, gagged by the theme it commands itself to express. A case of artistic phthisis.

Or, the suicide of the poem.

So Edgarpoe ceased to write poems. When he wrote his poetics he put it in prose. A poetics that I call also a prosaics, since it tries to govern his tales as well.

But the tales, fortunately, don't heed Edgar's theories. Except for these vapid fables, they *don't* blabber incomprehensibilities about the neverneverland of the disembodied intellect.

The tales rear up their frightened heads inside Poe's head,

those tales *written by his Imp of the Perverse!* That Imp, to whom *thought is anathema!*

He is the author of the tales of compulsive crime, of irrepressible self-incrimination, of murder, of suicide, of the self divided against itself.

And maybe the Imp of the Perverse is active, too, in still other sketches—as he was in the voyage tales and the detection stories—in which the intellect *seems* to be the storyteller.

But before I turn the page to Poe's tabloid tales of horror, I have a thought about his theory of the power of words.

If it was his undoing as a poet and a fabulist, the theory, as theory, was his making as a critic. Not in his own country, of course. Nor was that what he wanted. Was it too misbegotten of Poe to dream, to hope, at a time when Joseph Smith was receiving the Book of Mormon in an upstate New York pasture, when Mary Baker Eddy was about to codify her revelations and found the Mother Church of Christian Science—was it too outrageous for Edgar Poe to aspire to the leadership of the religion which *his* revelations expounded as true? The Religion of Art.

Feckless Edgar was foredoomed never to be a leader among men. His tetchy disposition; his acute *amour propre;* his propensity (despite his otherwise perfect Southern manners) to accuse everyone else of plagiarism; his occasional fits after taking a dram of whiskey or a glass of wine, a meagre dole of the demon sufficing to make him look an addicted debauchee—none of *these* characteristics is the stuff of which prophets were made, in the 1830s and 1840s, in these States. Besides, to follow, even to understand, Poe's new faith one had to be, or wish to be, an artist himself, a poet. Not the universal calling here, in the presidency of Millard Fillmore.

It took a *hypocrite lecteur* to get the message. From Poe to Valéry the line runs, first to his *frère,* Baudelaire, thence to his *semblable,* Mallarmé. And then, as I've said, by way of Laforgue and Corbière to Eliot and Stevens, and so back at last to this nation of numbskulls who mistook for Poe's work some of the mindless rhymes of Thomas Holley Chivers, a nation which exalted on pedestals secondrate poets like

Bryant and thirdrate scriveners like Willis and Drake—and neglected Poe.

The symbolist religion of art! The image of the artist as the autochthynous creator of his own universe—the perfect escape from the tyranny of time, from the baseness of the material life. The perfect substitute for that devotion to the spirit and *its* life which once was the business of the Christian Church to provide for the Western World, and which the world no longer takes as its business, having run away from its Father's business.

We are all runaways and orphans, inheriting a sterile life without spirit. For those of us who share the talent from which Poe with such pain extracted his perfect dreams of genius, his revelations of the power of art have a mesmerical effect. I think of Nabokov, creating the zany ratiocinations of Dr. Kinbote in *Pale Fire,* a plot it would take a Monsieur Dupin to disentangle, as it took such a one to create it. I think of Allen Tate, who imagines himself Poe's cousin; and of Poe's most sympathetic exegete, Richard Wilbur, who all his life as a poet has hovered on the edge of the bed of that seductress, autonomous Art, and who calls himself back to reality by the titles of his books—'*The Beautiful* Changes,' and '*Things of* This *World.*'

I think of myself. I too have been tempted to speak a distant star, to make a world *in my own image.*

Once, after I lectured on another poet whose soul is split between analytical intellect and feeling (I mean Robert Graves), a lady in the audience—this was at a university—introduced herself as a clinical psychologist and offered to test my perceptions (or was it apperceptions?) by a means of her own devising, one which she had already given to half a dozen other poets who had held the visiting lectureship before me. Half-skeptically I agreed, and soon she had set out, on a tabletop, three dozen sculpted figurines, or rather near-figurines. For they didn't really *resemble* things or persons, they *suggested* them. With a little cooperation from the imagination, or the unconscious, you could make yourself see that blob pinched in at the waist and bulbous above and below

as a woman, that other one as a man, that one as a child—
Not me, I said, you don't get me making those things into
Mother, Father, Sister. For the point of the game was for
the patient, or subject, to rearrange the objects and freely
associate out loud.

I associated as freely as my reservations permitted, and
spoke the proximate world on the tabletop.

Some weeks later the doctor had codified her interpretations. I remember one sentence in her letter: 'For a poet,
you have a strong reality principle.'

VI

Dull Realities

MONEY

'*Money money money*'
—Theodore Roethke,
'The Lost Son'
'*Money is a kind of poetry.*'
—Wallace Stevens

All right, Edgar, we've lingered long enough up here on Cloud
Nine. In the empyrean of this star you spoke, the air is *pretty
thin*. I cough, I gasp, I'm getting a confirmed case of phthisis
of the imagination.

What to do but grab hold of the dragline on your hoaxie
balloon and tow you down to this real world of ours. The
fact is, Idgar, the world is too much with us. The world's
too tough. Late and soon it refuses to be fried in your apocalyptic fireworks, just to singe us all into an afterlife of which
you dreamed. Each morning that's the real sun up there,
lighting these real streets where we, in our actual bodies,
awaken to endure a new day.

Reality. How can a writer deny it? What riches, in reality—
the search for material is over. The streets are paved, the
beds sheeted, with writers' gold! Pick it up—marriage and
money, society and sex, the rise and fall of the American
family, passion and politics. Look at all those glistering
themes!

And yet, until the advent of Henry James, who did? Who

but James Fenimore Cooper when he wasn't tracking the Last Mohican? Most of these themes are the very ones most assiduously avoided by Hawthorne, Melville, and Poe. When Mark Twain tried to stuff them into his books, his books exploded with imaginative indigestion (*A Connecticut Yankee*) or died of imaginative anemia (*The Prince and the Pauper*). Twain, like Poe, wrote prose lyricism—or satire; and the great themes of the nineteenth-century realistic novel came into his work primarily as satire, often to the detriment of that unity of effect which Poe regarded as the writer's first obligation and which Twain so rarely achieved.

I think of nineteenth-century fiction as itself the subject of a satire, a pictorial satire by Daumier or Grandville. I see a seesaw, on one end of which are crowded Jane Austen, Thackeray, George Eliot, Dickens, Balzac, Dostoievsky, Tolstoi, and Henry James; and on the other, way up in the empyrean, in the splendor of his loneliness sits the shade of Edgarpoe.

But I'm trying to drag Poe down to earth. Because, having spent a couple of years now browsing in his seventeen-volume *œuvre*, I've actually found some sketches in which he treats those great and by him otherwise neglected subjects, money and marriage, sex and society, politics, and the fashions of the day.

When Edgarpoe addresses the talents of his genius to the subjects which occupied the triple-decker novels of his time, you may be sure he finds a handle all his own by which to hold them. Despite the seeming incompatibility of such a subject as the mercantile ethic with such a theme as Beauty, Edgar can treat the one with a levity we recognize as already having been put to the service of the other. Now, in a bit of *fol-de-rol* called 'Diddling Considered as One of the Exact Sciences,' Edgarpoe, symbolist seeker of Beauty, merges into Hoaxiepoe in buckskins and endeavors to make us laugh.

Poe is usually faulted for his efforts in cap and bells. 'He took his own humor very seriously, always a bad sign,' said F. O. Matthiessen. The vote of his critics is, What an un-

funny man. Something black and sick about his clownish
sketches, his tasteless grotesqueries.

Yet they're surprised at his delighted review of *Georgia
Scenes*. Frontier horseplay doesn't seem to fit in very well
with the ideality of Poe's poems, or the ghoulish intensity
of his best-known stories. Yet what Longstreet so amusingly
wrote about had been equally a part, for a time, of Edgar
Poe's experience. Hadn't he written his foster father of a
fight between two scholars at the University of Virginia one
of whom had been expelled for having bitten off a chunk
of the other's arm?

Not very funny. But a true part of reality, the reality of
the American frontier.

And so is 'Diddling,' a different, more *ratiocinative* kind of
gouging.

'Diddling' has a *joie de vivre* not conspicuous in most of
Funny Edgar's efforts to tickle us. This isn't much of a story,
true, but Poe does propose a thoroughly cynical, caustic view
of human nature in America, and he then proceeds to illustrate it with a string of Yankee bargains already old in folklore
when he retold them. He tells, for instance, how an enterpris-
ing diddler can fleece the entire congregation at a camp meeting. Five years later, in 1849, Johnson Jones Hooper would
expand the motif in 'Simon Suggs Attends a Camp Meeting,'
a sketch which might be a familiar of every American's boyhood had it not been superseded by the chapter on a similar
subject in *Huckleberry Finn*. We know that Mark Twain
diddled Hooper out of his fame, but there's no proof that
Simon Suggs did the same to Poe—the yarn was already growing whiskers in the public domain.

Poe tells his diddling yarns with obvious *relish*, the joy,
in fact, of the diddler himself. For without that gratification
the diddler is merely a cheat, *'in petto.'* Poe calls this necessary quality of self-satisfaction 'the grin,' and he lists it as
the last among the diddler's requirements. 'Man,' he says,
'was made to diddle. This is his aim—his object—his *end*.'
And rightly considered, he says, 'Diddling is a compound,
of which the ingredients are minuteness, interest, persever-

ance, ingenuity, audacity, *nonchalance*, originality, impertinence, and *grin.*'

According to Poe, diddling is conducted primarily for, or from, the love of money. In this respect his diddler differs from Melville's marvellous characterization of the same type in *The Confidence-Man*. Melville's sharper diddled more for the love than the lucre—the love of separating men from their certainties, capturing the allegiance of their souls with arguments from the Apocrypha, or some other book not to be trusted. Melville made the diddler the type of his attack on the permissive liberalism, the lack of moral fibre, of his America. Poe has his own quarrel with America, one in which Melville's political and theological charges against his country's culture were inoperable because irrelevant. Poe's scorn is directed against a nation which refuses to support the profession of letters because too exclusively intent upon the making of money. Poe can see the tricks in that deck of cards, he can expose the credulity, chicanery, knavery to which American mankind is subject, and he does so with a scorn and relish sharpened by his bitter knowledge that this country of money-mad diddlers and their suckers had failed, had repeatedly failed, to provide one thousand persons willing to pledge five dollars per annum to support 'A Monthly Literary Journal To be Edited and Published in the City of Philadelphia by Edger A. Poe.' I quote a bit of Poe's 'Prospectus of The Penn Magazine':

> It shall be a leading object to assert in precept, and to maintain, the rights, while in effect it demonstrates the advantages, of an absolutely independent criticism—a criticism self-sustained; guiding itself only by the purest rules of Art; analyzing and urging these rules as it applies them; holding itself aloof from all personal bias; acknowledging no fear save that of outraging the right; yielding no point either to the vanity of an author, or to the assumptions of antique prejudice, or to the involute and anonymous cant of the Quarterlies, or to the arrogance of those organized *cliques* which, hanging like nightmares to American literature, manufacture, at the nod of our principal booksellers, a pseudo-public-opinion by wholesale. . . .

In respect to other features of the Penn Magazine. . . .
It will endeavour to support the general interests of the
republic of letters, without reference to particular regions;
regarding the world at large as the true audience of the
author. . . . Its aim chiefly shall be to *please*. . . .

The price will be $5 per annum, payable in advance, or
upon receipt of the first number, which will be issued on
the first of January, 1841. Letters addressed to the Editor
and Proprietor,

Edgar A. Poe.

Did anyone ever receive so worthy, so reasonable, so deserving and *necessary* a solicitation in the trashbin of his daily
mail? Editor A. Poe, I'd have reached at once for my quill
pen and my cheque book and sent by return post a draft upon
my account. . . . But no, America did not contain a thousand
citizens like me, citizens of the world, of the republic of letters. January first, 1841, came and went—without the appearance of The Penn Magazine, and Edgar A. Poe, our nation's
only *disinterested* magazinist, continued his life of fretful
bondage in the composing rooms owned and operated by,
and for the benefit of, scoundrels like Billy Burton of *Burton's Magazine*.

To be sure, Poe, with his characteristic bad luck, made a
grave miscalculation in his appeal to the public for support.
Like many Southern writers from John Pendleton Kennedy to
the Fugitive poets, Poe idealised and romanticized the plantation aristocracy as a class which would willingly become the
mother of the muses. To whom were Poe's appeals really
addressed? His former schoolmates in Richmond, his fellow
students at the University and his fellow Southern cadets at
the Military Academy, his sprinkling of acquaintances in the
professions among the Southern cities where he lived, did not
respond in any numbers to his call. The sons of the planter
class of the South were attuned not to poetry but to politics;
to rhetoric rather than to lyricism; to those very contests and
satisfactions of the temporal world which Poe ruled out of
the consideration of his art. True, their wives or daughters
indulged themselves in the cult of sentiment which so tinges

Poe's poems. But the ladies, though among his readers, provided insufficient patronage.

To identify social eminence, political power, and financial resources with intellectual authority and aesthetic taste seems a natural thing for the artist in search of unity. Those familiar with Yeats's views of the Irish aristocracy would do well to read the novels of Somerville and Ross, where the class Yeats hoped would foster virtue and the arts appear as a genial lot of hard-riding, hard-drinking, hard-gambling and hard-courting provincials with no more interest in the arts than has a high-spirited horse.

The result of Poe's miscalculation of the sensibility of the class to which he dreamed that he himself by rights belonged was, among other things, to keep him from ever addressing any other class of citizens in the United States who might, just possibly, have lent a more responsive hearing to his needs. Such a class were the New Englanders who supported Emerson, Hawthorne, Bryant, Whittier, Longfellow, and Lowell. But these transcendentalists and genteel bearers of the torch of Culture formed no part of Poe's public in the first place, nor could they have ever, since so much of his energy as a reviewer and controversialist went into attacking one after another of their avatars. Besides, except for Hawthorne all of these New England worthies were already by the time of the Mexican War lining up alongside the abolitionists. Poe seems never to have questioned the justice or propriety of the South's peculiar institution.

So when Edgar A. Poe, prospective editor of The Penn Magazine, deigned to depict the materialistic temper of his contemporaries, he had earned the right to take them off and put them down as he does in 'Diddling Considered as One of the Exact Sciences.' In his own way, and not for money (worse luck for him!), Poe made himself Jeremy Diddler incarnate.

So much so that, as I found out early in my life—as early as the first nightmare in which Miss Zenobia Psyche in the clocktower of the cathedral became myself being beheaded by the clock atop New Rochelle High—one can never be sure

when Poe is being serious and when he's putting us on. Because his put-ons are always serious, one way or another.

While Edgar was dreaming of Beauty and of founding a
magazine of his own—a dream that never went away, and
never came true—in 1848 the rest of the country also had a
dream. Gold had been found by a fool at Sutter's Mill, California, and what did America do but go mad in the search
for the gold which Legrand had so readily excavated upon
his successful ratiocinatory solution to the secret writing in
the pirate cryptogram. Poe does a send-up of the gold rush
in another sketch, 'Von Kempelen and His Discovery.'
    You have to be rather unwary to be diddled this time, and
I don't know whether anyone was. For Poe presents the discovery as a corrective to somebody else's alleged report
(false, of course) which he derided as having 'an amazingly
moon-hoax-y air'; what's more, the Von Kempelen of whom
he speaks is a descendant, by Poe's report, of the inventor of
Mäelzel's chess-player. Nonetheless, 'The following anecdote,
at least, is so well authenticated that we may receive it im-
plicitly.'
    Of course it's a complicated farandole, but the gist is this:
Von Kempelen, who was once a 'fellow-sojourner for a week
. . . at Earl's Hotel, Providence, Rhode Island,' with the
author, has returned to his native Bremen, where his doings
soon attracted the attention of the police. Busting into his
chamber in the Flatzplatz, they found the suspected counter-
feiter in a garret 'fitted up with some chemical apparatus,
of which the object has not yet been determined.' There's
a small furnace, and two crucibles, one containing molten
lead, the other, 'some liquid.' Nothing else remarkable, except that the prisoner's pocket contained a small packet of
'some *unknown substance*' mixed with antimony, and under
his bed they found a large trunk so heavy that three men
could not budge it. (I think of Legrand, Doc, and Jupiter
toiling in the pit!) Sure enough, it's filled with 'old bits of
brass.' Well, you know the rest. It was 'not only gold—real

gold—but gold far finer than any employed in coinage—gold, in fact, absolutely pure, virgin.'

But before we pursue to its end this satire of the Gold Rush we should inquire, what does money really signify to Edgar Poe? What does he mean by wealth and riches? No casual question, when one considers the contrast between the author's own life-long penury and not only the nearly total absence of paupers from his fictive personae but the prevalence among them of wealth, great wealth. Not only does Legrand dig up $450,000 of pirate treasure, and Dupin win his reward of 50,000 f.; there is Metzengerstein, living in his opulent castle, and Prince Mentoni in his palace; the widower of Ligeia 'had no lack of what the world calls wealth; Ligeia,' he says, 'had brought me more, very far more, than ordinarily falls to the lot of mortals.' Roderick Usher, too, lives on a scale of sumptuousness far beyond the lot of ordinary men. But of all these self-ruined and self-tortured millionaires, none is as rich, nor as happy, as Ellison, hero of 'The Domain of Arnheim':

> From his cradle to his grave a gale of prosperity bore my friend Ellison along. Nor do I mean the word prosperity in its mere worldly sense. I mean it as synonymous with happiness.

Now, that's a real surprise. Who had thought to find a happy character in a tale by Poe? The nameless friend who tells this tale continues, 'In general, from the violation of a few simple laws of humanity arises the wretchedness of mankind . . . it is not impossible that man, the individual, under certain unusual and highly fortuitous conditions may be happy.'

Which conditions? Well, among them, for Ellison, was a fortune, an *inheritance* nearly, but not quite, beyond calculation.

> Recourse was had to figures, and these but sufficed to confound. It was seen, that, even at three per cent., the annual income of the inheritance amounted to no less than thirteen millions and five hundred thousand dollars; which was one million and one hundred and twenty-five thousand per

month; or thirty-six thousand nine hundred and eighty-six
per day; or one thousand five hundred and forty-one per
hour; or six and twenty dollars for every minute that flew.

The minute particularity of these vast calculations (at only
three percent) may well bespeak poor Edgar Poe's pathetic
dreams of that lesser inheritance which was never to be his.
But if Ellison is happy, it is not merely because he owns all
this wealth. Having 'satisfied his conscience' with respect to
'individual charities,' Ellison was 'thrown back, in very great
measure, upon himself.' His own welfare, his spiritual welfare, devolves upon his character. And 'In the widest and
noblest sense he was a poet.'

This is to say that his riches are for Ellison not an end in
themselves but the means to fulfilling that noble sense in
which he is a poet. 'The fullest, if not the sole proper satisfaction of this sentiment he instinctively felt to lie in the
creation of novel forms of beauty.'

With an income of $26.00 per minute, Ellison is enabled
to create such novel forms. What he undertakes is nothing
less than the re-creation of nature, making landscape-
gardening into a species of poetic composition. Since
'arbitrary arrangements of matter constitute and alone constitute the true beauty,' he causes to be built an intricate
landscape wholly artificial in aspect, as free as possible from
the contours and features of nature. In the event this involves a 'united beauty, magnificence, and *strangeness*' to
produce 'a nature which is not God, nor an emanation from
God, but which still is nature in the sense of the handiwork
of the angels that hover between man and God.' It will be
seen that Ellison the landscape-gardener is very like Poe the
author of 'Al Aaraaf' and 'The Power of Words,' escaping
through artifice from nature, matter, and death. The angelic
landscape he constructs bears many resemblances to that
described in Coleridge's 'Kubla Khan,' with a winding river
which leads through strange and 'weird symmetry' toward a
crystalline pool 'as if dropped from heaven,' above which
towers 'a mass of semi-Gothic, semi-Saracenic architecture,

sustaining itself by miracle in mid-air.' This is without doubt
a benign vision of the same antinatural vista which, in 'The
City in the Sea' and in 'Dream-Land,' so appalled while it
enchanted its visitor.

Here, miraculously freed—perhaps by his prodigious
wealth, which makes all else possible—from the Imp of the
Perverse, Ellison with his God-like powers can without guilt
create a substitute for the material universe in which the
rest of us, poverty-stricken in pocket, are condemned to live.

If money makes possible the Paradise of Arnheim, this is
so only because its inheritor has the soul of a poet. What
is the worth of gold among a people whose lust for riches is
not a spiritual but a material hunger? Looking at his fellow
Americans in the year of the rush to Sutter's Mill, Edgar
found no Ellisons among that lot. In his account of Von
Kempelen's discovery, he tells us that the effect of the in-
novation was to depreciate the gold exchange, and immediately to increase the value of lead and silver! 'One thing
may be positively maintained—that the announcement of the
discovery six months ago would have had material influence
in regard to the settlement of California.'

So Poe, the starveling soul-poet, invokes man's age-old
alchemical dream of instant riches. But where Ben Jonson,
in *The Alchemist*, could maintain that

> this pen
> Did never aim to grieve, but better men. . . .
> He hopes to find no spirit so much diseas'd,
> But will with such fair correctives be pleas'd.

Poe seems to have had no such thought of satire as a corrective to the vices of his age. For Poe, satire serves to display
the follies of mankind—and the personal superiority of the
Artist-Genius to the generality of fools. The satisfaction in
Poe's satire seems personal, a testament of intellectual superiority, rather than, as is true of all the greater satirists of his
or any age, the exposure by reason of the vices which passion
(the humours of mankind) inflict on us so as to show men
how to amend their ways. It's not that Poe was too proud to

be other than contemptuous of mankind; it's merely that he had no cause to believe them capable of self-repair along the lines his intellect proposed as mandatory.

I wonder how much Poe was paid for 'Von Kempelen.' For 'MS. Found in a Bottle,' in 1831, he won a prize of $50 from *The Baltimore Saturday Visiter*. For 'The Gold Bug' he won a $100 prize from the appropriately titled *The Dollar Newspaper* in 1843. This last was, I think, the most he was ever paid at one time for any of his writings. Few were the days when that much gold could be found in the battered trunk under *his* bed.

POLITICS

Poe on politics! How about that? Yet Edgar, with his weekly deadline to meet, occasionally tried political institutions as a theme for authorial comment. In fact on several occasions he filled his column with just that sort of opinionating. Being Edgarpoe he didn't write ordinary journalism or set forth his withering views of the democratic dogma in the customary form. For so to do would be to compromise the originality of his own aristocratic genius with the very forms and thoughts designed by catchpenny scribblers to tickle the vulgar palate of that demagogic monster, the masses.

No, Poe could not do that, if only because the matter of his observations would make the masses roar with rage, should those masses come upon Poe's comment in a form which they would be inclined to take seriously—like an account of something factual, the report of an election, an opinion of a particular bill in the Congress, or the like. Was it to protect himself from enraged readers, or to obtain readers in the first place, that Poe made his political commentary in the form of science fictions, send-ups, Grotesques?

Whenever Edgar has a Great Message, he sends it to the reader in a letter—'MS. Found in a Bottle,' 'Hans Pfaall,' 'The Purloined Letter.' Now he does this again in 'Mellonta Tauta.' Only this time he signs it, 'Yours everlastingly, PUNDITA.' For here Hoaxiepoe impersonates a female—a female pundit, a Cassandra of the future, whose letter is dated 'On board Balloon "Skylark," April 1, 2848.' That's a thousand years after the date of its publication. As was true of Hans Pfaall's departure from this world, the exact date is April Fool's.

The foreign-sounding title of Pundita's letter appears elsewhere among the impostures of Hoaxiepoe. Appears in Greek characters as the epigraph to his still more futuristic sketch, 'The Colloquy of Monos and Una.' The phrase 'Mellonta Tauta' translates as *'These things are in the near future,'* a line, displayed with Poe's everlasting love of erudition, from the *Antigone* of Sophocles. You can see that in the midst of his flapdoodle Hoaxiepoe is being quite serious.

The first half of 'Mellonta Tauta' consists, inconsequently enough, of Pundita's amused account of the aborted condition of metaphysics among the ignorant 'Amriccans' a thousand years before her time. No need now to follow her argument into that cloudy region; what we're after is her account of the political institutions of that distant and misguided age. There's no unity of effect connecting Pundita's views of metaphysics with her political wisdom, save that the author of her epistle is impatient with all the stupidities he sees ruling the world in 1848. Stupid ideas, stupid institutions.

Like this one:

> The ancient Amriccans *governed themselves!*—did ever anybody hear of such an absurdity? . . . that they started with the queerest idea conceivable, viz.: that all men are born free and equal—this in the very teeth of the laws of *gradation* so visibly impressed upon all things in the moral and physical universe.

This absurdity leads to the next one—

> Every man 'voted,' as they called it—that is to say meddled with public affairs—until, at length, it was discovered that what is everybody's business is nobody's, and that the 'Republic' (so the absurd thing was called) was without a government at all.

What's more, they discovered 'that universal suffrage gave opportunity for fraudulent schemes, by means of which any desired number of votes might at any time be polled, without the possibility of prevention or even detection, by any party which should be merely villainous enough not to be ashamed of the fraud.'

No wonder Poe puts this in jocular, fabulous form.

So subversive a tract could not be issued in the administration of President Fillmore. It had to be predated 2848.

Not since Hamilton's 'The people, sir, is a beast' have we heard so antidemocratic, so prejudicial a prejudice, as *this*.

Pundita blabbers on against republicanism and philosophers, and says that

> a fellow named *Mob* . . . took every thing into his own hands and set up a despotism, in comparison with which the fabulous Zeros and Hellofagabaluses were respectable and delectable. This Mob (a foreigner by birth) is said to have been the most odious of all men that ever encumbered the earth. He was a giant in stature—insolent, rapacious, filthy; had the gall of a bullock with the heart of a hyena and the brains of a peacock. . . .

'Poe was always great,' wrote Baudelaire, 'not only in his noble conceptions but also as a prankster.'

But I think that underneath the prank he is in deadly, if cranky, earnest.

For he did the same thing again in 'Some Words With a Mummy.' Here the cancellation of TIME runs backwards. A group of savants prepares to dissect an Egyptian mummy, and just for kicks they first give the mummy an electric charge. The body stirs, kicks Dr. Ponnonner, awakens, and speaks its mind. Its name is Count Allamistakeo (Funny Edgar, at it again), and when informed of American mores, it—I'd better say he—opines in no uncertain terms. E.g.,

> We then spoke of the great beauty and importance of Democracy, and were at much trouble in impressing the Count with a due sense of the advantages we enjoyed in living where there was suffrage *ad libitum*, and no king.

He listened with marked interest, and in fact seemed not a little amused. When we had done, he said that, a great while ago, there had occurred something of a very similar sort. Thirteen Egyptian provinces determined all at once to be free, and to set a magnificent example to the rest of mankind. They assembled their wise men, and concocted the most ingenious constitution it is possible to conceive. For a while they managed remarkably well; only their habit of bragging was prodigious. The thing ended, however in the consolidation of the thirteen states, with some fifteen or twenty others, in the most odious and insupportable despotism that was ever heard of upon the face of the Earth.

I asked what was the name of the usurping tyrant.

As well as the Count could recollect, it was *Mob*.

Whether he spins the clock a thousand years forward or several thousand backwards, Poe looks upon the Great American Experience from a perspective which makes it seem vulgar, trivial, self-defeating.

Well, what had American democracy ever done for Edgar Allan Poe? He with his visions of demonic suffering, of heroic ratiocination, of a life on 'a happier star,' what had this nation of enfranchised voters ever done for his genius and its works? With his head full of the mysteries of the universe his belly was empty, his stove cold, his cupboard bare, his wife dying, his works rewarded at the same rate paid for newspaper fillers and magazine hackwork. The literary firmament was fully occupied by self-important New Englanders who puffed one another's moralistic twaddle, and Poe, a Southerner, was shouldered aside as not of their party.

Poe on politics thus far seems less a writer of stories than a hyperbolic pamphleteer without a party. He attacks institutions but doesn't create characters either molded by those institutions or believably reacting against them. Poe's opinions about the electorate resemble those of Fenimore Cooper, but Edgar wrote no *Chainbearer*, no *Satanstoe*, no *Home as Found*, no tale in which a character follows a career of actions determined by any political circumstance. Poe did, however, write a sketch about a popular hero, that is, the sort of personage whom a self-seeking, ignorant mob would elévate as its ideal. For some reason he called this sketch 'The Man That Was Used Up: A Tale of the Late Bugaboo and Kickapoo Campaign.'

The tale recounts the efforts of the narrator to learn all about 'that truly fine-looking fellow, Brevet Brigadier-General John A. B. C. Smith,' whom all applaud as 'a *remarkable* man—a *very* remarkable man—indeed one of the *most* remarkable men of the age.' Approaching one acquaintance after another for an account of the General's virtues, he hears nothing but the same slogans—'Great wretches, those Bugaboos—savage and so on. . . . Smith!—O yes! great man! . . .' Meeting the renowned hero himself, the narrator is disappointed by Smith's reluctance to expatiate upon 'the theme I had just then most at heart—I mean the mysterious circumstances attending the Bugaboo war,' but he does repeat the gist of Smith's conversation on other 'philosophical' matters.

In case you wonder why I give details of what looks a tedious parody of some unknown subject, let me allege that in 1839, when Poe was writing, the real identity of a hero of 'the Bugaboo and Kickapoo War,' a Brevet-General, was not obscure. (His now-secret identity was recovered to me by Ronald Curran.) Which general officer of the U. S. Army, fresh from triumphant campaigns against the redoubtable Winnebagoes, Menominees, Sioux, and Seminoles, lately the protector of the borders of Maine against incursions from New Brunswick, was the all-admired hero of the day? Why, General Winfield Scott. Winfield Who? Well, it's not Poe's fault that although Scott went on to still greater fame in exploits yet more valorous (as the *Encyclopaedia Britannica* reminds us) at Vera Cruz, Cerro Gordo, Contreras-Churubusco, Molina del Rey, and, above all, Chapultepec (1847–48), he nevertheless failed to win the presidency of the United States on the Whig ticket in 1852, and hence is all but forgotten a century later. Already in 1839, Scott was being bruited as a possible president and Whig. And that's what made so trenchant Poe's apostasy from the ranks of the hero's admirers in 'The Man That Was

Used Up.' For Edgar seems to have wondered what, exactly, were the intellectual qualifications of a redoubtable Indian fighter to become a president. When, in his tale, Brevet-General J. A. B. C. Smith speaks, the monologue goes like this: 'Man alive, how *do* you do? why, how *are* ye? *very* glad to see ye, indeed,' he would begin. From his first words we can infer that the glad-handing politician was a prominent character already in the fifty-eighth year of the Republic.

'There is nothing at all like it,' he would say; 'we are a wonderful people, and live in a wonderful age. Parachutes and railroads—man-traps and spring-guns! Our steam-boats are upon every sea, and the Nassau balloon packet is about to run regular trips (fare either way only twenty pounds sterling) between London and Timbuctoo. And who shall calculate the immense influence upon social life—upon arts —upon commerce—upon literature—which will be the immediate result of the great principle of electro-magnetics! . . .'

Here, in the full vulgarity of his spirit, is the Man of the Hour, the Man of the Nineteenth Century, equally devoted to Progress and the Machine. If, from Poe's day to our own, we have met him again and again in our literature, as Melville's Confidence-Man, as Twain's Colonel Sellers or Hank Morgan, as Lewis's Babbitt (to mention only the most obvious examples), his recurrence in fiction bespeaks his durability as a type of the national character. The words quoted above are about all that Poe's narrator gets from General Smith, so on them alone we base our judgment of this great leader of men.

But the narrator pays him a visit, and makes yet a further discovery. The hero, whose physical appearance had been exemplary in every feature, is found at his *toilette*—and here, to be sure, Edgar's buffoonery gets a bit out of hand. The Great Man is found to reside in a shapeless, squeaky-voiced mass of matter on the floor. As his Negro valet provides first one prosthetic leg, then another, then an arm, another arm, a set of teeth, a false palate, shoulders, a bosom, a wig, at last the well-known physique and physiognomy of Brevet-

General Smith take recognizable form. The old joke about the beauty who removed each of her physical charms before going to bed on her wedding night has been given a new and rather savage twist. The great valorous hero, whom the ignorant mob of Americans nearly deify despite their not knowing anything of his true character, proves to be a mechanismus, a puppet, himself a product of the very mechanical ingenuity whose mindless praise comprises his only philosophy.

THE SOCIAL ORDER

A country in which the business of government is turned over to every ignoramus, roughneck, and vulgarian, will produce national leaders after its own desires. To a man like Poe, whose analysis of the faults of democracy permits him to find allies in no party, life in the turbulent experiment of Jacksonian democracy must have had the charms of involuntary confinement in a madhouse. Where else would a rational man expect to find such a turnabout of his reasonable expectations?

Poe's reasonable expectations, as I deem them, were of course the expectable results of his upbringing on the one hand and of his intellectual independence on the other. Poe seems never to have questioned the hierarchy of social classes which was especially marked in Virginia. Nor would he, since by all rights (were rights only all) he, Edgar Allan Poe, belonged at the very top, or near it, of the pyramid. Poe was no humanitarian liberal, and he didn't care a fig that beneath that summit of society toiled and moiled the lower orders, the whole structure supported by the poor whites and Negro slaves. Few if any of even these lived lives of penury comparable to that of Edgar Allan Poe, so wrongfully denied his proper prerogatives.

In fact Penniless Edgar lived out his life in one rôle especially bitter in a country like ours, where, despite the magnitude of the star under which we are born, status is thought to be achieved rather than prescribed. That role is the Disinherited Aristocrat. Especially bitter, yet especially attractive too. How many Americans have found, in the face of their personal failures (in business, in love, in life) a great consolation in the knowledge that, were truth and justice seen to, they would be acknowledged as—the Lost Dauphin of France; or Napoleon; or the true Earl of Renwick, or the rightful Macleod of Skye. How enviable, the Irish, *all* of whom are the sons of the sons of kings! The motif of the Disinherited Aristocrat links Poe with Melville, with Hawthorne, with Mark Twain, all of whom were, like Edgar (the grandson of General Poe, Quartermaster in the Revolutionary Army), descended from forebears who had seen better days. In the case of those writers, all more in fealty to Christian doctrine than was Poe, this motif in their own lives had a way of becoming associated with Adam's Fall from the aristocracy of Grace. The Disinheritance of the Aristocrat was thus a paradigm of the fate of Man.

Poe's sense of his own uniqueness, his own genius, his own knowledge of what was true but not recognized by the mass of mankind who scorned his gift of that knowledge, made his lot both more bitter and more exalted than that of other Disinherited Aristocrats. The acuity of his intellect led him to construct a metaphysics which explained the entire universe, yet he couldn't raise a thousand dollars to start a magazine of his own. Poe's sufferings—I mean this time physical sufferings, actual hunger, the bite of the cold in unheated rooms, as well as the throbbing affront to his pride as a man of honor that he could provide no better for his invalid wife and devoted mother-in-law—might well have made the man a bitter misogynist. Yet everyone who had anything to do with him in the conduct of the magazines for which he worked has reported that his bearing was almost always amiable, his manners those of a Southern gentleman, and it was only when stricken by occasional bouts of drinking that he behaved in a way to embarrass his friends. His conduct under the influence has been more often deplored than described, but there seems to be no record that Poe ever behaved with physical violence toward others. His aggressive impulses were demoniac, but they seem to have been fully expressed either in his literary feuds and vendettas, in his caustic reviews of writers he deemed inferior, or directed in his fictions by a shaping literary intelligence which controlled them.

When a man is in the grip of a self-consistent system of thought of his own, of which the rest of the world is ignorant, the ordinary affairs of life, the arrangements of society itself, seem to him, as I've said, insane. This long prolegomenon is my way of introducing Edgar Poe's comment on those cracked arrangements, in his story 'The System of Doctor Tarr and Professor Fether.'

This tale does not say it is about America—in fact it is set in a southern province of France. Nor does it purport to be about society; it describes a visit to a *Maison de Santé*. Intrigued by a description given him by medical friends in Paris of a certain private madhouse, where Monsieur Maillard had won fame for the success of his 'system of soothing' lunatics, the narrator decides to go and see it. Under this system, 'all punishments were avoided . . . even confinement was seldom resorted to . . . the patients, while secretly watched, were left much apparent liberty, and . . . most of them were permitted to roam about the house and grounds in the ordinary apparel of persons in right mind.' In short, Maillard's system would give to lunatics the free self-expression which, in a later day, the 'system' of permissive child-rearing gives to children, which is also recommended (and sometimes tried) as a means of dealing with criminals, drug addicts, and other deviant persons. By a slight stretch of imagination we may provide further analogues from contemporary education and politics.

The visitor, approaching the madhouse where this system is practised, describes the view. It is distinctly reminiscent of several clichés from Gothic fiction:

> . . . a grass-grown by-path which, in half an hour, nearly lost itself in a dense forest clothing the base of a moun-

tain. Through this dank and gloomy wood we rode some
two miles, when the *Maison de Santé* came in view. It
was a fantastic *château*, much dilapidated, and indeed
scarcely tenantable through age and neglect. Its aspect inspired me with absolute dread . . .

This is very like the approach to the House of Usher. Nonetheless, the visitor plucks up his courage and at last is admitted to the hall. Monsieur Maillard informs him, however,
that the system of soothing has been abandoned. It had been
tried—'We did every thing that rational humanity could suggest'—but the danger was fearful. For instance, the practice
was to indulge the illusion of the patient; if a man thought
himself a chicken, so he was regarded—and was fed nothing
but corn and gravel. 'There is no argument which so touches
the feeble reason of the madman as the *reductio ad ab-
surdum*.' Another feature was to permit each patient to act
as a guardian of the others, for 'To repose confidence in the
understanding or discretion of a madman, is to gain him body
and soul,' as well as to economize on salaried keepers. All
these liberties, with no punishments, comprised the recently
abandoned system. Maillard offers his visitor a dinner with
choice wine, and they adjourn to the *salle à manger*.

There the scene has 'an air of oddity.' Patients are dressed
in outmoded fashions, in ill-fitting gowns, with immodest
displays of bosoms and arms. The table is surprisingly opulent, indeed, 'Never . . . had I witnessed so lavish, so waste-
ful an expenditure of the good things of life. There seemed
very little taste, however, in the arrangements.' The conversation takes rather an interesting turn as the diners one after
another expatiate on the queer cases who used to inhabit the
asylum. One such inmate thought himself a teapot; another,
a donkey; yet a third maintained he was a cheese and begged
his friends to slice him. Another mistook himself for a bottle
of champagne, another for a frog, and so on. Each speaker,
describing these freaks of fancy, would demonstrate to the
visitor what the one-time patient did to exhibit his lunacy.
All the while a motley orchestra is attacking its instruments,
producing cacophonous noises. One young girl tells of a

patient who thought clothes were to be taken off, not put on—and she proceeds to strip off her garments. Several diners leap forward to prevent her—when there are screams and yells from another chamber. Monsieur Maillard confides that sometimes the lunatics in their cells get up a yell in unison. The system by which they are confined there is that of Professor Tarr and Doctor Fether. The visitor is ashamed to admit he has never before heard of these experts.

The dinner continues, and so do the drinks. No doubt it is one glass too many of the Clos de Vougeot which brings Monsieur Maillard to admit that which the astute reader has already guessed. (Again Poe has used to some advantage the obtuse narrator.) Is it the wine, or is it the Imp of the Perverse which leads Maillard to confide how the 'system of soothing' worked so well that 'one fine morning the keepers found themselves pinioned hand and foot, and thrown into the cells where they were attended, as if *they* were the lunatics, by the lunatics themselves, who had usurped the offices of the keepers.'

Just as Maillard is in the midst of describing how he plotted the rebellion, persuaded his fellow patients to become his accomplices, imprisoned the keepers and made free with the wardrobe, the jewels, and the wine-cellar of the *Maison*, there is a loud commotion. The locked door is smashed from outside and the scene dissolves in 'the most terrible confusion.' There enters 'a perfect army of what I took to be chimpanzees, orang-outangs, or big black baboons.' These, we learn when things are sorted out, are the actual keepers of the asylum, escaped from their dungeon. Dr. Maillard, the originator of the soothing system, had himself a few years earlier become insane and was made a patient under his own system. 'A madman is not necessarily a fool,' he had told his visitor, and so, discovering what license its liberties permitted, he took advantage when he could, and with his mad confederates tarred and feathered his keepers. *That* comprised the system of Doctor Tarr and Professor Fether.

Poe seems to have been innocent of the work of de Sade, and yet how cleverly and closely he anticipated the produc-

tion of Peter Brook. In our own time *Marat/Sade* has enacted on stage and screen the political allegory of society as a
madhouse run by its inmates. As far as I know, nobody in
Poe's time or since has ever regarded his presentation of the
same insight as anything more than a *bagatelle*.

But Poe's *bagatelle* is set in France, so why do I think it
has anything to do with his being a Disinherited Aristocrat
among the Americans described by Pundita and the revived
mummy, when General J. A. B. C. Smith might run for election? I think Poe tells us this when he identifies the tune
which the mad musicians play at the moment when their
keepers burst through the door. During 'the whole of the
uproar,' they performed, 'if not exactly in tune, at least with
an energy superhuman,' the strains of *Yankee Doodle!*

VII

Grotesques and Arabesques

'Of my country and of my family I have little to say,' says
the narrator of 'MS. Found in a Bottle.' The teller of
'Berenice' confesses, 'My baptismal name is Egaeus; that of
my family I will not mention,' while Poe in 'A Tale of the
Ragged Mountains,' writes of his chief character, 'Of his
family I could obtain no satisfactory account.'

These anonymous and unfamilied heroes can of course be
explained away as the self-projections of their orphaned and
disinherited author. Yet this does not sufficiently account
for the denial to so many of his characters of a patrimony or
a name. Knowing Poe, knowing the *underlying consistency*
of all of his work (I italicize the phrase, as he would have
done), is there not likely *a philosophical necessity* for certain
of his characters to step into our consciousness as though un-
sired? I thought perhaps Poe kept this reason out of sight in
some subterranean chamber, entombed like so many of the
victims in his tales, allowing it to work upon us only indirectly
as he says allegory best operates. Then, quite by chance—like
Monsieur Dupin or the husband of Ligeia or the narrator of
'The Raven'—plucking from the bookshelf of an obscure
library (it was the Reference Room in the collections of the
Royal Borough of Kensington, in Horton Street, W.8) a
volume of unworldly lore, I came, in Porphyry's *On the Life
of Plotinos*, upon the following curious passage:

> Plotinos, the philosopher our contemporary, seemed
> ashamed of being in the body

So deeply rooted was this feeling that he could never be induced to tell of his ancestry, his parentage, or his birthplace.

Birthplace, parentage, ancestry—these are the attributes of body. To the soul they are inessential accidents. And the direction of Poe's mind, the thrust of his imagination is— may I restate the obvious?—away from the body and toward the spirit, away from the 'dull realities' of this world, toward the transcendent consciousness on 'a far happier star.' His protagonists are all attempting to get out of the clotted condition of their own materiality, to cross the barrier between the perceptible sensual world and that which lies beyond it. And so they undertake hazardous voyages, either into the stratosphere or to the moon; or by descending into dungeons and vaults in the earth; or down maelstroms in the sea toward the center of the very world. Others cross the bourne between our life and another by breaking through the barrier of silence and speaking from beyond the grave. Some achieve this posthumous eloquence as the result of a mesmerical suspension of mortality; some, consuming inordinate amounts of laudanum, take the trip on drugs. Still others have already arrived at the desired condition of immaterial existence and speak to one another, in 'Colloquies' and 'Conversations,' as disembodied shades.

But for those Poe stories in which the characters are still alive, it may be inessential, indeed distracting, to establish a recognizable place as the locus of the action, as it is to provide the participants with a realistic station in life or a family. How many of Poe's tales (bar 'The Gold Bug' and 'A Tale of the Ragged Mountains') can be said to take place in the South, or for that matter in the United States, or, by the evidence of their texts, in the nineteenth century? Still, I do not propose that *all* of his fictions are suspended in time and unfixed in locus. In many both place and time are indeed specific. These on inspection prove to be either his detection tales (which most concertedly of his serious fictions do explore a real world), or his grotesques. Satire, the prevailing grotesque tone, is for Poe a lower exercise of the imagination than those fictions which discover the truths of the soul.

Hence the buffoonish tone of those sketches which treat of dull realities. Hence the tone of excitation, the breathless terror and ecstatic fixation in those tales which explore the soulscape rather than the social milieu in which a soul is fated to exist.

Everyone knows that Poe himself points to such a division between his tales by giving his volume in 1840 the double title, *Tales of the Grotesque and Arabesque.* Poe scholars agree that A. H. Quinn correctly identified the source of these odd terms in Poe's critical vocabulary as Sir Walter Scott's essay, 'On the Supernatural in Fictitious Composition,' *Fortnightly Review* (1827). Much has been made over the exact meanings of 'arabesque' and 'grotesque,' and whether we can apply them only to the tales in the 1840 volume or use them as pigeonholes in which to sort out all of Poe's fictions. Although Poe in his criticism is forever, as we have seen, making rigid distinctions, this particular pair of terms has made for as much confusion as clarification of his intentions. A reordering of the works is in order.

I take 'grotesque' and 'arabesque' to indicate two fundamentally different intentions on the part of the fictioneer. Roughly stated, a grotesque is a satire, an arabesque a prose equivalent of a poem. The terms themselves, as used by Scott—and presumably by Poe—derive not from the vocabulary of literature but from that of art, décor, architecture. In this they resemble that parent term, Gothic, of which they are, for Poe, subdivisions.

In an art work, *grotesque* signifies the depiction of monsters in an elaborate, foliated setting; while *arabesque* refers to an intricate pattern, geometric in design, which does not reproduce the human form—this latter element deriving from the Mohammedan injunction against the reproduction in a work of art of that divine image, the human body. *Arabesque* thus links Poe's practice as a writer of Gothic tales with the desired condition toward which his imagination ever impels him: renunciation and transcendence of the body. It connects also with his interest in that other Romantic craze, Arabiana, already touched on in such poems as 'Al Aaraaf' and 'Israfel.' The intricacy of pattern in an arabesque corresponds to Poe's desire, or need, to reveal by complex and elaborate concealments of his theme. There is no *human form* anywhere in Poe's arabesques; but their intricate patterns of abstraction create a synthetic and harmonious—though often horrifying—experience, a consistency.

When a compulsive theoretician of literary form draws the terms of his distinctions from another art, the fact seems both worthy of notice and an invitation to inference. There is evident an irreconcilable difference in both the intention and the mode of operation between a work of fiction and a pictorial or three-dimensional art form. A fiction, as Poe elsewhere says repeatedly enough, requires a plot, indeed hinges upon its plot; and what is plot but the management of a human action in time? But painting, architecture, décor—the arts to which the terms *grotesque* and *arabesque* are more properly applied—have nothing to do with plots or actions, they are concerned with the arrangements of elements in space. Such arts are essentially static, devoid (usually) of human content, and constitute expressions by a shaping aesthetic sense of its chosen materials. The reasons may readily be inferred why Poe's fictions so often resemble *tableaux vivants*, his *tableaux vivants* so readily becoming *tableaux morts*.

I propose to disregard Poe's use of these terms only for the tales in his 1840 volume, but rather to regard them as indicative of two of his principal commitments of the imagination in his fiction. (Always excepted from these considerations are his tales of ratiocination, in which, to be sure, elements of both the grotesque and the arabesque appear.) By an inductive analysis of Poe's stories, such as he himself (I would like to think) might desire us to make upon his *œuvre*, I intuit the following criteria for his tales of the

Grotesque and the Arabesque. (Henceforth I shall capitalize them as generic nouns, as Poe did in his title.)

A Grotesque is not debarred from representing a real person, but it must do so in a caricature, making monstrosities of realities. Consequently we discover that all of Poe's Grotesques are set in contemporary time, and many are satires of recognizable persons and events. (E.g., the send-up of General Winfield Scott in 'The Man That Was Used Up'; the put-down of the Gold Rush in 'Von Kempelen and His Discovery'; the attacks on contemporary government and philosophy in 'Some Words with a Mummy' and 'Mellonta Tauta.') Poe's Arabesques, however, are set in unspecified time and in imaginary places (as is true of 'Ligeia,' 'The Fall of the House of Usher,' 'Berenice,' etc.). In the Arabesques there are a very few characters—a narrator, two or three others —but the Grotesques may have a cast of a dozen characters or more, although there is no effort to give these personages more than one dimension.

While the two modes seem mutually exclusive, Poe on examination proves often to have written an Arabesque and a Grotesque on the same theme. His variable sense of gravity enables such divagations to appear in his work. How often haven't we wildly swung between ecstasy and revulsion, between hoax and revelation, between flapdoodle and the sublime! Some may think this proof of Poe's instability, his inability to control his tone. Or perhaps his Imp of the Perverse leads him to mock in Grotesques the achievement of his own Arabesques, as though to put his work beyond the reach of parody by others. Consider. What is 'A Predicament,' that preposterous parody—ostensibly—of a *Blackwood's* story, but a parody—in fact—of Poe's own (and as yet unwritten) 'The Pit and the Pendulum'? And speaking of his 'Imp of the Perverse,' what other than that Imp made him turn the other way and write 'The Angel of the Odd'— a laborious spoof of a simpleton prone to take too many drams, who comes thereby to the frustration of great expectations. Yet again, what is 'Some Words with a Mummy' but a send-up of the very theme taken seriously in 'Mesmeric

Revelations,' although to be sure that itself was a hoax to
begin with—a hoax of serious intent. But then again, *all* of
Poe's hoaxes have a serious intent, somewhere. 'Thou Art
the Man' is such a hoax (the narrator knowing the solution
all the time), and it is a version, in the mode of frontier
humor (the native Grotesque) of the detection theme presented more seriously, more skillfully, and in a more cosmo-
politan vehicle in 'The Purloined Letter.' 'The Masque of
the Red Death' is one of Poe's most memorable Arabesques,
parodied, so to speak, by a Grotesque on the very same
theme, 'King Pest.' And, as the present chapter will indicate, other such pairs of linked dissimilars include 'Eleonora'
and 'Loss of Breath'; 'Ligeia' and 'The Spectacles'; 'The
Cask of Amontillado' and 'The Premature Burial.'

What characterizes the Arabesques is their exploration
of extreme psychological states—the narrators or chief characters are often madmen, or persons who undergo some ex-
cruciating suffering of the soul. Insofar as the Grotesque is a
mode of satire, it depends on a rationalistic view of experience as the norm against which the recorded monstrous defec-
tions be measured; but in the Grotesques the ratiocinative
power leads not to the perception of ecstasy, as in the tales of
detection and exploration, but rather to the exposure of the
idiocy of the monstrous world.

Yet a further inference from Poe's duplicity in the treatment of so many of his themes is this: Chief among his
themes is duplicity itself. The doubleness of experience. How
can we tell the reality from its mirror, the world from its
picture in a work of art, the image from the image of the
image? Poe, whose entire enterprise is a desperate effort to
unify our existence on this suffering globe of shards, himself
sees that all of our passions, intuitions, thoughts, are susceptible of inversion, may become their opposites, so that
ecstatic transcendence may be lodged in the heart of a hoax.
Identity itself, the very vessel of perception, may be fatally
flawed, fatally broken in twain. One of Poe's themes is the
fate of the man haunted by his own double, his anima, his

weird. Which is the real consciousness, the 'I' who speaks or
the doppelgänger who pursues him?

SEEING DOUBLE

Had I not been thus prolix, you might either have misunderstood me altogether, or, with the rabble, have fancied
me mad. As it is, you will easily perceive that I am one of
the many uncounted victims of the Imp of the Perverse.

Thus speaks Hoaxiepoe in his earnest guise as truthsayer.
It is evident, if only from the sentences just quoted, that the
author is aware of deep cleavages in his own self—or, in the
terminology of his time, in his soul. He appears, to himself
as well as to others, as both sane and mad; as both a civil
workaday person who keeps appointments and earns his
wages, and as a victim of the Imp of the Perverse. This Imp,
it will be recalled, is that principle which compels us to 'act,
for the reason that we should *not*. . . . Nor will this overwhelming tendency to do wrong for the wrong's sake, admit
of analysis, or resolution into ulterior elements. It is a radical, a primitive impulse.'

Poe speaks here with unexampled knowledge of the hidden self within the self. In 'The Imp of the Perverse'
he summons the courage so to expose his secret sinfulness
only because, like J. Alfred Prufrock, he speaks from across
a bourne from which no traveller returns: it is his gallows
confession, his confession of his confession of his motiveless
crime, a crime which had been perfect except for his double
compulsion to perform that which he should not do: first to
murder his victim (no details are given as to any injury the
victim may have done him), then, 'as [he] reflected upon
[his] absolute security,' to confess—to rush down the street
crying aloud his guilt—which had otherwise been undetected.
Curiously, the mode of the murder's commission was suffocation: he substituted for his victim's night-candle a poisonous
candle of his own devising. Curiously again, when apprehended, 'I turned—I gasped for breath. For a moment I ex-

perienced all the pangs of suffocation. . . .' Everything is
doubled, as the punishment fits the crime.

Who, or what, is this Imp of the Perverse but a portion
of the ego separated out from the rest, which seeks the destruction of that from which it is separated? The fact that it
may seek its own destruction too does not deter it from its
calamitous purpose. Life is on a collision course with death;
the death-wish betrays, whenever it can, the life instinct.
This seems madness, the mind undoing its own self-
protective calculation by an uncontrollable, 'a radical, a primitive impulse.'

This impulse is so primitive, so uncanny, so terrifying that
in 'The Imp of the Perverse' it appears only as a malignant
force impelling the protagonist. He cannot objectify it as a
character. But if this impulse to undo one's own security be
considered in a comic rather than a terrifying aspect—as
comedy is so often the obverse of terror—it can easily be ob-
jectified in a ridiculous guise. Stripped of its terror, it can
make us—make author also—laugh, though to be sure its effect
upon the self from which it has separated itself is every bit
as disastrous as was that of the Imp of the Perverse, whose
grotesque double is the Angel of the Odd. In Poe's sketch
of that title, the protagonist—the primary self—is a perfectly
ordinary homme moyen sensuel, to whom appears a ridiculous
personage who comments upon his thoughts and plies him
with drink. This Angel of the Odd, speaking in the Dutch
dialect Poe had borrowed from Irving for 'Hans Pfaall,' is a
personage constructed from a rum puncheon, kegs, bottles
and a funnel. At his urging the narrator gets so drunk that
he snoozes past the hour on which his fire insurance expired.
Having missed the deadline for signing its renewal, he
awakens to discover, naturally enough, that his house is on
fire—and now he becomes temporarily blinded, is deserted
by his fiancée, decides upon suicide, dives into a river,
changes his mind, then rushes over a precipice—from which
he is saved by his 'grasping the end of a long guide-rope,
which depended from a passing balloon.' This is perhaps more
silly than amusing, yet what does it burlesque but the very

themes of self-destruction and escape from reality which elsewhere comprise the ballast of Poe's more serious tales?

Between them, 'The Imp of the Perverse' and 'The Angel
of the Odd' state in outline form, as it were, many basic
postulates of Poe's *donnée*: the division of the self, the destructive opposition of the death-wish and the life-wish; fear
of death, blindness, suffocation (all, as Freud repeatedly
shows, surrogate forms of castration-fear and fear of impotence); the unanticipated eruption of aggressive impulse, and
of self-incrimination; the incurable addiction to drink (or
drugs) which speeds the self-destructive impulse on its way;
and the wish-fantasy of escape from all of these predicaments.

Some of this obsessive material becomes clear, because
handled with masterful intelligence, in the story 'William
Wilson.' The name William Wilson, as the narrator tells us,
is a *nom pro tem*. The chosen disguise reveals that its bearer
is, in his own view, self-begotten: he is William Wilson,
William son of his own *Will*. He has, that is, willed himself
into being—willed the self we meet, the one that survives its
murder of its double. It's not entirely clear whether, at the
end, as William Wilson sees his own bloodied face in a mirror where a moment earlier no mirror stood before, he does
survive the murder of his doppelgänger, or whether he speaks
his lurid confession from beyond the grave. If he survives,
he does so in a condition of madness which his exacerbated
prose style embodies and reveals:

Let me call myself, for the present, William Wilson.
The fair page lying before me need not be sullied with
my real appellation. This has been already too much an
object for the scorn—for the horror—for the detestation of
my race. To the uttermost regions of the globe have not
the indignant winds bruited its unparalleled infamy? Oh,
outcast of all outcasts most abandoned!—to the earth art
thou not forever dead? to its honors, to its flowers, to its
golden aspirations?—and a cloud, dense, dismal, and limit-
less, does it not hang eternally between thy hopes and
heaven?

These, as W. H. Auden was the first to notice, are the accents of lunacy—these triple iterations, these rhetorical inflations, these rhodomontades in which luxuriates an abandoned soul —accents which Poe gives his narrator as a means of establishing his character. True, in the body of the tale William Wilson does not rant and rave in three-decker clauses. Indeed, he tells his doomed screed with a reasonableness, a clarity, a perspicuous control of his own narrative which cannot fail to involve the reader in his fate. Unlike the narrator of 'The Tell-Tale Heart' ('why *will* you say that I am mad?'), the possibility of his own dementia never occurs to William Wilson. He is sane, he is cool, he is fully aware of his own doings. But there is one circumstance in his life he can only report, for he himself does not understand it. It is an urge to do evil: 'a sudden elevation in turpitude whose origin alone it is my present purpose to assign.'

What follows is the autobiography of 'William Wilson.' Its chief events are recognizably based upon two periods in Edgar Poe's own life, his boyhood schooldays at Stoke Newington in England and his misadventures at the gaming tables while a student in the University of Virginia. But these schoolboy remembrances are conflated in a tone and style of Byronic intensity. Indeed the shadow of Byron tinges this tale, for, as Arthur Hobson Quinn points out, Poe drew upon Irving's sketch 'An Unwritten Account of Lord Byron' (published in 1836) in its design.

Little did Poe know it, but in 'William Wilson' he made *so easy* Griswold's mission of calumniating his character! Not content with reproducing in William Wilson's history these two well-publicized episodes from his own life, he also assigned to his fictitious narrator *his own birthday!* The 19th of January, 1813. Or, in its first printing (1839), the 19th of January, 1811. (Poe kept moving his birthdate forward, in successive magazine biographies, in order to seem younger than he was. So, it appears, did William Wilson.) But to be scrupulous about it, Poe didn't actually say that it was *William Wilson* whose birth-date coincided with his own. He makes William Wilson say that 'My namesake was born

on the nineteenth of January, 1813 [or 1811]—and this is a
somewhat remarkable coincidence; for the day is precisely
that of my own nativity.' By this time, William Wilson, the
bully and scourge of the other boys at Dr. Bransby's dismal
school, is himself the victim of the one among them who
resists 'the imperiousness' of his disposition. This lad, by yet
another singular coincidence, is also named William Wilson.
(I shall hereinafter call him Wilson².).

William Wilson is tormented daily as Wilson² coolly imi-
tates his manner, dress, and speech, though the one defect,
the only one, in Wilson² is that he cannot speak louder than
a whisper. Nevertheless, *'His singular whisper, it grew to be
the very echo of my own.'* What is further curious is that
none of the schoolboys but Wilson himself seems aware of
the mocking and sarcastic harassment inflicted upon him by
Wilson². William at last is driven to try to murder his tor-
menting double: he approaches, by stealth, at night, the
sleeping Wilson². As he looks upon his victim he feels
'a numbness, an iciness of feeling. . . . gasping for
breath. . . .' For he is struck by the identity of the victim's
appearance with his own. He flees, quitting the bedchamber,
the school, this phase of his life.

Quickly to sum up the rest of the tale, William Wilson
passes from Dr. Bransby's through Eton, from Eton to Oxford, by now possessing 'rooted habits of vice . . . soulless
dissipation.' Now he arranges to cheat a lord of his patrimony
with a fixed deck of cards. (No doubt Edgar here remembers
his own *losing* at cards while at Virginia, in consequence of
which debts he had to leave the University.) Just as he is
about to clinch the trick, there seems to enter the dimly lit
room that familiar stranger who is his nemesis. 'Who and
what was this Wilson?—and whence came he?—and what
were his purposes? Upon neither of these points could I be
satisfied. . . .' William Wilson is his own obtuse narrator.
Though he thinks himself as clever as might a Monsieur
Dupin, he never acknowledges what is obvious to the reader
—what Poe had made inevitable by giving this tale for epi-

graph these lines (which he made up, T. O. Mabbott says, but attributed to Chamberlayne's *Pharronida*),

What say of it? what say CONSCIENCE grim,
That spectre in my path?

Wilson[2] exposes William Wilson, forcing his immediate departure from Oxford in disgrace. But, he learns, 'I *fled in vain*. My evil destiny pursued me as if in exultation,' pursued him to Paris, to Vienna, Berlin, Moscow. At last, William Wilson attends a masked ball in Naples, intent upon seducing the young wife of the Duke his host. There, too, in a costume exactly like his own, masked in black as he himself is, he sees his nemesis approach. In a frenzy Wilson drags his double into a little antechamber, and 'getting him at mercy, plunged my sword, with brute ferocity, repeatedly through and through his bosom.' Looking up, he discovers now a mirror where the wall had heretofore seemed blank, and 'as I stepped up to it in an extremity of terror, mine own image, but with features all pale and dabbled in blood, advanced to meet me with a feeble and tottering gait.' But no—

It was Wilson; but he spoke no longer in a whisper, and I could have fancied that I myself was speaking while he said:

'You have conquered, and I yield. Yet henceforth art thou also dead—dead to the World, to Heaven, and to Hope! In me didst thou exist—and, in my death, see by this image, which is thine own, how utterly thou hast murdered thyself!'

Utterly murdered thyself! What is CONSCIENCE, after all, but that part of the ego which regards the rest as an object *which it can judge*. The part so regarded is the less developed, the more infantile, regressive, narcissistic. The more primitive, the more uncontrolled, incivil, aggressive. But how can the evil-doing part of the ego survive the murder of its own judging half?

'William Wilson' is perhaps the most vivid and memorable of Romantic tales of the divided self. In its psychological probing, and in the success of its objectifying the twin irrepressible impulses *to do evil* and *to judge oneself*, it makes Stevenson's *Dr. Jekyll and Mr. Hyde* seem naïve. For how much closer to the inadmissible truth is Poe's resolution than Stevenson's, who makes the better of the two selves destroy its evil-doing double. In Poe's own country the only thing like 'William Wilson' is by that other demon-haunted genius, Mark Twain. But where Poe's tale is taut with demonic intensity, there is a wonderful hilarity in 'The Facts Concerning A Recent Carnival of Crime in Connecticut,' in which Mark Twain, tortured by his Calvinist conscience, outwits his tormentor—and murders him. Then he is free to slay enemies, cheat widows, and freely indulge that wayward, mischief-loving self whose life had been a perpetual pang of suffering thanks to Conscience.

But in Poe's 'William Wilson' the duplication of the self is more complex, the emotional logic more complicated. If William Wilson's double is his conscience, he is also his Imp of the Perverse. Which is to say that each half of the split ego has its own Imp of the Perverse—Wilson himself is such an Imp to Wilson[2], the first Wilson revelling in obliquity in acquiescence to a deep impulse in himself which outrages the moral imperative represented by Wilson[2]. On the point of succeeding in his outrageous vices—bullying the schoolboys, tricking Lord Glendenning into cutting a marked deck, seducing the Duchess Di Broglio—what makes Wilson fail but the betrayal of his impulse to do evil by his equally uncontrollable impulse to judge himself? No wonder he has no hope of Heaven at the end, for whichever Wilson he acts as, the other will arise to torment him. All the more damning because there's no vestige in Poe's tale of the damnatory Calvinism which in later life drove Mark Twain to the point of despair. When the Imp of the Perverse triumphs and rules unchallenged, as at the end of 'William Wilson,' that much of the self which survives is condemned to madness in the house of woe.

MURDER!

Despite the strength of the death wish among Poe's characters, only in one tale does any of them literally commit suicide. In 'The Assignation' (one of Edgar's earliest Arabesques, begun as a parody of the *Blackwood's* type of Gothic tale), there are not one but *two* suicides: the Prince Mentoni and the Marchesa Aphrodite both perish by their own hands, at the stroke of the same hour on the clock. As the clock ticked on, Poe became more circumspect and skillful in the treatment of his pervasive theme. He puts a mask upon red death, as it were, and contrives at least two disguises for the self's will to destruction: (a) by dividing the ego into a self and a double, he enables one to murder the other in a dramatization of the suicide-wish; (b) without resort to such doubling, Poe contrives that the self undergo obsessive and repeated, *but involuntary,* mortal dangers, particularly by accidental and premature entombment. Such is the heavy burden of his putatively factual-autobiographical sketch, 'The Premature Burial.'

But there's yet a third device in Edgar's handling of his guilty secret and his secret guilt. To wit, (c), in which he doubles his character and then arranges for one self to *murder the other by burying him alive.* Such is the case, most memorably, in 'The Cask of Amontillado.' To understand, as fully as we must, who does what to whom, and why, when Montresor leaves Fortunato chained to the one wall with another, newly plastered, before him, let us consider Poe's affection for the motif of the premature burial. (It. will recur also in 'The Black Cat,' and 'The Fall of the House of Usher'; and, with variations, in 'Berenice' and 'Ligeia.' We have already seen Poe's fondness for conferring deathlike states upon the living, as in 'Monsieur Valdemar' and 'Mesmeric Revelation,' as well as for bringing the dead back to life, as in 'Some Words with a Mummy.')

'There are certain themes,' he writes, 'of which the interest

is all-absorbing, but which are too entirely horrible for the
purposes of legitimate fiction. . . . To be buried alive is,
beyond question, the most terrific of these extremes which
has ever fallen to the lot of mere mortality.' This 'ultimate
woe' requires that 'the severity and majesty of truth sanctify
and sustain' the author's presentation thereof. In this way
Poe invokes the cloak of truth-telling, as had Defoe, Swift,
and Richardson before him, for subjects and motives so different from his. What ensues in 'The Premature Burial' is
a catalogue of suppositious occasions on which an unfortunate
person, thought to be dead, was buried alive. Some were rescued from their vaults or tombs, one or two were later dis-
interred and discovered in the postures of horrible awareness
of their terrifying predicaments: '. . . Thus she remained,
and thus she rotted, erect.'

At the last, the truth-teller tells of his own experience, of
which the foregoing were but simulacra. Being subject to
epileptic seizures, it is not surprising he should be obsessed
by the fear of being buried while in a trance. He even has
had his family vault 'so remodelled as to admit of being readily opened from within.' No wonder he has made a scrap-
book of every occurrence the world over of the accident he
most fears. On one occasion—the last which his tale recounts
—he seemed to awaken in a closely confined wooden space,
all dark . . .

> there came suddenly to my nostrils the strong peculiar
> odor of moist earth. . . . I was *not* within the vault. I had
> fallen into a trance while absent from home—while among
> strangers—when, or how, I could not remember—and it was
> they who had buried me as a dog—nailed up in some coffin
> —and thrust, deep, deep, and for ever, into some ordinary
> and nameless *grave*.

This seems as horrifying as the worst of the other predicaments Poe has bestowed upon his tortured narrators—groping
in the pit, lying bound beneath the pendulum, whirling in
the maelstrom, being stabbed by one's double. It is just here,
at this point, that 'truth' intervenes, to turn horror to mere

nightmare and to restore the bright light of rational exposition to a circumstance too dreadful for the soul to bear. The
narrator of 'The Premature Burial' screams and attracts the
attention of strangers who 'restored [him] to the full possession of [his] memory.' Now he recalls that he had gone
to sleep in the narrow cabin of a sloop bearing a cargo of garden mould. It was no more than that, and the terror is completely explained away. His tortures, he concludes,

> were inconceivably hideous; but out of Evil proceeded
> Good; for their very excess wrought in my spirit an in-
> evitable revulsion. My soul acquired tone—acquired temper.
> I went abroad. I took vigorous exercise. I breathed the free
> air of Heaven. I thought upon other subjects than Death.
> . . . I read no 'Night Thoughts,' no fustian about church-
> yards—no bugaboo tales—*such as this*. In short, I became
> a new man, and lived a man's life.

Poor Eddie. What this rather labored sketch is trying to tell
us is, 'I *wish* I could thus easily rid myself of these obsessive
hallucinations.' Calling 'The Premature Burial' a bugaboo
tale, Eddie admits that he cannot shake himself free from
the long shadow, the gasping breath, the feeling of fatal and
foetal enclosure.

If he cannot be free from it, though, he can figure out *how
best to make use of it* in his ratiocinative-ecstatic-horrific
tales. By means of whose telling he can all but control the
terrors that shake him to the marrow of his soul.

Doomed to live in his own time, Poe had to be his own
alienist. In 1844 there was no physician in America who
could have given Poe a better understanding of his terrors
than he himself so painfully arrived at. A century later he
could have read about such things in Dr. Karl Menninger's
study, *Man Against Himself*. He might have found a real-
life counterpart to the sufferer in his own 'The Premature
Burial':

> One recalls the extraordinary career of Harry Houdini
> (Ehrich Weiss) who was particularly fond of extricating
> himself from apparently inextricable situations,

and here Menninger quotes from an article about Houdini
in *The Psychoanalytic Review,*

> straightjackets, all manner of manacles, chains, handcuffs,
> prison cells, chests, hampers, glass boxes, roll-top desks, and
> even iron boilers. With his arms thoroughly secured he
> leaped from bridges, suspended head downward by block
> and tackle he loosened himself from meshes of constricting
> apparatus. He allowed himself to be chained and buried
> in six feet of earth, to be locked in steel vaults, to be nailed
> in huge packing cases. Once, breaking free after an en-
> deavor lasting over an hour, he said, "The pain, torture,
> agony, and misery of that struggle will forever live in my
> mind." His variations on the escape act were endless, noth-
> ing being too bizarre, tedious, or difficult so long as the
> principles of a constraining force were present.

Was there ever so close a reenactment of Poe's most horror-
struck fantasies? Houdini's escapes recapitulate the predicaments of Poe's hapless balloonists, the fears of his epileptic,
the fates of his voyager Pym and of Madeline Usher. Of
Houdini, Menninger continues,

> His most dramatic escapes were from coffins buried under-
> ground and from chains while under water.

But what does it all mean? Why did Houdini seek out, as
though impelled by some principle of perversity, situations
so claustrophobic and predicaments so difficult of egress?

> Coupled with this, unconsciously, is the fact that he had an
> extraordinary attachment for his mother which strongly af-
> fected his entire life . . .

And the author in *The Psychoanalytic Review* opined that
'almost every stunt staged by Houdini represented a form
of pseudo-suicide.' Now, Menninger himself concludes that

> We have no right then to dismiss the significance of a par-
> ticular method of committing suicide [or pseudo-suicide]
> as meaningless. In the light of clinical experience we know
> with a fair degree of definiteness what some of these sym-
> bols, and hence these methods, mean. . . . Such fantasies

may be accompanied by a strong sense of guilt and there is a well-known (concomitant) conception of the womb, or entry into the womb, as being something terrible. This we recognize in the nature of the mythological representations of entering life hereafter—the dog Cerberus, the terrible river Styx, purgatory and so on.

Alas the poor psychotic imagination, to which everything that counts for anything becomes both itself and its opposite: Death is an image of birth, birth of death, and suicide and murder partake of each other's character in the throes of the struggle between Eros and Thanatos, the id and the superego, the self and the world.

'The thousand injuries of Fortunato I had borne as best I could, but when he ventured upon insult, I vowed revenge.' So begins the narrator of 'The Cask of Amontillado,' who, like the Ancient Mariner in Coleridge's *Rime*, has but this one tale to tell—and that fifty years after the event. But what injuries Fortunato had done him, or what insult, he never reveals. These offenses are as mysterious, as shrouded, or—as we now say—as repressed as the crimes committed by the mysterious stranger in Poe's sketch 'The Man of the Crowd'; as rancorous and secret as the wound given Monsieur Dupin by the Minister D——. All we are given is this miscreant's name: Fortunato. The injured party who revels in the perfection of his revenge is Montresor.

Mon*tresor*. *Fortun*ato. Are these not synonymous? When Montresor leads Fortunato down into the farthest vault of his family's wine-cellar, into a catacomb of human bones, is he not, like William Wilson, conducting his double thither? My treasure, my fortune, down into the bowels of the earth, a charnel-house of bones.

But if Fortunato is Montresor's double, he is not, like Wilson[2], his conscience. Indeed, Fortunato appears a pathetic adversary. When first seen—as in the *dénouement* of 'William Wilson' and 'The Masque of the Red Death,' it is during carnival—he is wearing motley, cap and bells, and is quite drunk. No difficult thing for Montresor to play upon his enemy's vanity as a connoisseur of wines (Fortunato would seem already a victim of the Imp of the Perverse, masquerading as the Angel of the Odd). Montresor easily cajoles him down into the vault to taste his newly purchased Amontillado. As Montresor feverishly walls up the crypt into which he has chained the hapless Fortunato, the last sound he hears is the jingling of his bells. At this, he says, 'My heart grew sick—on account of the dampness of the catacombs.' For fifty years no mortal has disturbed his handiwork, the wall of bones and stones behind which the remains of Fortunato, still chained to the rock, stand now. (Like the unfortunate lady in 'The Premature Burial,' he has rotted erect.)

But has not Montresor walled up himself in this revenge? Of what else can he think, can he have thought for the past half-century, but of that night's vengeance upon his enemy? His freedom to do otherwise stands chained in the dank vault with Fortunato.

A somewhat different thesis is maintained by Mme Bonaparte. She finds the wine-cellar—the long, dark, dank tunnel of human remains—to be an obvious, indeed an importunate, symbol of the maternal womb and the entrance thither, and Montresor, leading Fortunato ever deeper to effect his execution, is committing the murder of his father-figure in the act of possessing the mother's body. The fact that the names of the two characters are interchangeable synonyms may seem to buttress this assertion.

Come to think of it, how can we deny the thesis? But, on thinking further, how can we accept it as a full exposition of the narrator's horrible purpose, his malignancy, his compulsion fifty years ago so to act, his obsession now to confess his action? Considering the persons, circumstances, and objects in this very brief tale in connection not only with the universal significations which psychiatric studies place upon them, but also the equally universal significations they attract to themselves as members of Poe's *œuvre*, some further notions come symbiotically into play.

If, as I maintain, the two are doubles, it is doubtless of

some moment that one, Montresor, is in full possession of
his wits, acts ruthlessly according to his premeditated plan,
and exercises aggressive and total power over the other. That
other, Fortunato, on the contrary is from the start befuddled
by both vanity and inebriation; acts on sudden impulse; as-
sumes good will where Montresor is malice incarnate; and
suffers as the passive, total victim of his adversary's malign
cunning. The aggressor is presented as aggrandized by his
victory, the victim as already degraded and ridiculous (as
well as pathetic) in his sufferings.

His ridiculousness is symbolized by his costume: 'The man
wore motley. He had on a tight-fitting parti-striped dress,
and his head was surmounted by the comical cap and bells.'
These are the bells whose jangling is the last sound Montresor hears from behind the wall of Fortunato's tomb. Now,
the cap and bells are of course everywhere acknowledged as
signs of the Fool, but why is the Fool so crowned? The cap
needs no description—we immediately see it as the bent coni-
cal foolscap of tradition, perhaps with a pompom, tassel,
or bell at the very tip, while the bells would likely be
bunched in clusters above each of the wearer's ears. Anyone
familiar with the Fool's antics in folk pageantry will not miss
his personification, particularly around the head, of the male
member. The Fool is man's lustful nature made absurd and
comical. If Fortunato is Montresor's double or the image of
his father, he is made to appear ridiculous in motley because
he also represents the all but irrepressible stirrings and strivings of Montresor's own sexual nature. Thus 'The Cask of
Amontillado' is, whatever else it may be, a screed of psycho-
machia, in which the calculating intellectual principle cleverly tricks, entraps, immobilizes and extinguishes the body.
What were the injuries and insults of Fortunato upon Montresor? Among others, they include the denial by the former
to the latter of that transcendence, that beatitude, which
cannot be known to the soul still harassed and enslaved by
passion.

So by interring Fortunato, Montresor at once has symbolically slain his own father and rival for his mother's affec-

tion, and forever interred his own passion, his own fertility, his own vitality. This narrator has indeed acted in accordance with—has indeed become—his Imp of the Perverse. But is he liberated thereby to experience the transcendent bliss which the insults of Fortunato had denied him? Not a bit of it. He too is dead to the world, immobile, chained to the rock of his one guilt-ridden act of aggression against Father and Self. This is the horrible truth he did not learn until he had experienced it.

And how appropriate it is that such a dreadful aggression against the self be enacted in a place which cannot but suggest the mother's womb, in its aspect of the terrifying: a charnel-house of bones, the family vault. Here is the undoubted source of Montresor's/Fortunato's being.

Poe seems as fixated as his Montresor, but not as successfully has the author himself interred his own vitality-principle. If he tells essentially the same tale over and over, he yet tells it differently every time. This must be the distinction, in art as in life, between symbol and real action. Symbolic action can repeat itself with variations till the end of time, but a real act of this obsessive kind is as much a prison for the actor as was Montresor's murder of his double, than which he has no other tale to tell.

MADNESS!

There are no parents in the tales of Edgar Poe, nary a Mum nor a Dad. Instead all is symbol. And what does this total repression of both sonhood and parenthood signify but that to acknowledge such relationships is to venture into territory too dangerous, too terrifying, for specificity. Desire and hatred are alike insatiable and unallayed. But the terrible war of superego upon the id, the endless battle between conscience and impulse, the unsleeping enmity of the self and its Imp of the Perverse—these struggles are enacted and reenacted in Poe's work, but always in disguise.

Take "The Tell-Tale Heart," surely one of his nearly perfect tales. It's only four pages long, a triumph of the art of economy:

How, then, am I mad? Hearken! and observe how healthily —how calmly I can tell you the whole story.

When a narrator commences in *this* vein, we know him to be mad already. But we also know his author to be sane. For with such precision to portray the methodicalness of a madman is the work not of a madman but of a man who truly understands what it is to be mad. Artistic control is the warrant of auctorial sanity. It is axiomatic in the psychiatric practice of our century that self-knowledge is a necessary condition for the therapeutic process. Never using the language of the modern diagnostician—which was unavailable to him in the first place, and which in any case he didn't need—Poe demonstrates the extent of his self-knowledge in his manipulation of symbolic objects and actions toward ends which his tales embody.

The events are few, the action brief. 'I' (in the story) believes himself sane because he is so calm, so methodical, so fully aware and in control of his purpose. Of course his knowledge of that purpose is limited, while his recital thereof endows the reader with a greater knowledge than his own. 'The disease,' he says right at the start, 'had sharpened my senses. . . . Above all was the sense of hearing acute. I heard all things in the heavens and in the earth. I heard many things in hell.' Now of whom can this be said but a delusional person? At the same time, mad as he is, this narrator is *the hero of sensibility*. His heightened senses bring close both heaven and hell.

His plot is motiveless. 'Object there was none. Passion there was none. I loved the old man. He had never wronged me. He had never given me insult. For his gold I had no desire.' The crime he is about to commit will be all the more terrible because apparently gratuitous. But let us not be lulled by this narrator's lack of admitted motive. He may have a motive—one which he cannot admit, even to himself.

I think it was his eye! yes, it was this! One of his eyes resembled that of a vulture—a pale blue eye, with a film over it. Whenever it fell upon me, my blood ran cold; and so by degrees—very gradually—I made up my mind to take the life of the old man, and thus rid myself of the eye for ever.

And a paragraph later he reiterates, 'It was not the old man who vexed me, but his Evil Eye.'

Nowhere does this narrator explain what relationship, if any, exists between him and the possessor of the Evil Eye. We do, however, learn from his tale that he and the old man live under the same roof—apparently alone together, for there's no evidence of anyone else's being in the house. Is the young man the old man's servant? Odd that he would not say so. Perhaps the youth is the old man's son. Quite natural that he should not say so. 'I loved the old man. He had never wronged me. . . . I was never kinder to the old man than during the whole week before I killed him.' Such the aggressive revulsion caused by the old man's Evil Eye!

What can this be all about? The Evil Eye is a belief as old and as dire as any in man's superstitious memory, and it usually signifies the attribution to another of a power wished for by the self. In this particular case there are other vibrations emanating from the vulture-like eye of the benign old man. Insofar as we have warrant—which I think we do— to take him as a father-figure, his Eye becomes the all-seeing surveillance of the child by the father, even by The Father. This surveillance is of course the origin of the child's conscience, the inculcation into his soul of the paternal principles of right and wrong. As such, the old man's eye becomes a ray to be feared. For if the boy deviate ever so little from the strict paths of rectitude, *it will find him out.*

Poe, in other tales, seems to be obsessed with the eye to the point of fetishism. In 'Ligeia' it is the lady's eyes which represent, to her husband, the total knowledge embodied in her person. By synecdoche the eyes become that which he worships. But the old man's eye is endowed with no such spiritual powers. Come to think of it, it is always referred to in the singular, as though he had but one. An old man with one all-seeing eye, an Evil Eye—from the plausible to the superstitious we pass in the text; perhaps further still to the mythical. One-eyed Odin, one-eyed because he sold his other *for knowledge.* Yet the knowledge in a father's (or a father-figure's) eye which a child most likely fears is the suspicion that he has been seen in a forbidden act, especially masturbation, or some other exercise of the libido. That above all seems to the young child to be forbidden, and therefore what an all-seeing Eye would see. Yet this old man's ocular power is never so specified. What is specified, though, is the resemblance of his one eye to that of a vulture.

Vulture, vulture. Everywhere else in Poe's work, in Poe's mind, vulture is associated with TIME, and time is associated with our mortality, our confinement in a body. The vulture-like eye of an aged man is thus an insupportable reminder of the narrator's insufferable mortality. Could he but rid himself of its all-seeing scrutiny, he would then be free of his subjection to time.

All the more so if the father-figure in this tale be, in one of his aspects, a Father-Figure. As, to an infant, his own natural father doubtless is. As, to the baby Eddie, his foster-father may have been. Perhaps he had even a subliminal memory of his natural father, who so early deserted him, eye and all, to the hard knocks experience held in store. So, the evil in that Evil Eye is likely a mingling of the stern reproaches of conscience with the reminder of his own subjection to time, age, and death.

To murder the possessor of such an eye would be indeed to reverse their situations. In life, the old man seems to the narrator an absolute monarch, a personage whose power over him, however benignly exercised, is nonetheless immutable. Such exactly is the degree to which a murderer dominates his victim. And so it is that the narrator does not merely do the old man in. No, he stealthily approaches the sleeping old man, in the dead of night, and ever so craftily draws nearer, then plays upon his sleeping face a single ray from his lantern. A ray like the beam of an eye. This he does each

night for a week—that very week in which he was never before
so kind to him during the waking hours, when the old man
had his eye working.

Upon the eighth night I was more than usually cautious
in opening the door. A watch's minute hand moves more
quickly than did mine. Never before that night had I *felt*
the extent of my powers—of my sagacity. I could scarcely
contain my feelings of triumph. To think that there I was,
opening the door, little by little, and he not even to dream
of my secret deeds or thoughts.

This miscreant is full of the praise of his own sagacity, a
terrible parody of the true sagacity of a Dupin or a Legrand.
For what he takes to be ratiocination is in fact the irresistible
operation of the principle of his own perversity, the urge to
do secret deeds, have secret thoughts undetected by the otherwise ever-watchful eye of the old man. He is so pleased to
have outwitted that eye that he chuckles—and the old man
stirs, then cries 'Who's there?' The room is pitchy black, the
shutters drawn for fear of robbers. Now the old man is sitting
bolt upright in bed, 'listening;—just as I have done, night
after night, hearkening to the death watches in the wall.'

The old man must have realized what was happening,
what was about to happen, for

> Presently I heard a slight groan . . . not of pain or of
> grief—oh, no!—it was the low stifled sound that arises from
> the bottom of the soul when overcharged with awe. . . . I
> knew it well. I knew what the old man felt, and pitied him,
> although I chuckled at heart.

And then, breaking the darkness and the silence, he spots
his ray directly 'upon the vulture eye.' 'Now, I say, there came
to my ears a low, dull, quick sound, such as a watch makes
when enveloped in cotton.' This is the sound, he says, of the
old man's heartbeat.

Excited to a pitch of 'uncontrollable terror' by the drum-
beat of his victim's heart, he gives a shout, flings wide the
door of his lantern, and drags the old man to the floor. Then

he suffocates him under the mattress. 'His eye would trouble me no more.'

Now, quickly, methodically, the murderer completes his work. 'First I dismembered the corpse. I cut off the head and the arms and the legs.' Then he places all between the beams under the floorboards. These he deftly replaces so that no eye could detect a thing. He had made care to catch all the blood in a tub. 'Ha! ha!'

Death by suffocation—this is a recrudescence of the favorite mode of dying everywhere else in Edgar Poe's tales of the dying, the dead, and the doomed. Illness is invariably phthisis; what character draws untroubled breath? Such sufferings seem inevitable to the imagination of a writer whose memory is blighted by the consumption which carried off the three women he most loved. But there is yet another reason for the young man's choosing to suffocate the eye which he could not abide. As is true of dreamwork, the vengeance is meted out thrice: he extinguishes the eye, he suffocates the old man, he dismembers him. I think these three terrible acts are disguises of each other.

In its aspect of getting rid of the Evil Eye, this murder is a more intense and violent form of blinding. And the symbolic content of blinding has been self-evident since Oedipus inflicted it upon himself as a partial remission for what the *lex talionis*, more strictly applied, would have required. In striking the Evil Eye of the old man, the young madman strikes, symbolically, at his sexual power. Nor does this contradict the other significations I have suggested for the ocular member. As the source of conscience, of surveillance of the boy's sexual misdemeanors, and as the reminder of his subjection to his own body, the eye derives some of its powers from its linkage, in imagination, with potency.

But what has suffocation to do with this? Only that the inability to breathe is an equivalent of impotence, of sexual impotence. By inflicting this form of death on the old man, the youth is denying his elder's sexual power.

And cutting off the head, the arms, the legs? These amputations, too, are symbolic castrations.

The 'I' is nothing if not methodical. He leaves nothing to chance.

No sooner has he replaced the floorboards—it is now four o'clock—but there is a rapping at his door. Neighbors, hearing a scream, had called the police. He explains that the scream was his own, *in a dream*. Then—why does he do this?—he invites the police into the house, to search and see for themselves, saying that the old man was away in the country.

I led them, at length, to *his* chamber. I showed them his treasures, secure, undisturbed. In the enthusiasm of my confidence, I brought chairs into the room, and desired them *here* to rest from their fatigues, while I myself, in the wild audacity of my perfect triumph, placed my own seat upon the very spot beneath which reposed the corpse of the victim.

At first all is well, but as they sit, and chat, his head begins to ache, he hears a ringing in his ears. It grows in volume, *'a low, dull, quick sound . . . as a watch makes when enveloped in cotton. . . . hark!* louder! louder! *louder!'*

He could escape the Evil Eye, but not 'the beating of his hideous heart.'

Of course it was his own heart which the murderer heard beat. Would he have heard it, had not his Imp of the Perverse commanded that he lead the police to the very scene of the crime? Or was this Imp, whose impulse seems so inexplicable, his own conscience, inescapable as long as his own heart should beat, demanding punishment for the terrible crime he had wrought? Thus he is *never* free from the gaze of the old man's clear blue eye.

VIII

The Marriage Group

'A SERIES OF MERE HOUSEHOLD EVENTS'

Edgar Poe is a prose-poet of love, an analyst and dramatist in his tales of the deepest of all attachments, the passion of a man for a woman. Recalling that this is the very emotion which, in 'Al Aaraaf,' barred the spirit Angelo from Heaven, it may come as a surprise to be told that Poe is a great love poet. In his prose. But it is so.

What he writes on this theme will not readily be confused with the efforts of others. For who besides Poe has so clearly felt (whether he consciously understood it or not is beside the point, so vividly is the feeling expressed in his tales), the intense symbiosis between love and hatred? Here, as everywhere, Edgarpoe looks into the dark glass of his soul, and sees doubly. His tales of courtship, marriage, and life in the resulting love nest are *something else* indeed from those of any writer before him. Few since have dared, or have sought the courage to dare, to look with so pitiless a gaze so deeply into their own souls. Love is seldom as simple or as happy as is popularly hoped. And Poe, who in these tales of love, courtship, and marriage, if nowhere else, fulfilled the behest described in his own *Marginalia*—to write a book called 'My Heart Laid Bare,' in which the *truth* be told— discovered ways to tell the nearly insupportable truths of his own soul. A soul in perpetual torment, for, as we shall see, its dispositions of feeling were such from birth—or from

before birth—that there could have been no satisfactory fulfilment of its insatiable longings. Such, in outline, was the
tragedy of Edgar Allan Poe. Such, in brief, is the human condition also, more or less, although, to be sure, most of us are
enabled to transfer our attentions to the substitutes which
this life offers for the impossible Archetypes of the erotic
imagination. Yet does he not speak to our condition who
cannot permit his imagination the freedom of such transference? Poe is a haunted man, haunted by the recrudescence,
in daydream or in dream, of the spectral love-object whose
image, imprinted on the proverbial film of the deepest reel
in memory's storage-bank, neither life nor language can ever
actually assuage. The ghost that will not be laid.

Because there may lurk such a ghost within us all, Poe,
in his weird tales of love, plucks not only the wild chords
of his own sufferings but also touches a universal heart-
string. And so he explores the reciprocities between love and
hatred, between the acceptance of another person as the actual fulfilment of an erotic ideal and *the need to destroy* that
same person as the betrayal of the ideal with whom she has—
by a horrible error, a fatal mistake of the lover's being—been
so invested: this too is part of the love-knot tied and disen-
tangled by that victim of Cupid, Edgar Poe. Not everybody's
valentine, though Edgar offers 'The Black Cat,' one of his
explorations of these emotions, as 'a series of mere household events.' Yet even this matter-of-fact narrator calls his
narrative 'the most wild yet most homely,' and assures us that
he is not mad. These things may seem beyond belief, he says,
but,

> Hereafter, perhaps, some intellect may be found which
> will reduce my phantasm to the commonplace—some in-
> tellect more calm, more logical, and far less excitable than
> my own, which will perceive, in the circumstances I detail
> with awe, nothing more than an ordinary succession of
> very natural causes and effects.

In short, however grotesque are the elements in the design
of the ensuing Arabesque, they will declare themselves in

an intelligible order to a ratiocinative mind of sufficient power.

Once again we are faced with a problem in detection. As in 'The Murders in the Rue Morgue,' the crime is the murder of a woman. And, as in 'The Purloined Letter,' the culprit is identified from the start. The problem here is, from his confession *to deduce his motive*.

The narrator of 'The Black Cat' is a husband, yet his wife is never named. It is as though she has no name, or he cannot remember it, or he dare not speak it. Nearly everywhere else we have seen Poe bestow upon the beloveds, fiancées, and brides of his poems and tales the most euphonious and original cognomens: Eulalie, Ulalume, Helen, Annabel Lee, Ligeia, Morella, Madeline, Berenice. But this wife has no name.

It is she who suggests, to the narrator who is so tender toward his pets, the old superstition that a black cat is a witch in disguise. As in 'The Tell-Tale Heart,' where the belief in the Evil Eye is introduced to make more spooky the power of the old man's gaze, here too folklore is pressed into the service of Poe's plot. Wife suggests, but husband may in truth believe, that black cat=witch. This, and other evidence soon to be introduced and offered in the present brief, lead me to suggest that, in the synoptic and evasive glossary of this tale, witch=wife. Ergo, black cat=wife.

In this story we are told all about the narrator's feelings —first of affection, then of loathing—for his cat, but of his attitude to or relations with his wife we learn next to nothing. The relation with the cat begins as mutual love, the cat (Pluto by name) cuddling up against him, he petting and fondling Pluto. Then the demon of intemperance (the Imp of the Perverse disguised as the Angel of the Odd) takes possession of the man. He becomes a drunkard, he curses his wife, he strikes her, and gradually he conceives absolute detestation of the affectionate cat. Becoming panicky at his unpredictable behavior, the cat bites his hand. Now enraged, he seizes the poor thing and with his penknife carves out one of its eyes.

Even for so horrible a misdeed he feels, when sober, inadequate remorse. The awful wound heals, and the cat, as
before, continues to seek his companionship. His disgust and
loathing grow. He can stand its importunities no longer—he
hangs the creature by the neck, from a tree in the garden—
'hung it *because* I knew that it had loved me, and *because*
I felt it had given me no reason of offence.'

That very night his house goes up in flames. All is destroyed
save one wall, and on that wall, newly plastered, is imprinted
by fire the image of the cat hanging from its noose. The narrator is much surprised by this graphic preservation of the
crime which he forbears to cite as the cause of his disaster.
He figures out an unlikely rational explanation for this phenomenon (the details of which are irrelevant to my purpose
here).

This would seem to be the whole story of the black cat.
But no, in the manner of dreams which haunt the dreamer
over again, there is a recrudescence of the black cat—the narrator becomes aware, in a gin mill one night, of *another* black
cat, whose provenience no one knows, sitting atop a barrel.
This creature attaches itself *to him*, follows him home, and
he becomes aware that it is the spitting image of Pluto[1], even
to its lacking one eye. His wife is delighted with the new cat,
but he notices that a splotch of white hair on its breast grows
in time to resemble the outline of a *gallows*. Pluto[2] habitually
climbs, claws embedded in its master's clothing, 'to my
breast.' 'At such times,' he says, 'although I longed to destroy
it with one blow, I was yet withheld from so doing . . . by
absolute *dread* of the beast.'

One day, with his wife he goes down the steep cellar stairs
on some errand. The cat follows, nearly tripping him head-
long. In exasperation he grabs an axe and raises it, 'forgetting
in my wrath the childish dread . . .' His wife impulsively
tries to stay his hand (her Imp of the Perverse?). 'Goaded
by this interference into a rage more than demoniacal, I with-
drew my arm from her grasp and buried the axe in her brain.'
(His.) 'She fell dead upon the spot without a groan.'

Is narrator overcome with remorse, prostrated with grief?

Does he weep, does he lament the terrible accident? Not at all. 'This hideous murder accomplished, I set myself forthwith, and with entire deliberation, to the task of concealing the body.' This hideous *murder!* As though he can now admit it had been his unacknowledged purpose all along. How more plainly, without violating the dynamics of his tale, could Poe have told us that from the first the cat had been but a displacement of the wife! Now the murderer, methodical as the madman who smothered the old fellow with the ever-watchful eye, must contrive to dispose of the body. As had that other youth, he considers 'cutting the corpse into minute fragments'; like him, this murderer also thinks of putting the parts beneath the floorboards. But no, he chooses instead (like Montresor) 'to wall it up in the cellar.' And this he neatly does. Now he notices that the cat is nowhere to be seen.

> It is impossible to describe, or to imagine, the deep, the blissful sense of relief which the absence of the detested creature occasioned in my bosom. It did not make its appearance during the night.

Which creature? Is it the cat whose absence by night delights his bosom with blissful relief? Not a word does he say of his feelings at the simultaneous disappearance from his bed and bosom of his wife. Well may we understand the tranquillity of this narrator's sleep when with one blow he has removed from his life both the real and the surrogate source of his terror.

Let us leave him sleeping blissfully for the moment, while we consider some curious features of this 'series of mere household events.' A frightened cat would be likely to scratch its owner, but narrator is goaded to cut out its eye not by a scratch but by a *bite.* But see, there's more to chew on here than at first glance appeared. As Mme Bonaparte intuited, identifying the cat's mouth as the feared *vagina dentata.* Very good, and not as absurdly unlikely as may at first appear. Let me expatiate a moment on teeth and mouths, eyes and other members, as we meet them and the narrators who are fixated upon them in Poe's tales. I got to thinking, why did this narrator wait until the cat bit him, rather than go into his tantrum when scratched?

The answer may be right before my eyes, but I've become so arduous a Poe-taster that I can't help but follow a slightly devious chain of clues. There is another of Eddie's love stories in which much is made of teeth, the teeth of Berenice, who, as was true of Poe's own wife, Virginia, is the cousin of the poor fellow who tells their tale. Egaeus, her fiancé, says, 'Of Berenice I . . . seriously believed *que tous ses dents étaient des idées. Des idées!* . . . ah, *therefore* it was that I coveted them so madly.' This seems kinky in the extreme, *particularly* when he violates the poor girl's grave to rip the teeth from her mouth. But isn't this fetish of the unfortunate Egaeus rather like that of Ligeia's husband for that lady's *eyes?* As Egaeus describes the presentiment by which he first becomes fixated upon the teeth of Berenice we see the correspondence between these features further explicated:

> The eyes were lifeless, and lustreless, and seemingly pupilless, and I shrank involuntarily from their glassy stare to the contemplation of the thin and shrunken lips. . . . The teeth!—the teeth!—they were here and there, and everywhere, visibly and palpably before me; long, narrow, and excessively white, with the pale lips writhing about them.

And these teeth represent *des idées*. Now the mouth is not usually thought of as an *intellectual* organ, while the eye conventionally has this designation. Still, when we wish to say that we comprehend something, we may say we have digested it, or chewed it over, or ruminated thereon. But the weird images in Poe's love tales reach below the level of linguistic formation to establish the similitudes they make of certain bodily parts.

Consider in what ways mouth and eye resemble each other. Each is an orifice in the body, surrounded by lips or lids which seem to open and close by a will of their own. Each is lubricated with a fluid of its own origin, and each leads inward—toward the stomach, toward the brain, toward the mysterious interior of the living creature. The thought may occur which other orifice of the body—of the female body—these two, in the respects just mentioned, might be conceived to resemble. And let us propose, for the purposes of this investigation, a male ratiocinator who is rendered incapable of referring to, of dealing with, of describing, of touching, that female part—rendered so by a fear, a terror, a hysteria so pervading that he must obsessively dwell on what he cannot bring himself to touch. How then can he respond to his inescapable need? The human being is a devious creature. Imagination can offer substitutes for the forbidden fruit. Poe's narrators are compelled to see, to bite and taste, that forbidden fruit, not aware of what it is. This is not to say that the reader (and perhaps even the author, at that level of deep awareness at which he exercises artistic control over his fantasies) is not aware. Maybe our awareness remains mostly subliminal. At any rate these terrible tales touch some deep resonance in us, or we should not read them at all.

So complete is the working-out of these strange similitudes, these symbolic substitutions, in Edgar Poe's imagination that when he exercises artistic control upon the obsessive materials a whole set of related correspondences come into play. *Ses dents étaient des idées* . . . Just as the vagina is the entrance to the mysterious womb, the unifier of all life, so is the eye to that all-synthesizing ratiocinator, the brain; and the teeth to the all-digesting stomach, in which the womb is lodged. And now, perhaps, the bizarre intellectualization of the courtship of the Poetagonists—the mental giganticism attributed by them to Morella and Ligeia—comes clear.

For reasons we are still attempting to fathom, Poe was never able directly to treat of his obsessive longing to be reborn in the womb, the re-entrance into which becomes, as a result of his terror, an image of death, so that prenatal bliss and life after death are images of one another. Images of that primary unity to which the soul tends, for which it agonizingly pines. Let me not equivocate, the reason for this evasion, for its repression and sublimation is everywhere evident. Such thoughts as these cut too close to the bone, they verge

all too closely upon the forbidden lust of the id—the lust the
ego usually rejects and tries to repress and control—for its
own maternal original, the interuterine life before birth.
Therefore this longing is everywhere disguised. By shifting
the object of fascination from the unmentionable and terrifying vagina to the mouth or the eye, and by substituting for
the attributes of the unifying womb those of the unifying
mind, Poe is able to pursue, in masquerade and charade, the
object, and the consequences, of his obsessional love-
attachment.

So when the narrator undertakes to do injury to the
hitherto inoffensive cat, he repays its having given him a little
bite—by cutting out its eye. The bite, the bite . . . given by
the creature in fear . . . might this not be a hysterical and
aggressive form of a caress? For indeed the mouth is an organ
of caressing, and biting a means of erotic excitation. Eating
one another. Isn't this excitation what the narrator of this
household tale is so terribly afraid of? The removal of the
offender's eye is clearly a substitute excision (in another
disguise) of the same organ which terrifies him—the eye a
substitute for the teeth, the teeth a substitute for the female
part. This intricate series of substitutions enables us to be
reminded of the most archaic code of *justice*. For such a crime
the exaction must be an eye for an eye, a tooth for a tooth.

The hanging of the black cat comes next. Princess Bonaparte considers the hung cat to be not in fact the victim of
the impenitent narrator, but the penis of the impotent author. The cat is so emphatically a wife-substitute, though,
that I find it difficult to think it at the same time a penis-
substitute. I prefer to think that hanging can represent
female impotence as well as male, and that Poe's mad narrator is displacing onto the surrogate for his wife, whose passion, whose clutching bites and embraces menace him, the
impotence which he himself cannot escape.

With the appearance of the second cat we know we are
in dream-land. The mark on its throat—a gallows—may be
seen only by the narrator. The *lex talionis* is beginning to
close its noose around his own throat. The whole tale, he tells

us at the outset, is his gallows confession. He is about to be hanged. Then, indeed will *he* be impotent, like the cat.

Oh, the *dénouement*. As in 'The Tell-Tale Heart,' the blissful murderer's repose is interrupted by a clamor at the door. The police arrive. Once more the culprit invites them to tour the premises. Yet again he leads them to the very spot behind which is concealed the incriminating corpse. 'And here, through the mere frenzy of bravado, I rapped heavily with a cane . . . upon that very portion of the brickwork behind which stood the corpse of the wife of my bosom.' How audaciously does this fellow defy—or should we say invite—his fate!

> But may God shield and deliver me from the fangs of the Arch-Fiend! No sooner had the reverberation of my blows sunk into silence, than I was answered by a voice from within the tomb!

Strong arms rip down the plaster, and there, perched atop the head of the already rotted and erect corpse, 'with red extended mouth and solitary eye of fire, sat the hideous beast whose craft had seduced me into murder, and whose informing voice had consigned me to the hangman.' Tooth and eye, eye and tooth. The concentric circle of this man's fate has tightened in the noose around his neck—yet another terrifying image of that which in his imagination has been represented by mouth, teeth, eye-socket, and eye. An 'I' for an eye.

AVERSIONS

Think not that Edgar is so terrified of nuptials that he cannot joke, in his fashion, on this head. The maidenhead. Where his nightmarish tales of murdering the beloved '*because* I knew that it had loved me' are terse with the economy of a perfectly calculated symbolism, his knockabout burlesques and farces are prolix. The narrators of these Grotesques like to laugh and laugh, or try to make us do likewise,

for as long as someone is laughing they do not have to surrender to the hysteria their comical predicaments disguise.

Take the case of the youth in 'The Spectacles,' a Grotesque
on that most romantic subject, courtship, or rather, love at
first sight. Simpson, as he calls himself though of French
descent, having changed his name to gain an inheritance, is
only twenty-two, handsome, well-apportioned, but he has
very weak *eyes*. Indeed he can scarcely see. But vanity pre-
cludes his wearing glasses. Therefore, from a distance—from
his box at the opera—he beholds and is smitten by the
ethereal beauty of a woman, Madame Lalande. I won't try to
recapitulate the machinery of this rather tedious spoof; let
it suffice that there are in fact two Mmes Lalande, and when
Simpson's friends realize that he has set his heart not on the
lithe young French woman but on her elder companion of
the same name, they conspire with that lady to play a trick
on the self-willed suitor. He pays assiduous court to this
Mme Lalande, and she, surprisingly, requests that he vow
to wear spectacles. He gallantly promises to do so, as a favor
to her, after their wedding. As you can see, the stage is set
to prove how blind is love.

After the midnight wedding, in their carriage, young
Simpson, obedient to his vows, dons his glasses—and finds
he has married a shrivelled old be-rouged, be-powdered, be-
wigged and padded old woman of eighty-two. His bride is
the female counterpart of The Man That Was Used Up!
The body is a piece of machinery.

But that's not the end of Simpson's discomfiture. Replying
to his expostulations, Mme Lalande—Mrs. Simpson—delivers
herself of her genealogy and that of her descendants, and it
comes to the young man that he has married his own great-
great grandmother!

But keep on laughing, for the last paragraph resolves these
embarrassments. The ceremony, like his courtship, has been
a joke. His friends plotted it all, one of them impersonated
the priest, so the wedding was no wedding. And the finale
brings this near-sighted lover a bliss perhaps beyond his
deserts: he gets to marry the other Mme Lalande, the *really*

young, really beautiful companion of her great aunt of the same name.

So he doesn't have to marry his great-great grandmother. He marries his cousin. Even if we smile at Poe's impostures, aren't we struck by the consanguinity which afflicts his suitor? How curious that his faulty vision leads so precipitously toward incest! And the happy resolution only mitigates somewhat the closeness of the attachment of his heart for a member of his mother's blood.

A cousin, not so many times removed as is Mme Lalande[2] from Simpson, is the object of desire for the suitor named Egaeus, he of the fixation upon the teeth of Berenice. The tale that bears her name is an Arabesque whose terror complements the jocose knockabout of 'The Spectacles.' Egaeus and Berenice never know their nuptial day, for the lady falls sick, wastes away, and on a certain black day is found apparently dead. No time is lost in hurrying her body to its tomb. It is on that night that her now demented lover, acting in a trance, violates her grave—he remembers shrieks— and awakens when a horrified servant tells him of the spoliation of Berenice's tomb—something about her being *still alive* when the teeth were ripped from her mouth.

The disease which afflicted Berenice at first appeared to be the consumption to which Poe's ladies are so vulnerable, but her final fit nonetheless proved an epileptic seizure. As was so comically foretold in 'The Premature Burial.' Like the husband of 'The Black Cat,' Egaeus has murdered the one who loved him most—and has pulled the teeth from the mouth whose writhing lips obsessed him.

Nightmare horror and death thus cheat Berenice and Egaeus of the peaceful consummation of their love. In fact we have yet to follow one of Poe's suitors to the marriage bed. (I leave out of account the pillow talk of the nameless wife and husband in 'The Black Cat.') What, for Poe-people, is life like after the wedding? That is the burden of another of his hilarious comedies, 'Loss of Breath.'

Hilarious because the husband discovers, on the morning after their wedding, as he launches a string of vilifications

against his new bride, that he cannot speak them—because
he has lost his breath. Not for nothing is his name Mr. Lackobreath. Nor should we be surprised that he discovers, among
his wife's effects (in which he searches *for his lost breath*)
'a number of *billets doux* from Mr. Windenough.' He also
finds 'a set of false teeth, two pairs of hips, an eye.' Alas, it
appears Mr. Lackobreath has married the wrong Mme Lalande after all.

Is there any meaning to this laborious jocosity? It is well
established that, on the oneiric level of conceptualization,
which Poe seems to have had accessible to his imagination
almost at will, whether he committed himself to the Arabesque or the Grotesque mode, ability to breathe is interchangeably connected with sexual potency. It is quite clear
from the details of Poe's sketch that Mr. Lackobreath has had
his ability to breathe taken from him on his nuptial night.
Mr. Windenough would seem able to breathe with ease, with
impunity. For a dozen frenzied pages Mr. Lackobreath suffers
the consequences of his loss—he is taken for dead; he is dis-
figured, his nose and ears are cut off (as though loss of breath
weren't sufficient a symbolization of what ails him), he is
crushed, battered, and at last—what else should we expect?—
put in the tomb while conscious still, though still out of
breath. He seems to enjoy his premature inhumation, especially when he discovers that the vault also contains his rival.
This tale runs itself into the ground and isn't really very
funny; Lackobreath exacts some breath from Windenough,
they at length are liberated from the tomb—but the curious
part is, there's no further word in the story about Mrs. Lackobreath. She drops out of sight, out of mind, and the tale
concludes with some of Funny Edgar's dreary comicality in
the pompous, philosophical line. In short, hysteria takes over
and the source of the difficulty is quite repressed. Regaining
his ability to breathe, Lackobreath is content with that literal power. It is as though speech, talk talk talk were all the
potency he desires. Like Montresor, he cannot stop himself
from telling his tale.

I HAVE BEEN FAITHFUL TO YOU
IN MY FASHION

The very thought of a consummated marriage struck Poe's imagination with terror. As is plain from 'The Spectacles' and 'Loss of Breath,' he was beset by redoubled fears of committing incest and of connubial non-performance—equally damned if he did and damned if he didn't. Poor Edgar responded by aggressively exhibiting himself to the view of the curious world. But such self-exposures proved a sort of send-up, like his voyages to the moon and into the maelstrom. Appearing in motley, Edgar commits burlesques so broad that the object lampooned can't be the author at all, but some other poor forked carrot with no more human reality in him than has the butt of a joke.

Still, not all the stories in Edgar Poe's 'Marriage Group' are burlesques, the modern writer's approximation of fabliaux. No, these appear only in Poe's monogamous tales. When he contrives a plot involving not merely the marriage of a hapless Poetagonist but his *remarriage* also, then the gears, rods, and pistons of Poe's fictional *frisson*-machine shift from the bump and clatter of his Grotesques to the wilder, smoother rhythms of Arabesques. Then, then, his theme becomes too serious altogether for flummery or the release of fears in raucous laughter. Then, the fears are instead indulged, luxuriated in. They are savored, they are enjoyed.

Of the tales I have in mind, the finest and most fully articulated is surely 'Ligeia.' (Others include 'Morella' and 'Eleanora.' The theme itself was one Poe had early tried to use in poetry, producing only the bathetic 'Bridal Ballad.') And of all of Poe's tales 'Ligeia' has been among the most frequently examined and explained, though to be sure its explainers seem to me systematically to have missed the point of the story, being diverted by whatever system of thought they attempt to impose on it. Controversialists in the learned journals have savaged one another over such questions as

whether 'Ligeia' is a tale of vampirism (drawing on the long
roster of vampire fiction, legend, and belief) or a story of
transmigration of souls (this involves the long history of soul-
displacement in literature and fable). One scholar has recently proposed that in marrying Ligeia ('I met her first and
most frequently in some large, old, decaying city near the
Rhine') the narrator commits himself to Continental Romanticism; after Ligeia's demise, when he remarries Lady
Rowena Trevanion of Tremaine, 'fair-haired and blue-eyed,'
a girl apparently from Cornwall, narrator succumbs to the
false lure of British Romanticism; in the end, however, his
first and truer love reasserts her claim upon his intellectual
fealty. I admit a case can be made for this. You'd be hard
put to guess how convincing that case is, but if you've recently *read* Poe's 'Ligeia,' you may feel (as I do) that this
theory about its 'meaning' is too clever by half.

It's incontestable, though, that Ligeia herself is associated,
in Narrator's mind, with *knowledge*. She is described, admired, adored, nay, worshipped, not so much for what she
looks like, or for who she is, but for *what she knows*, what
contemplation of her boundless mind makes Narrator (he
nowhere names himself) think that he knows. The Beloved
as Wisdom-Figure. One thing, though, which he *doesn't* know
is rather surprising: 'And now, while I write, a recollection
flashes upon me that I have *never known* the paternal name
of her who was my friend and my betrothed, and who became the partner of my studies, and finally the wife of my
bosom.' Husband, Husband, what, O what did you and your
friend, your betrothed, the partner of your studies and the
wife of your bosom talk about during the long hours in seminar which comprised your courtship? Did you never think to
ask her her paternal name? Ah, Edgarpoe, you don't becloud
our clear view of this romance with your obfuscations. You
knew that name well, too well for remembrance. You caused
yourself to pretend it was forgotten.

Deep as is his love for Ligeia, deeper still is a certain knowledge she possesses and represents to her adoring husband.
Into this knowledge she seems to promise to initiate him. Nor

should this surprise us, who have met Ligeia before—at least
we have already met a *spirit*, if not a lady on the Rhine, who
possessed that rather singular cognomen. The chief appeal of
the name 'Ligeia' to Edgarpoe was, I think—I have tried to
think as he thought and to hear with his ear—its chief appeal
is, this is the only conceivable feminine name (assuming it to
be such) which rhymes with the Great Key Word, *Idea*:

> Ligeia! Ligeia!
>   My beautiful one!
> Whose harshest idea
>   Will to melody run . . .
>
> .   .   .   .   .   .
> Ligeia! wherever
>   Thy image may be,
> No magic may sever
>   Thy music from thee,

—as we remember from 'Al Aaraaf,' where this lady appears
as the disembodied embodiment of Intellectual Beauty. In
the tale, all her melodious wisdom seems to Husband to be
concentrated in the expression of her eyes—

> How for long hours have I pondered upon it! What was it
> —that something more profound than the well of Democ-
> ritus—which lay far within the pupils of my beloved? What
> *was* it? I was possessed with a passion to discover . . .
>   There is no point, among the many incomprehensible
> anomalies of the science of mind, more thrillingly excit-
> ing than the fact—never, I believe, noticed in the schools
> —that in our endeavors to recall to memory something long
> forgotten, we often find ourselves *upon the very verge* of
> remembrance, without being able, in the end, to re-
> member . . .

So, it appears, the knowledge all but revealed in Ligeia's
luminous eyes is *something already known but forgotten*, a
not-quite-vanished memory of some primal condition, anterior
to this life. 'I was sufficiently aware of her supremacy,' says
Husband, 'to resign myself with a child-like confidence, to
her guidance through the chaotic world of metaphysical in-

vestigation,' knowing that 'I might at length pass onward to the goal of a wisdom too divinely precious not to be forbidden.'

Already we have the clues in hand to trace the parameters of an Archetype. The Archetype of the Fall of Man. Here are the elements: a Beloved Woman, Forbidden Knowledge, an irresistible compulsion to possess the latter by possessing the former. But we must not think that Poe is going to give us a Fortunate Fall. It is already subliminally clear that the forbidden wisdom, sought here under Ligeia's all-knowing tutelage, by the process of remembering back before the beginning of one's present existence, is of the same kind as that intellectual destination toward which the mariner hurtled, half unwitting, in 'MS. Found in a Bottle': 'It is evident that we are hurrying onward to some exciting knowledge—some never-to-be-imparted secret, whose attainment is destruction.'

Ligeia's husband comes closer than did the mariner to defining that forbidden secret, since he has taken a cram course from his wife. 'I have spoken of the learning of Ligeia: it was immense. . . .' She epitomizes all knowledge, all wisdom, all learning. She is also the epitome of ideality, or spirit, a quality imparted to Husband by the haunting expression of her eyes. No merely human eyes, however lovely, ever held such mysteries, such clues to the unifying spirit which invisibly presides over the wayward chaos of our mortal world:

And (strange, oh strangest mystery of all!) I found, in the commonest objects of the universe, a circle of analogies to that expression.

He finds analogies to the sentiment aroused within him 'by her large and luminous orbs' (a term more apt for the moon than for the eye)—analogies in a growing vine, in 'the contemplation of a moth, a butterfly, a chrysalis, a stream of running water.' 'I have felt it,' he adds, 'in the ocean—in the falling of a meteor. I have felt it in the glances of unusually aged people. And there are one or two stars in heaven. . . .

I have been filled with it by certain sounds from stringed instruments, and not infrequently by passages from books. . . .'

In short, this is an anatomy of the universe, passing from the lowliest individual plant and animal lives through the life-giving element (water), into the outer spaces of the stars and meteors, thence beyond the fixities of matter into the existence of the spirit (in the 'unusually aged,' such as the crew of the spectral ship in 'MS. Found in a Bottle'), and thence still farther outward to the music of the spheres, culminating in pure thought, as recorded in 'passages from books.' What a gaze had Ligeia! *Quels yeux!*

As I think again of this progression of analogies, it looks this time as though the *same ethereal quality* pervades the living creatures, inanimate things, the heavenly bodies, man's own sensations and his thought. By further analogy all of these are interchangeable with one another, partaking of the same ideality by which they resemble Ligeia's wondrous gaze. This interpenetration of the organic and the inorganic is perceptible only to the most highly organized sensibility, felt only by the most suprasensient nervous system, one in which the reactions of the body have become infused with the motions of the soul. Ligeia, it would seem, doesn't even have to make an effort so to perceive the world around her, it is her nature to make such perceptions visible to those—to one in particular—who truly love her, and who worship the reflection of her wisdom in her eyes.

The interpenetration of organic and inorganic, of matter and spirit by each other's essence, is dramatized again in 'The Fall of the House of Usher' and proves a principle of existence itself in 'Eureka.' There we will find that matter and spirit differ not in essence but in degree; their essence is in fact the same. This abstract postulate is essential to Poe's universe; because he really believes it to be true, both the terrors and the ecstasies of his tales are necessary and not to be avoided. But such speculations, in 'Ligeia,' are merely hinted at, presented analogically, referred to a still deeper, more secret mystery which they merely reflect.

Ligeia's husband, as we have been noticing, adores her, worships her, feels unworthy of her love, stands to her as a child before its mother, as an acolyte before his priestess. In fact Ligeia is herself a condensation of several relationships familiar in Romantic literature, as also in the literature of 'Romance . . . that spirit which . . . presided, as they tell, over marriages ill-omened.' Ligeia is both her husband's Muse and Sacred Mother. Now it is clear why Husband has never dared to ask her or remind himself of her 'paternal name'; for if he did, he would have to face up to its being the same as his mother's. Nor would her married name be any better —hence we never learn *his* paternal name—since married to him, she bears the name of *his* father.

As Muse, as Mother-Figure, Ligeia resembles in several aspects that mythical abstraction come to life in a particular woman whom Robert Graves has revived yet again in our time and called The White Goddess. The algolagnic heroine is indeed a persistent visitant of literature, and in Ligeia we have Poe's fullest representation of 'La Belle Dame Sans Merci.' It is typical of Poe that her beauty is incarnate in an intellectual principal which unifies sensation and thought, matter and spirit, and—as we shall see—life and death. These are the gifts comprising her knowledge both sacred and forbidden, and intrinsic with her love at once all-giving and all-demanding. A dangerous woman to lose your heart to.

And this paragon of superhuman and metaphysical virtue is no seraph, as in 'Al Aaraaf,' but indeed a woman, 'most violently prey to the tumultuous vultures of stern passion,' a passion which her luckless husband quails to see in 'the miraculous expansion of those eyes which at once so delighted and appalled me.' Now, *vultures* (or condors), wherever met in Poe, signify, as in 'Sonnet—To Science,' our enslavement to Time in this real world where flesh is carrion. Passion, as we know from 'Al Aaraaf' and 'The Colloquy of Monos and Una,' is the affliction of an impure nature, one not sufficiently devoted to the transcendence of its own fallen state to be worthy of inhabiting the paradisal star where purer spirits dwell. And Ligeia herself is 'a prey to the tumultuous vultures of stern passion.' It begins to seem as though this Muse and Sacred Mother is also an impassioned woman, covetous of her lover's body, desirous of his being prey to an equally tumultuous passion—for her.

But Poe was impotent. We have seen the evidence. We have the diagnosis from his psychiatrist, Dr. Princess Bonaparte. Professor Krutch anticipated her findings with his more cursory examination of the patient. I have to find their findings acceptable. The problem, in the story, in which the feckless husband represents some of the fantasies of Edgar Allan Poe, in this: What can an impotent lover do when his beloved is aroused to 'the tumultuous vultures of stern passion'? A very interesting question, since he makes *her* the prey of the vultures, whereas in fact (were any of this a fact) she would make *him* the prey of her passions. Which would make *her* a vulture. Alas, what can he do?

He can solve everything by wishing her dead so hard that she dies. Apotheosized by both a 'passage from books' and a poem on her lips, the poem of her own composing. Poe, always concentrating all the resources of his prose to the production of a unified effect, had prepared for the event. Perhaps, in Ezra Pound's phrase, he had 'over-prepared the event.' A passage from a book appears as epigraph to the tale. The same passage reappears at the end of the paragraph which itemized all the things, from chrysalis to the music of the spheres, of which Husband thought while gazing in Ligeia's 'divine orbs':

> And the will therein lieth, which dieth not. Who knoweth the mysteries of the will, with its vigor? For God is but a great will pervading all things by nature of its intentness. Man doth not yield him to the angels, nor unto death utterly, save only through the weakness of his feeble will.

Quoted from Joseph Glanvill, according to Poe; though according to Edward Davidson the locus of such sentiments in Glanvill's work 'has so far escaped detection' (*Poe: A Critical Study*, p. 77). No matter whether the attribution be apocryphal or not; Glanvill, 'whom,' says Saintsbury in his history of English literature, 'the echoing magnificence of a sentence from him, prefixed to Poe's "Ligeia," may have made known to many more than have read him in his originals,' provided Poe with as much glamor as Poe bestowed on him. For by attributing the above-quoted doctrine to Glanvill, Poe associates it with the seventeenth-century scholar who upheld both the objective study of Nature (he was an early defender of the Royal Society) and the truth of witchcraft (in *Sadducismus Triumphatus*). Not only does this suggest to the reader that he may take his pick, for all it matters, between science and witchcraft, reason and belief, to account for the anthropomorphism of the passage. It suggests also that Ligeia's wisdom encompasses all of the contrarieties and antinomies suggested by Glanvill's intellectual and supernatural pursuits.

Ligeia is apotheosized by a poem—her own poem—whispered by her dying lips. Dying, she wishes most of all for life; living, she had written a poem in which the angels watch a troupe of mimes act out 'the play [that] is the tragedy, Man / And its hero, the conqueror Worm.' The Worm is Death, imagined by Ligeia as a serpent which writhes and devours men, amid

> . . . much of Madness, and more of Sin
> And Horror, the soul of the plot!

All this is done by actors emulating 'God on high' and

> Mere puppets . . . who come and go
> At the bidding of vast formless things
> That shift the scenery to and fro,
> Flapping from out their condor wings
> Invisible Woe!

The poem is a condensation of the tale, and the philosophy —if it can be called one—which it presents tells us that life is an unassuaged disaster, an unequal battle between mankind and inexorable Death, enacted for the amusement of angels who make no move on man's behalf although the horror of the show makes even these angels 'pallid and wan.' Although *this* is life, Ligeia herself would rather live than die; and dying, she affirms (for the third time in the tale) the epigraph Poe claims to have borrowed from Glanvill:

> 'O God!' half shrieked Ligeia, leaping to her feet and extending her arms aloft . . . 'O God! O Divine Father! —shall these things be undeviatingly so!—shall this conqueror be not once conquered? Are we not part and parcel in Thee? Who—who knoweth the mysteries of the will with its vigor? Man doth not yield him to the angels, *nor unto death utterly*, save only through the weakness of his feeble will.'

Even as she repeats again the sentence from Glanvill, 'She died.'

I must confess that Ligeia's performance as a poet casts a bit in doubt, for me, her prowess as Giantess of the Intellect. Assuming, that is, that she really is, as Husband thinks, equally gifted in all things. I mean, the author of 'The Conqueror Worm' is hardly as divine a singer as Husband thought. Her poem, to be blunt about it, is a piece of fustian, not a patch on Blake's 'O Rose, thou art sick,' a mere eight-liner which suggests far, far more than it says. 'The Conqueror Worm,' on the contrary, says right out all that it could suggest, nor do its banal rhythm or obvious imagery leave anything—*anything*—to *our* imagination. So I take Ligeia-as-Poet as putative. Anyway, the poem is really only the prelude to her last words. Glanvill's.

Those words imply that if death is but a failure of our will, then our will can triumph over death if only volition be strong enough—that is, as strong as God's. For, as Ligeia half-shrieked, 'Are we not part and parcel in Thee?' So then, if we are, why can we not *will ourselves not to die?*

Or do Ligeia's last words mean, *We can will someone else not to die.* Ligeia, as everyone knows, comes back to this life again, taking over—*quel frisson!*—the body, the very corpse, of her husband's *second wife.* When Rowena is on her deathbed she arises and totters into the center of the chamber, looking, breathing, seeming for all the world like the Lady Ligeia. Although Rowena Trevanion of Tremaine was slight and fair-haired and Ligeia had been statuesque and dark, Rowena, dying, becomes raven-haired and tall, tall as Ligeia. Is this Ligeia willing her own metempsychosis, or is it her husband wishing her back to life-in-death a second time?

But we have left Husband bereft, after her first dying. We must see what he does with his life thereafter.

He's a rich widower now, for 'Ligeia had brought me far more, very far more, than ordinarily falls to the lot of mortals.' With this wealth he purchases an old abbey in England, and although prostrate with grief he somehow finds the energy completely to redecorate the interior of this capacious structure. The language here is revealing. The exterior of the abbey and its situation are described with almost every adjective in the Gothic repertoire: wildest, least frequented, gloomy and dreary grandeur, savage aspect, melancholy and time-honored memories, utter abandonment, remote and unsocial region, verdant decay. To this diction of the decadence wrought by ruin and time is joined the diction of decadence wrought by the human will, as Husband now describes the fitting-out of the interior in 'a display of more than regal magnificence':

> Alas, I feel how much even of incipient madness might have been discovered in the gorgeous and fantastic draperies, in the solemn carvings of Egypt, in the wild cornices and furniture, in the Bedlam pattern of the carpets of tufted gold.

In the midst of all this wild opulence he 'had become a bounden slave to the trammels of opium,' and the description that follows is wilder still, as though the very architecture partook of the distorted involutions of his opium dreams. He describes the bridal chamber into which he led 'the fair-haired and blue-eyed Lady Rowena Trevanion, of Tremaine':

> . . . and here there was no system, no keeping, in the fantastic display, to take hold upon the memory. The room

lay in a high turret of the castellated abbey, was pentagonal in shape, and of capacious size . . .

It is a bizarre jumble of window-glass from Venice, a ceiling carved in Semi-Gothic, Semi-Druidical devices, from which hangs a Saracen censor, flickering over the Eastern ottomans and the Indian bridal-couch 'with a pall-like canopy above.' In each of the five corners stands a huge sarcophagus, 'but in the draping of the apartment lay, alas! the chief fantasy of all': as the visitor to the apartment moved to the center of the room, 'he saw himself surrounded by an endless succession of . . . ghastly forms . . . giving a hideous and uneasy animation to the whole.'

Some readers have taken the décor in Lady Rowena's bower to represent Poe's ideal conception of the well-appointed chamber. But how different is this grotesque medley of sinister shapes, gloomy devices, and psychedelic shadows, from the tranquil bower of dreams in the Faubourg Saint Germain where we found Monsieur Dupin. No, Ligeia's successor and Husband are in a bower which externalizes the narrator's disordered mind, as does the earlier dream-chamber of Prince Mentoni in 'The Assignation,' that 'apartment whose unparalleled splendor' made the observer 'dizzy with luxuriousness' as 'the senses were oppressed by mingling and conflicting perfumes.' Mentoni's chamber anticipates the remarried husband's:

> In the architecture and embellishment . . . the evident design had been to dazzle and astound. Little attention had been paid to the decora of what is technically called *keeping*, or to the proprieties of nationality. The eye wandered from object to object, and rested on none . . .

Yet, in his 'Philosophy of Furniture,' Poe had created an ideal décor in which '*Repose* speaks in all' of the 'effects,' and where a single lamp with 'a plain crimson-tinted ground-glass shade,' hanging from the ceiling, 'throws a tranquil but magical radiance over all.' True, this chamber is, to our taste, rather opulent and it resembles in many particulars both the dream-bower of Mentoni and the bridal chamber made for

Rowena. But the difference is all in the disarrangements there
of the elements which are harmoniously unified in 'Philosophy
of Furniture.' These disordered chambers are, like Poe's landscapes and the geography of his voyages, the projections outward into objects of the mind that both perceives and creates
them.

Into such a chamber the husband now conducts his new
bride. In so gloomily sinister a fashion has he furnished it
that even he must ask, 'Where were the souls of the haughty
family of the bride, when, through thirst of gold, they permitted to pass the threshold of an apartment *so* bedecked,
a maiden and a daughter so beloved?' The room which poor
Rowena has entered is at once three *loci*: her bridal bower is
her death chamber, and both, as I've said, are really in the
mind—indeed, they *are* the mind, of the narrator.

What a marriage. Here, in this very chamber, he says, 'I
passed, with the Lady of Tremaine, the unhallowed hours
of the first month of our marriage.' He notes with pleasure that
his wife 'shunned me and loved me but little'; for his part,
'I loathed her with a hatred belonging more to a demon than
to man.' Now he can think of nothing but—Ligeia:

> Ligeia, the beloved, the august, the entombed. I revelled
> in recollections of her purity, of her wisdom, of her lofty—
> her ethereal nature, of her passionate, her idolatrous love.

And now he tells us that he's a habitual opium-eater. 'In
the excitement of my opium dreams,' he says, he calls aloud
Ligeia's name, 'as if, through the wild eagerness, the solemn
passion, the consuming ardor of my longings for the departed,
I could restore her to the pathways she had abandoned—ah,
could it be forever?—upon earth.'

Need we be surprised that Ligeia is soon to reappear? Or
that Rowena, so injured and insulted by Husband, will soon
fall sick—with *the very same wasting disease* that carried off
Ligeia? Or that once taken ill, Rowena will be terrified by
the illusory movements of sinister shapes swirling about her?

We are now at the point in the tale where the unbelievable
is about to happen. Unbelievable, that is, if you can believe

any of what has happened thus far. The fact that we stay with Poe clear to the end, that despite the pompous inflation of style and the grotesqueness of situation and event, we read him through with enough suspension of disbelief to be ready for his final *frisson*—all this bespeaks Poe's success in mastering his obsessional materials by imposing upon them a coherent and necessary literary form. We give 'Ligeia' enough credence not in spite of its stylistic grotesqueries but because of them. Poe, as we know, could write as clearly and as perspicuously as Defoe when he wanted to. But who would tolerate the plain style of Monsieur Dupin's sidekick in the mouth of Ligeia's husband? Each tells his own tale in the language, in the rhythms, in the rhetoric most appropriate to his own character. And that character is, for Poe, embodied in his mental, or as Poe calls it, his 'psychal' state. The state of mind of the narrator in 'Ligeia' is one of terrible, nearly insupportable exacerbation; he is living out compulsive fantasies which obtrude upon the opium trances in which he has sought refuge. But let's not mistake for this distraught and, I think, technically insane narrator, the mind of Edgar Poe. For it is Poe, with his equally tortured sensibility, who has exercised his intellectual and artistic faculties—has exhibited them in the fullness of their control—to make us aware of the mental disorder of his character, the husband of both Rowena and Ligeia.

Meanwhile, back in the deadroom, Rowena must die. She must recapitulate the death of Ligeia while Husband, half narcotized, looks on, helpless to save her from her death. Indeed, he may have caused, may be causing it. Does he really murder Rowena? Some critics have approached this tale with the delicacy of the Prefect of Police, and disputations among them argue such points as this, as well as whether the tale is a ghost story or a love story (whose?). Besides, does Ligeia reappear in Rowena's body because *she* wills to come back to her husband, or because her husband wills her return? Roy Basler concluded that Husband poisons Rowena and imagines the rest. Mme Bonaparte identifies everybody in the tale, as is usual with her, with real persons: Husband=

Edgar; Ligeia=Elizabeth Arnold; Rowena=Virginia Clemm but also Frances Allen. Were we to take Mme Bonaparte as literally as she takes Poe, would we have any right or reason to take either of them seriously?

Let there be light. If my mythologized interpretation of Ligeia as Muse and Mother-Goddess has any merit, then it follows that Rowena is the poor mortal woman whom the adept of the Mother Goddess loves, as a substitute or surrogate for the aforesaid Divine She. Her eyes do not fascinate Narrator; he barely mentions that they were blue—the wrong color, since Ligeia's orphic orbs were dark. She is all flesh, all flesh; no wonder he turns from her with loathing and 'a hatred belonging more to a demon than to man,' takes dope, and dreams of the unifying, tranquillizing, ethereal qualities of his lost tutelary spirit. And even Ligeia had become lost to him because, spirit though she was, she was also a mortal body, decaying, and 'a prey to the tumultuous vultures of stern passion.' Rowena resembles Ligeia only at the lower end of the spectrum of possible correspondences. Rowena rises to Ligeia-like spirituality only at the moment when she passes from life into death. Then, and only then, Ligeia's spirit passes into Rowena's body, and she looks like Ligeia. Several times, Narrator has examined her *eyelids* during her death-throes. Now, at the final moment, he at last mentions her *eyes*:

'Here then, at last,' I shrieked aloud, 'can I never—can I never be mistaken—these are the full, and the black, and the wild eyes—of my lost love—of the Lady—of the LADY LIGEIA.'

Terror, terror, terror grips us the first time we read this tale. A strange numbness at the heart, a willingness to be frightened at the very moment we would dismiss the spectre as a story-teller's audacious imposition. But we don't dismiss the imposition, we give in to the sensation of being terrified as though revelling in a voluptuous excitation. Why are we unwilling or unable to see through this most horrible trick of Hoaxiepoe's? Or, if able to see through it, unable to free ourselves from illusions exposed as illusions? Is it because we are reminded of something we are on the verge of remembering but cannot?

Later, after many readings in which the tale of 'Ligeia' has never lost its power to move me, I have asked myself what is the composition of that feeling which grips me now, as ever before, when I retrace the fantastic dreams of this narrator imagined by Edgar Poe. I recognized that terror contributes but half of the power that numbs the heart and makes the hackles rise. The other half comes from pity, pity, pity.

How sore, how mortal was the wound that left the *persona* through whom Poe speaks so bereft that after his first and primal love he could know no other? So overwhelmingly is he possessed by that first love that, should *he* choose to succeed the 'raven-black' hair and brilliant black eyes of Ligeia with 'the fair-haired and blue-eyed' Rowena, it first seems to him 'a moment of mental alienation' when he betrayed his first love's memory by leading to the altar his second, so different in aspect. Then his love for her turns to hatred and loathing, a loathing and hatred he had unconsciously anticipated by decorating her bridal suite as a psychedelic torture-chamber. Whether the three drops of red liquid which fall into Rowena's wine-glass are *really* emanations from the spirit of the jealous Ligeia, or are poison placed there by the husband in his opium jag, or are his wild remembrance of the bloody sputum of the author's dying mother, Rowena must die—if indeed she ever lived save as a wraith in the guilt-haunted imagination of Ligeia's acolyte who could love no one, love nothing, but the almost-remembered actuality of Ligeia. Whether Rowena be wraith or woman, how can she sustain her own beauty, her own features, the color of her own eyes and hair, in the imagination of a lover who is so completely imprisoned by his first, his only, his only possible devotion?

It seems impossible to doubt that the prototypes of these experiences in the tale were the death of Eddie's mother, his guilty transference of love to Mrs. Allan, then later to various childhood sweethearts and at last to poor Virginia Clemm,

each of whom died in the same lingering way and seemed
no doubt to Edgar to be a resurrection of her predecessors
only to re-enact her predecessors' death. Poor, poor Eddie
Poe. But these hapless accidents of one miserable scrivener's
biography are in 'Ligeia' successfully mythologized, universalized, raised to the level of archetype. Strange though the
combination seems, in Poe, of ideality with necrophilia, here
he has imagined a condition of blessedness, its loss, the loser's
search for its recurrence in another love-object, the intensifi-
cation of that love into hatred for its substitute and longing
for the lost love, and a final apotheosis in which the lost love
seems to reappear.

Erotic interest is all but completely censored, is quite subsumed in Ligeia's metaphysics. Despite the one allusion to
her 'stern passion,' there is no physical contact mentioned
in either of Narrator's 'marriages.' This delicacy, or squeam-
ishness, fooled several generations of readers into thinking
that Poe was a spiritual writer—if they didn't take him for a
fiend. Of course we can now read Poe with less prejudice,
and so we recognize that it is this suppressed erotic intensity
which throbs and shudders throughout the tale. When
Rowena is in her dying hours, Narrator cries,

> But why shall I minutely detail the unspeakable horrors
> of the night? Why shall I pause to relate how, time after
> time, until near the period of the gray dawn, this hideous
> drama of revivification was repeated; how each terrific re-
> lapse was only into a sterner and apparently more irredeem-
> able death; how each agony wore the aspect of a struggle
> with some invisible foe. . . . Let me hurry to a conclusion.

Are these the throes of the dying body struggling to live, or
of the living body struggling to die? What other experience
does this description suggest than the repeated, excited violation of the body in successive, spasmodic orgasm? Death
is usually a metaphor of sexual experience, all the more so
for Poe because his own nature did not permit him to know,
nor did the prurient mores of his class and time allow him
to describe, sexual union in a normal way. Through the psy-

chic identity of sexual extinction with death itself, Poe is enabled imaginatively to 'possess' the beloved by experiencing the moment of her bodily dissolution.

I have already mentioned similarities between 'Ligeia' and 'The Assignation.' In that story there are other interesting analogies to this one besides the décor of the dreamer's chamber. 'The Assignation' is a tale of a consummated love—the consummation comes in the simultaneous suicides of the lordly dreamer-lover and his forbidden beloved, the Marchesa Aphrodite. Here, in this early tale, are some of the nascent images which will exfoliate in 'Ligeia.' The Marchesa, whose given name identifies her at once as indeed a Love Goddess, is, like Helen in the famous poem, and like Ligeia, described as having hyacinthine hair and hands of marble. These associations link all three beloved women with classic beauty, with the ideal purity of the ancient world, with the dignity of the earliest age of myth and epic. The Prince Mentoni achieves perpetual union with his Aphrodite by dying into her death. Ligeia's husband is not so fortunate, his beloved dies before him, and he must somehow summon her back, wish herself to will herself back, into life. But this cannot be. All that can be managed, while men suffer in their bodies and their spirits are tortured by the vultures of passion and the passage of time, is to bring her back to the instant of her leaving, as she slipped beyond the veil of the beyond. Closer than this we cannot come in this life to the mysteries of a knowledge which is forbidden to mortality, forbidden with a tabu as intense and as absolute as that which makes impossible a grown son's desire for the all-consoling love which as an infant he felt lavished on him by his mother, and which makes unthinkable his reciprocation.

Thus as fiction, as myth, as psychological archetype, the pattern of imagined action in 'Ligeia' is not only fantastic but self-consistent—and true, in its kinky way, to human experience as well as to the accidents of one particularly blighted life. Yet the myths of antiquity and the psychology of today do not fully elucidate this singular imaginative construct. For Poe, death is a metaphor of sexuality—and of something more.

It is the multiple associations of death in Poe's work which lend his tales their particular fascination, their concatenation of terror and sublimity inextricably intermingled.

Death is personal extinction, the obliteration of this particular bundle of sensations and memories, and therefore terrifying. Death is also deliverance from the memories and sensations in which this particular person, this particular combination of atoms divided from the unity whence they came, is imprisoned—and thus death is welcome. Death is the necessitous apocalypse in which all divided creation hurtles toward instantaneous reunion in the oneness from which it had been sundered. Thus death, the most feared, is also the bringer of deliverance in a metapersonal ecstasy. But that is another story, as we see in the *Narrative of Arthur Gordon Pym* and in *Eureka*.

IX

Body of the World:
NARRATIVE OF ARTHUR GORDON PYM

Had Poe been able to write according to the truth of his own theories (as he pretended, in 'The Philosophy of Composition,' to be able to do), he would have written one and only one superpoem, a success, instead of his fifty failures in verse and his seventy tales of the grotesque and arabesque and detection. Despite his avid and feverish efforts, over and over again, he was unable to unify in a single work his knowledge, his terror, his transcendence. Three of these attempts, however, are more ambitious even than his other writings. One is his only extended work of fiction, a prose romance nearly ten times the length of his customary tales. Another is his effort to explain the nature of the universe in terms as scientific as they are imaginative. And the third is his most concentrated story, 'The Fall of the House of Usher,' a distillation of all his thought into one memorable nightmare. I cannot escape from the demon that has drawn me deeper and deeper into the vortex of Poe's mind without grappling, at last, with these three works. There, if anywhere, may be discovered the final knowledge toward which all of Poe's work leads us. Whether it be visionary, or the bitterness of dregs, I'll quaff his dram to the end.

These three compendia of his themes—*Pym, Eureka,* 'Usher'—each edges inexorably toward apocalypse, the unavoidable condition of wisdom, by a different route. In *Narrative of Arthur Gordon Pym* we go clear around the earth, upon the sea; this is the Total Voyage of Discovery, hinted at and sketched in earlier journeys into maelstrom and in the journal cast adrift in a bottle. Here is the discoverer exploring the body of this world, exploring it with his own body.

In *Eureka* the discoverer is the mind, and what is explored is not merely this world but the entire universe. Here indeed the mind at last is 'Out of Space, / Out of Time.' In 'The Fall of the House of Usher,' however, we are back in our own finite world, striving to escape from our imprisonment. If *Pym* and *Eureka* may be schematized as exhibiting the Hero, the Discoverer, in his aspect, respectively, of Body and Mind, in 'Usher' we meet him as a Soul. Not a disembodied soul, but, alas for him, a bodied one. As we shall see.

Of course these terms, these faculties, appear in all three tales, for if Poe is never as unified and as all-comprehending as he wishes to be, neither is his psychological method of rationally ordained splits as divisive as he proposes. Thus Arthur Gordon Pym, embodying body, has also a mind and in fact both his body and mind exist in order to contrive a certain initiation for his soul—an initiation, through sensient experience into knowledge, a knowledge that proves beyond both sensation and thought. So even as Poe's unification splits asunder, his divisions unify. Let's ship out with Pym on his doomed, irreversible voyages.

Narrative of Arthur Gordon Pym begins—and is this not appropriate?—with a departure from *Edgartown*. While the place-name on Martha's Vineyard make possible this coincidence, many readers have noticed a further euphonic similarity between the name of the protagonist and that of the author of this narrative. We see that what is being sailed away from is the self, the ego. This is a voyage of discovery, of exploration, into the great unknown. Indeed it proves in the end to be a voyage beyond the final veil of existence. Unlike the journeys of the Norse seaman into the maelstrom or of the author of 'MS. Found in a Bottle,' Pym's last trip is undertaken *on purpose*. But the voyage through the veil is not the immediate end in view for Arthur Gordon Pym, it is only the last of many voyages in his narrative. He sails in no fewer than five vessels, and his tale is a harrowing sequence of entombments alive, mutiny, and murder; of survival through hurricane, starvation, and cannibalism; encounters with dangerous beasts and savage tribes. Most of these motifs are duplicated and reduplicated in a fashion like that of dreamwork. They seem obsessive, as Pym escapes from horror in order to endure horror yet again. And as is the case in Poe's other journey tales, at the height of his sufferings there is an excitation of the soul, a condition near ecstasy. Although Pym is a ratiocinator, full of learned and interesting disquisitions on seamanship, geology, and language, and he proves to be an observant recorder of the flora, fauna, and primitive customs on the islands of Antarctica, he remains through most of his narrative a passive character, one to whom things happen. His 'thought' is essentially rationalist, not, like that of Monsieur Dupin, intuitive. Pym goes on being naïf and unknowing in the midst of his adventures. He does not recognize where he is going or why—that is for the reader of his narrative to comprehend.

It has been charged by critics that the *Narrative* is shapeless and chaotic, a sprawling mass of compulsive repetitions which betrays its author as an obsessive neurotic, not an artist at all. I would not hold that Poe is everywhere in full control of what he writes, but that he desperately tries to control what is almost beyond control. And that struggle to master the uncontrollable is the very theme of Pym's *Narrative*.

It is objected, for instance, that the same horrible misadventures are repeated *ad nauseam*. Why so many voyages, so many entombments, and so forth? Let us reconsider Pym's five departures to see if the very redundancy of the action is not an embodiment of meaning in the *Narrative*.

With his drinking companion Augustus, Pym first sets out, at midnight, for a brief sail in his little sloop, the *Ariel*. As Harry Levin and Leslie Fiedler have said, Augustus is an alter ego of Pym's; later in the tale, another, more ambiguous reflection of the self appears in the character of Dirk Peters, the dwarf half-breed. Now, however, it is Augustus, the re-

spectable New Englander with a weakness for drink, who in
effect lures Pym to undertake a midnight sail as a lark, then
proves too drunk to manage the helm. As a result their sloop
is crushed by a whaler. Many readers have noticed that Pym's
sloop bears the name of the boat from which Shelley was
drowned. Here, indeed, Augustus *nearly* drowns in a whirlpool and Pym is impaled underwater and nearly decapitated.
So the lark ends in disaster, but the disaster ends in rescue.

Pym and Augustus's second setting-forth is no more au-
spicious and just as impulsive. This time Pym runs away
from home, disowning his grandfather as he sneaks aboard
a ship of which Augustus's father is captain. Now the tricky
lads contrive, at Augustus's suggestion, that Pym be concealed as a stowaway. Augustus leads Pym through a winding
tunnel amidships into a coffin-like box in which he is to lie
until they are at sea. Thus Pym assents to an action the implication of which is that he is to be entombed to be en-
wombed, buried to rise again—as though to a new destiny.
The instigator of these devices, Augustus, seems to be not
only Pym's alter ego but also, perhaps, his Imp of the Perverse; for in the event, none of his seemingly sensible plans
comes out as proposed. He has cast Pym into direst jeopardy,
to which course Pym has enthusiastically consented.

Pym assents here, as everywhere else, not by any witting
design, for he cannot see at any point what is to follow. Indeed what follows *is* his destiny, whose seemingly malign
promptings he must fulfill unawares. Pym's destiny is of
course seated in his unconscious, whence it rises again and
again to dominate, in terror and in ecstasy, his feckless life
of putative choices. This power of the unwitting to dominate consciousness, the unwitting with its feelings deeper
than those the mind can imagine it could choose between,
this power that surges with uncontrollable energy and directs
body and mind toward ends it will not articulate or disclose,
is what Poe elsewhere identifies as the Psyche. It is what we
acknowledge as the id whose behests cannot be transcended
or escaped. In *Narrative of Arthur Gordon Pym*, the narrator

is as helpless in its grasp as are his vessels in the tidal currents of the sea.

In making their plan the two conspirators had taken for granted, as well they might, the stability of the ship's government. Who could foresee that no sooner was the *Grampus* out of harbor than mutineers would seize the ship, murder most of the crew, cast Captain Barnard adrift, and block up the escape hatch of Pym's secret compartment? In the subterranean allegory of psychomachy which throbs beneath the surface of Pym's *Narrative*, these events signify the subversion of civil rule, of the restraints of the superego. When Pym, after terrible frights and sufferings, emerges at last, he beholds a ship in which his alter ego Augustus is the slavey of the murderous mutineers, and they in turn are divided into rival factions. Both factions are headed by characters of a primitive race. The Negro cook is the bloodthirsty leader of the revolt, hacking white men to death; he is opposed by a strange creature, half Oskarora Indian, half white, named Dirk Peters, who is as dwarfish and misshapen as the Negro Pompey in 'A Predicament'; he resembles also Hop-Frog, whose revenge upon king and court was incendiary, and perfect.

In the event, Dirk Peters, Augustus Pym, and another seaman are the sole survivors of the *Grampus*. Then in adventures similar to those of Coleridge's Ancient Mariner, they drift through tropical seas aboard her helpless hulk. Hoping for deliverance from an approaching ship, they are appalled to see—to *smell*, first—that she is a ship of the dead, and that they are heading where she leads. Starving, with a horror from which there is no escape, they agree to draw lots so that the body of one may sustain the lives of three. The fourth seaman is the luckless choice, and, revived by their awful feast, Pym and Peters thrive. But Augustus, injured in the mutiny, sinks as his wound turns gangrenous. At last Pym and Peters are the sole survivors. And as Peters throws Augustus's body overboard, the putrified leg comes off in his hand. Poe is never at a loss for the detail still more ghastly than all the horrors that have gone before.

Dirk Peters now completely displaces Augustus as the alter ego of Pym. What does this substitution mean? Pym's first double was white, handsome, impulsive, and rationalistic. It was Augustus who made the plan for Pym's stowing away. His name, in fact, associates Augustus with both the Age of Reason and with C. Auguste Dupin. Now the wound he suffered in the anarchic struggle has festered and he has died and been submerged in the sea. In his place remains the Indian half-breed, ugly, dwarfish, the bald pate on his scalp filled in with a patch of bear's fur. Peters is incredibly strong, crafty, and resourceful—a more atavistic alter ego, surely; one better equipped to help Pym survive the unspeakable dangers which yet await him. But Dirk Peters is himself a part of those dangers.

It has been pointed out, by Marie Bonaparte, Levin, and Fiedler, that the color symbolism in *Pym* is a clue to one of its subterranean meanings. White is a color of mystery, awe, annihilation, as is the case in *Moby-Dick*. Black is also the color of mystery and terror, and of annihilations from which Pym, with the aid of Peters (himself half-white, half-dark), is saved. The sly and treacherous savage race on the island to which comes the ship that rescues Pym and Peters, this tribe who trick the entire crew into being buried in an avalanche, are not the Polynesians one would expect to find in the southernmost seas, but barbaric Negroes with woolly heads, thick lips, and coal-black skins. These savages regard whiteness as tabu, they worship the Arctic bear, fall speechless with terror at the sight of a white pocket handkerchief, yet they detest the white men who intrude upon their wretched economy. Using the conventions of the contemporary mariner's voyage tale, which Melville would soon put to his own purposes in *Typee*, *Omoo*, and *Mardi*, Poe constructs his narrative so that the submerged allegory comes clear. At the very gates of the sought-for deliverance into annihilation in the whiteness of the cataract of the seas lurk the black figures of terror and savagery, who menace the self with a meaningless destruction.

To be buried alive on the island would mean that Pym is

deprived of the final exaltation at the end, where, with Peters in his canoe, he is drawn onward by the current through the luminous veil:

> And now we rushed into the embrace of the cataract, where a chasm threw itself open to receive us. But there arose in our pathway a shrouded human figure, very far larger in its proportions than any dweller among men. And the hue of the skin of the figure was of the perfect whiteness of the snow.

It is incontestable that Poe's island of Tsalal represents in one aspect the American South. This land that resembled a bale of cotton with its brutal pickaninnies is conceived out of Edgar Poe's most atavistic fears. The only known allusion to Negroes in all of Poe's correspondence is his accusation to John Allan that 'You suffer me to be subjected to the whims & caprices, not only of your white family, but the complete authority of the blacks—these grievances I could not submit to.' Appearances of Negro characters in Poe's tales are occasionally comic stereotypes of the Mr. Bones variety (Jupiter in 'The Gold Bug') or, more often, grotesquely deformed (Pompey in 'A Predicament'); or else deformed and simian creatures are associated with Negroes, as is the orang outang in 'The Murders in the Rue Morgue,' and Hop-Frog and the ape-like costumes he contrives for his victims. The same is true of the tarred and feathered escapees from the madhouse in 'The System of Dr. Tarr and Professor Fether.' Fairly close to the surface of his mind, Poe reflects that side of his Southern background which associates the Negro not, as did Mark Twain, with nobility in chains, but with violence, cruelty, lust, bestiality. As opinions about the real world these associations are scarcely civil. But Poe does not offer them as descriptions of life in Richmond. With his terrible gifts of self-knowledge and self-revelation he shows us 'the power of blackness' as the images projected upon the external world by the atavistic impulses of the alienated self.

I can't agree with Leslie Fiedler that Poe's imagination moved southward in this *Narrative* because he associated a

trip in that direction with his mother's taking him in infancy
from Boston to Richmond. Nor do I think it likely that the
white sea around the black island represents breast milk fed
the infant Eddie by a Negro mammy—Edgar after all was
the child not of a plantation lady but of a itinerant actress.
Still, it is certain that all the images toward the end of the
tale are the inescapable impressions of *the regressive imagination*. Poe's imagination regressed toward two opposite yet
complementary conditions, conditions here represented by
characters, colors, geographical features, in short the hy-
pothesized reality of Pym's adventures. He regressed toward
white, and toward blackness; toward such comforting, maternal images as the warm white water and the womblike
vortex, and toward such frightening bogeys as the brutal
black savages and the tomblike inhumation under the landslide they contrived to kill the white explorers. He regresses,
in short, toward both dying and being reborn, toward the
extinction of consciousness and the realization of a supra-
consciousness in the moment of the self's annihilation.

Such a duplication of the regressive object into its complementary yet opposite ends is a characteristic of Poe's mind.
His dualistic imagination summoned up Pym's double, not as
a single doppelgänger but, as we have seen, itself split between Augustus and Dirk Peters. (Pym's grandfather, whom
he disowned on the dock at Edgartown, was named 'old Mr.
Peterson.') There are similar alternatives in the tone and the
style of the tale—indeed, these are purposefully varied in a
pattern of contrasts, similar to that in Poe's other tales of
voyages by sea and into the sky. Passages of nightmarish terror are followed by lucid expositions of natural phenomena.
In the midst of the mutiny aboard the *Grampus*, Pym pauses
to give a careful explanation of the seafaring term 'lying-to.'
The horrible encounter with the ravening seagull which
dropped on the deck of the *Grampus* a piece of human flesh
torn from a cadaver on which it had perched aboard the spectral ship, giving that corpse a semblance of life, is followed
by a chapter of tender solicitude wherein Pym and his three
companions attempt to ease each others' sufferings. This in

turn precedes a terror yet more atavistic, their drawing of lots to choose the victim of their hunger. Cannibalism is a prelude to their rescue by the ship *Jane Guy*. Ashore on the island of Tsalal, although menaced by savages Pym gives an anthropologist's account of their way of life. Escaping from the natives' effort to bury them alive, Pym and Peters explore the rock fissure in which they had been hidden, and Pym describes the nature and shapes of the clefts with a geologist's attention to detail.

This accuracy, the comfort of intellectual prowess, is no protection against the inevitable danger which at once ensues. Indeed, the prospect of further exploration stirs up in Pym's mind an excitement which proves premonitory of a new terror—for of course the discovery which Pym seeks is inextricable from the horrors which afflict his body and the terrors which shake his soul:

> . . . presently I found my imagination growing terribly excited by the thoughts of the vast depths yet to be descended, and the precarious nature of the pegs and soapstone holes which were my only support. It was in vain I endeavoured to banish these reflections, and to keep my eyes steadily bent upon the flat surface of the cliff before me. The more earnestly I struggled *not to think*, the more intensely vivid became my conceptions, and the more horribly distinct. At length arrived that crisis of fancy, so fearful in all similar cases, the crisis in which we begin to anticipate the feelings with which we *shall* fall—to picture to ourselves the sickness, and dizziness, and the last struggle, and the half swoon, and the final bitterness of the rushing and headlong descent. And now I found these fancies creating their own realities, and all imagined horrors crowding upon me in fact. I felt my knees strike violently together, while my fingers were gradually but certainly relaxing their grasp. There was a ringing in my ears, and I said, 'This is my knell of death!' And now I was consumed with the irrepressible desire of looking below. I could not, I would not, confine my glances to the cliff; and, with a wild, indefinable emotion, half of horror, half of a relieved oppression, I threw my vision far down

into the abyss. For one moment my fingers clutched convulsively upon their hold, while, with the movement, the
faintest possible idea of ultimate escape wandered, like a
shadow, through my mind—in the next my whole soul was
pervaded with a *longing to fall;* a desire, a yearning, a passion utterly uncontrollable. I let go at once my grasp upon
the peg, and, turning half round from the precipice, remained tottering for an instant against its naked face.
But now there came a spinning of the brain, a shrill-
sounding and phantom voice screamed within my ears;
a dusky, fiendish, and filmy figure stood immediately beneath me; and sighing, I sunk down with a bursting heart,
and plunged within its arms.

I had swooned, and Peters had caught me as I fell . . .

What is this but the very same situation, the identical
images, which Poe used to define the subject of his sketch,
'The Imp of the Perverse'! That subject—who could forget
it?—is the longing of the perpetrator of a perfect crime to
reveal his own iniquity. It is *the longing of the living body
to die,* of the organic to become inorganic, of the differentiated consciousness in the agony of its separateness to experience the frightening ecstasy of its reintegration into the unity
from which it has been exiled—the unity of personal annihilation. It is a metaphor of a metaphor; for the unstated desire,
which appals with an intensity exactly equal to that with
which it is longed for, is the desire for ultimate regression,
extinction at the source of life. I began by noticing the euphony between the names Arthur Gordon Pym and Edgar
Allan Poe; now I must acknowledge the accuracy with which
James Cox has suggested another way to crack the code of
Pym's name: as an anagram of IMP. It is Pym's perverse
spirit of self-annihilation which is the spring propelling all his
perilous adventures. Thus Poe had unflinchingly seen beyond
the pleasure principle three-quarters of a century before
Freud, in another terminology, defined the meaning of his
Imp.

The passage on the fear of falling is but one of many pre-
lusive to the final sentences I have already quoted, that pas-

sage about the cataract into which the travellers' canoe is irresistibly drawn. Let me cite its images once again—'And now we rushed,' Poe writes, 'into the *embrace* of the cataract,' where a chasm *'threw itself open* to receive us . . .' What in the vertiginous passage was described with terror as a failure of the ego to direct the mind, here is given with wonder, as a condition of nature itself. There is no thought of avoiding the cataract, no thought of assenting to it; there is no thought at all. And—'there arose in our pathway a shrouded human figure'—note that Poe doesn't designate its sex, only its size —'very far larger in its proportions than any dweller among men. And the hue of the skin of the figure was of the perfect whiteness of the snow.'

This series of phrases, of 'of' phrases, is the perfect syntactical epitome of the action, an endlessly regressive series of phrases disappearing into each other until there is nothing left to say or see but Nothing.

This final passage, which seems to describe annihilation, proves, as I've said, to imply rebirth. (From the terms in its description—*embrace, threw itself open*—one could hypothecate that the shrouded figure is feminine rather than male, as the tale-teller plunges into the vortex.) The way to actual annihilation lay in all those entombments from which Pym was so miraculously saved.

Although Pym is sometimes completely alone (when buried, entombed, trapped in a narrow space below decks), he always escapes from jeopardy and is usually companioned, at first by Augustus, then by both Augustus and Peters, then, after Augustus's death, by Peters. Leslie Fiedler maintains, as is his wont, that Peters is the 'dark spouse' in Pym's fantasy of miscegenated homoerotic love. But the emotional logic of the tale must be verily wrenched to support such an interpretation. I respond to these characters in a different way, a way I think truer to Poe's own response. Augustus, being the rational, Prefect of Police side of Pym's mind, is debonair when in town, full of stratagems and clever plans (plans too clever by half), but unwittingly he leads Pym toward his destiny of disastrous suffering. Immediately after the cannibal feast (which subsequent events—the direct rescue of the survivors by the *Jane Guy*—prove to have been unnecessary) Augustus sickens and dies. This is as much as to say that that part of Pym projected outward as Augustus—the workaday reasoning mind, the civil social creature—can neither abide nor survive the horrors which it is yet the fate of Pym's body and soul to experience in his not yet fully conscious search for absolute truth. From this point on Pym's companion and double is the resilient dwarfish savage, dark Dirk Peters, whose Christian name (if he be a Christian) means *dagger*, like the weapon with which he slew the sacred Arctic bear.

Like Melville's Ishmael, Pym alone survives to tell the tale. True, Peters survives too—indeed, as we learn from Poe's 'Note' appended to Pym's *Narrative*, Peters outlives Pym. But he has no tale to tell, and so cannot provide the information in the missing chapters which Pym failed to supply before his 'late sudden and distressing death.' Although Peters is inarticulate there, he represents the dark, the savage, the primitive sufficiency dwelling within the self. Indeed, the self survives because it is dependent upon his powers. But the ego cannot surrender to those principles which Peters embodies, lest it become, like him, torpid and brutish. We might instance a further parallel to Poe's contrivance of splitting the self in Hawthorne's division of the complete psyche in 'The Birthmark' between Aylmer, the intelligence, and Aminadab, the brutish understrapper down in the laboratory, on whose dogged cooperation the intellectual is dependent.

On Peters, then, Pym depends in his extremities, falling into his dark double's arms in his vertiginous drop from the cliff, being protected by Peters's strength from wild beasts, being rescued from entombment in the chasm by Peters's exertions. Yet as the two of them drift in their canoe, with a captive Tsalal blackamoor, toward the ultimate vortex of the world, first the savage perishes from fright, then Peters grows more and more torpid ('I knew not what to think of his apathy'). It is Pym and Pym alone who witnesses the revelation of the white superhuman figure at the brink of the chasm. In the regressive dream-imagery of this narrative, the self sails ever further back into time, into its own experience, casting off its rational dealings with the world, outlasting its own instinctual savagery, until at the end, the triumphant intuitive self welcomes its seeming annihilation. Unlike Monos or Una in their 'Colloquy,' Pym does not define the experience he is just about to have as the story ends. Instead the conclusion of his tale embodies it.

There remains the slight question of what that ending actually means. Does Pym perish in the white spray? If so, how come we find him alive and well in New York City in July, 1838, having, he tells us in the 'Introductory Note' to his *Narrative*, returned from his South Sea adventure by way of Richmond, Virginia, where it was only the urging, he says, of 'Mr. Poe, lately editor of the Southern Literary Messenger,' which convinced him to commit his memoirs to print. Indeed, says Pym, he consented to do this only on the condition that 'the name of Mr. Poe [be] affixed to the articles in the table of contents of the magazine,' so as to present his truths in the guise of another's fictions.

Those critics who think this ending an imposture—for how could Pym have survived to tell the tale?—have opined in ignorance of a theory of the circulation of the oceans which Poe, like many other Americans in the 1830s, took seriously. This was the then-famous Symmes notion, popularized by the magazine-writer Jeremiah Reynolds, who also wrote an account (which Melville read) of a white whale in the Pacific, and whose name Poe would call while in his dying fit. The Symmes theory proposed that the currents of the seas all poured through a vortex at the South Pole, emerging at the North Pole and re-circulating around the globe. Once this idea is entertained, it is evident that Pym and Peters need not perish when their canoe hurtles into the vortex. No, like the fisherman in the maelstrom, they have gone down into the vortex and have been cast up alive.

But if Pym is back among mankind in Richmond and New York, what sort of a hoax have he and Mr. Poe played on us with their impositious cataclysm at the end of the MS.?

Hoaxiepoe, at it again! He presents his balloon hoax as fact, his Pym's cup of truth as fiction. *But*—it is we, not he, who decide that the arctic mist shrouds the annihilation of Pym's consciousness. Suppose we reconsider that. Suppose we remember that in this tale everything that happens is repeated, is *itself* a repetition of what has gone before *and* a precursor of that which is to come: all those departures, entombments aboard and ashore, all those vertiginous moments, those awakenings from horror into ecstasy into horror into yet further excitations of the soul . . . Suppose that we suppose the tumble into the maelstrom to be, not the *actual end* of Pym's individual existence, but a *premonitory simulacrum* of that end! For after all, were that end the real end, the veritable holocaust which awaits the world and which the world awaits, Pym would not be arranging with Poe to publish his book. He'd be conversing on Al Aaraaf with the likes of Una and Monos, and the world in which his body had suffered the humiliations, the mortifications, the putrefactions of mortal existence, would have become a dead cinder. Instead, Pym (with Peters, his durable savage self) enters the womb of the world itself, from which he was born, and is reborn.

X

The Mind of God, OR
'WHAT I HERE PROPOUND IS TRUE'

Eureka: A Prose Poem is Edgar A. Poe's masterpiece. He knew it; he said so himself. But a *prose* poem? How can a poem, which must be metrical, and not more than a hundred lines long, and should have as its subject the death of a beautiful woman, and express this subject as *indefinitely* (and therefore as *spiritually*) as possible, and be based on the hypnagogic repetition of a melancholy, single-word refrain, be made in prose? In prose of demonstrative clarity, with hypotheses, proofs, and explanations of those proofs, one hundred and thirty pages in extent? A poem in such prose, whose treatment has neither meters nor refrains, and whose subject has no death of a beautiful woman—but instead the birth, death, and rebirth of the entire universe!

History has not been kind to either Edgar A. Poe or his *Eureka.* The latter is scarcely ever read nowadays save by Poefessors, who have to read everything in order to write anything about Poe. True, *Eureka* has been reprinted at least once in a popularly priced paperback textbook, so that students, too, could have a try at understanding the universe. This was the selection of Poe's writings prepared by W. H. Auden in 1950. The students who used it are now themselves old enough to be parents of other students, who, if their teachers use Auden's edition, will have no such chance to read *Eureka.* In the *second* edition of Auden's *Selected Prose and Poetry* of Poe, there is no *Eureka.* I detect—in

fact I accuse—the intervening hand of some educationist-
editor at Rinehart, who substituted for this unique reprinting
of a masterpiece a few more of Edgar's chestnuts, readily
available in a dozen other paperback selections.

Of those who have read *Eureka*, nearly everyone is taken
in by Poe's subject and treatment, and so, I do believe, misses
his point. *Eureka* is appraised as a treatise on astrophysics.
But what is it other than a master code-breaker to Poe's
œuvre?

Some readers, some critics and exegetes, to be sure, have
recognized its centrality as an exposition of Poe's ideas. But
even they can easily take *Eureka* the wrong way, as I think.
Poe's tales are nowadays sometimes read as partial statements
of *Eureka*'s philosophy. Critics apply its doctrines to Poe's
stories, as though the tales were written in order to explain
the conceptions which *Eureka* explains. There is indeed a
relationship between *Eureka* and Poe's obsessional searches
for nearly-remembered knowledge in his tales of voyages and
marriage. Certainly his detective heroes are nothing if not
scientifically intuitive in their scrutiny of clues. But what
would happen if, instead of applying *Eureka* like an astrolo-
ger's dream-book to the plots of the tales, we read *Eureka*
itself as one of those tales? A tale which is a poem.

This tale uses cosmogony as its materials, the terminology
of science as its diction, but is itself neither a scientific
treatise nor, despite Poe's protestations, is it in fact a description of the universe. It is the ultimately depersonalized
and mechanical characterization of the psychic rhythm of
existence. The faculties most intensely engaged in the creation and exposition of the cosmogony in *Eureka* are intuition
and ratiocination—the very cast of mind we find in Poe's
active heroes, Monsieur Dupin and Legrand, whose powers,
and the perspicuous expository style used to exhibit them,
are, so to speak, now engaged to crack the great cipher of
appearances and to detect the true pattern of that greater
life of the Universe of which the life of man is but an individuated and fragmentary example. What Dupin demonstrates about human action, Poe himself, as author of *Eureka*,

demonstrates about all existence: the hidden rhythm of its processes, of which intuitive thought itself is the closest approximation.

   Is it not surprising that the poet who, in his early 'Sonnet —To Science,' characterized that branch of intellectual research as a 'True Daughter of Old Time,' a monster begotten of the carrion-devouring, vulturish parent, driving the soul to seek solace on 'some happier star,' now should himself write a treatise seemingly on astrophysics? There must be an explanation to this contretemps, one which intuitive ratiocination will reveal. Perhaps it is this: the proportionate relationship between *Eureka* and the astrophysical theories upon which it draws is equal to the square of the difference between physics and metaphysics. *Eureka* is a treatise on meta-astrophysics. It uses the scientific information, the best such information, available to Poe in 1848—he draws heavily and, to all appearances, accurately, with sympathetic understanding, upon a number of reputable writings by recent and contemporaneous astronomers. He is especially in debt to Alexander von Humboldt, author of *The Cosmos*; indeed, in a show of indebtedness rare for one whose critical writings seem paranoiac in tracing the plagiarisms (real or suspected) of others, Poe dedicates, 'with very profound respect,' his *Eureka* to his predecessor. In its pages he quotes, supports, or argues against the writings also of Leibnitz, Laplace, Comte, Lagrange, and Herschel. Where, and when, and how, one cannot help but wonder, did Edgar Allan Poe, whose every week was a desperate struggle of the scrivening pen against starvation, find or make the time to read, much less to master, these complex and mathematical discourses on the sun, the moons, the planets, the stars and the galaxies?
   If this present treatise on the work of Poe has any validity, it posits Q.E.D. to the proposition that for him, *Vida es sueña*, and everything, every thought, every feeling, every instinct which he had and felt and followed to its predestined end, was, somehow, an expression of an interior, even of an

anterior, life, to which he, more directly and more intensely than most other men, was attuned. The same must be true for his meta-astrophysical researches. Poe made himself a soi-disant astronomer because this was an inescapable extension of the necessary pattern of his own convictions.

Much though he draws from the great astronomers of the day, and close—intuitively close—though his deductions and hunches come, in some instances, to more recent scientific theory, Poe's *Eureka* nonetheless is not, as I have said, a work of science. It is instead a closed system of logical induction in which hypotheses about existence are tested first by their internal coherence within the terms given. Such coherence once established, then evidence is marshalled from scientific predecessors who actually observed the qualities or processes really extant in the world they purport to explain. It suited the encapsulated quality of Poe's thought that he could make of these scientific hypotheses an entirely mental construct: 'We thus establish the Universe on a purely geometrical basis.' This sounds mathematical enough, but it is really a proposition which uses a mathematical vocabulary to establish an *aesthetic* principle. We have seen the unitary compulsion in Poe's theories of both poetry and fiction: all elements must tend toward the production of a single effect. I have had occasion to call Edgar a mechanician of literature, and his theories a program for the production of verbal contraptions. As a metaphysician he will prove no less entranced with mechanical process.

Indeed, in *Eureka*, so rarefied, so distant it would seem, from the concerns and cares of the ordinary American, it may be that Poe most closely approximates the commitment of those ordinary, Philistine fellow citizens to a conception, unacknowledged by most of them, of a mechanical universe. The entire universe as a huge coherent contraption! Of course there is a heavy overlay in such a notion of the rationalism of the eighteenth century, with Newton's watchmaker God in the wings. The difference is, for Poe, God is not a watchmaker who winds a perfect timepiece and lets it tick into eternity. For Poe, God *is* His own creation, which is the product of His will, and far from going through the same diurnal rounds forever, Poe's universe (*après* Humboldt, Herschel, et al.) is the embodiment of an eternal and recurrent process, ever changing. An eternal return.

Emerson said that 'A foolish consistency is the hobgoblin of little minds.' But for Poe, no consistency can be foolish. For Poe,

> Symmetry and consistency are convertible terms. A thing is consistent in the ratio of its truth—true in the ratio of its consistency. A *perfect consistency* . . . *can be nothing but an absolute truth.*

Which is about what we might expect from the mind that was so fascinated by the mystery of 'Maelzel's Chess Player.' Although Poe is absolutely serious in the body of his *Eureka* (there is a Hoaxiepoe introduction, to which I shall return), it just may come to pass that, taken in a metaphysical sense, his masterpiece—I say this in all admiration of his accomplishment—proves a sort of hoax after all. A hoax on him. For, as we shall see, the universe defined in *Eureka* can be taken to be a sort of Maelzel's chess game: a perfectly coherent, apparently mechanical and mathematical series of processes, with no visible agent at the helm—yet, secreted inside the mechanism whom do we find pulling the strings and wires, pushing the buttons and pedals that make it swell away from and then rush, returning inward, toward primal unity, but . . . I forbear to name him, it is too impious. I take refuge in a quotation. From Poe:

> As our starting point, then, let us adopt the *Godhead.* Of this Godhead, *in itself,* he alone is not imbecile—he alone is not impious who propounds—nothing. '*Nous ne connaissons rien,*' says Baron de Beilfield—'*Nous ne connaissons rien de la nature de l'essence de Dieu:—pour savoir ce qu'il est, il faut être Dieu même.*'—'We know absolutely *nothing* of the nature or essence of God:—in order to comprehend what it is, we should have to be God ourselves.'
>
> '*We should have to be God ourselves!*'—With a phrase

so startling as this yet ringing in my ears, I nevertheless
venture to demand if this our present ignorance of the
Deity is an ignorance to which the soul is *everlastingly*
condemned.

So let's not be too surprised or shocked when we discover,
later in this chapter, that the prime mover of the universe
isn't all that different from our own soul.

But I am leaping ahead of our author. I have plunged *in
medias res* into the middle and the end of his *Eureka*. If we
begin at the beginning of this impressive work of ratiocination, we discover that it resembles Poe's other tales of discovery. Like his science-fiction stories, *Eureka* begins with a
send-up, a fictitious and satirical *letter*. This is a lengthy and
rather buffoonish attack on those outmoded metaphysical
processes, the '*de*ductive or *a priori* philosophy' practiced by
'a Turkish philosopher called Aries and surnamed Tottle,'
whose 'most illustrious disciples were one Tuclid, a geome-
trician [Euclid], and one Kant, a Dutchman'; and also 'an
entirely different system, the *a posteriori* or *in*ductive,' invented by 'one Hog' [i.e., Bacon]. Alas for these labored
puns, a kind of namebasting which seems painful in Poe,
though when Mark Twain, in Sandy's interminable speeches
in A *Connecticut Yankee*, works the same vein of humor, we
laugh indulgently. Of course, Twain is funning with anach-
ronisms, putting into the mouth of a sixth-century peasant
lass the names of modern familiars. But isn't Poe doing the
same before him? For the epistle in which we find these
malaprops is supposed to have been written in the year 2048,
and was found a thousand years earlier, 'corked in a bottle
and floating on the *Mare Tenebrum*.' Yet we're not inclined
to grant Poe the same indulgence; rather, we feel about his
puns as he felt about Thomas Hood's, whose puns, writes
Poe in the last entry in his *Marginalia*, 'are the weak point
of the man . . . they leave upon us a painful impression;
for evidently they are the hypochondriac's struggle at mirth
—the grinnings of the death's head.' Not that Poe's genius,
like Hood's, is merely 'the result of vivid *Fancy* impelled by
Hypochondriasis'; in Poe's case we must substitute Imagina-

tion for Fancy, and for hypochondria, a philosophical conviction of the impossibility of knowing happiness in this life. Yet his puns are terrible.

If we've been reading Poe with diligence and care, we pretty soon recognize which of his personae is responsible for this belabored *humour noir*. Who but Pundita! The same speaker of puns who cast part of her journal adrift while in her balloon flight in 'Mellonta Tauta' (the Sophoclean title, remember, recurred as the motto to 'Monos and Una': 'These things shall come to pass.').

Several commentators have taxed Poe with what they term the mismanaged interpolation of an extrinsic and satirical letter into a serious discourse, on the grounds that the radical shift in tone, from Pundita's burlesque to the straightforward seriousness of the main body of *Eureka*, and then again to ecstatic passage of revelation at its conclusion, fatally contradicts Poe's own requirement that the design of a work have unity. That seems logical enough; having met such a would-be hilarious letter in 'Mellonta Tauta' and 'Hans Pfaall,' they cannot admit it to have a legitimate place in a work which propounds what is true. As for me, I welcome it here; for experience has taught me that Poe the Pundit's distinctions of genre are never as absolute as he maintains. His hoaxes are all serious beneath the surface, his serious writings seldom resist the temptation to impose on the reader, for Hoaxiepoe and Edgar the Metaphysician are one and the same, a regular practitioner of that aesthetic which keeps the reader off balance and always on the defensive against the superior cunning of the author. Besides, there may be room in a study of the Universe for a little levity at the expense of those who have misunderstood its design. For their number is legion.

Furthermore, Pundita's letter isn't entirely a joke. Its hoaxie humor serves two serious purposes. One is to demarcate the metaphysics to come from the errors of Aristotelian deduction and Baconian induction. The other is to establish both the villains and the heroes of *Eureka*'s plot. The villains (is that too strong a term?) are the philosophers of error; the heroes the metaphysicians, both methodical and intuitive, who have limned the true nature of Being. Of these, Newton is the methodical thinker whose researches are able to verify what the real hero of the piece, Kepler, was able to arrive at intuitively. Kepler is the Monsieur Dupin of universal metaphysics, surpassed in that branch of intuitive ratiocination only by Edgar Allan Poe.

Once the hoaxie introduction is past, Poe settles down to a radically different style of writing: faultless exposition, the patient yet uncondescending demonstration of a seamless web of argument by a mind which *takes pleasure* in the exercise of its own considerable powers. I don't doubt that the whole of *Eureka* began in Poe's boyhood wonder at the vast extent of the visible universe. On this he brooded for nearly forty years, fortifying his speculations with the far-flung readings in the astronomical authorities I have mentioned. Now he sets forth the premises of his own interpretation of their speculations, and recounts the progress of their arguments and his own, with the delight of an athlete at the top of his form. Were I ever to produce a textbook for science students, I'd certainly borrow the dozen pages of *Eureka* in which Poe describes the *size* of our universe, and compares to its seemingly vast expanse the infinite extent of space between the known galaxies of stars. I know of no passage in either scientific or imaginative writing which conveys with as much accuracy as awe the wonderstruck realization of the illimitable hugeness of the outer spaces. From these considerations Poe naturally passes to the question they imply:

> Let us take the opportunity of referring to the difficulty we have often experienced . . . in comprehending why chasms so totally unoccupied and therefore apparently so needless, have been made to intervene between star and star—between cluster and cluster. . . . The considerations through which, in this Essay, we have proceeded step by step, enable us clearly and immediately to perceive that *Space and Duration* are one.

Space and Time are identical! Each is merely a convertible dimension of infinity! But doesn't this proposition have the

look of a certainty without actually being one? It is arrived
at by a process of reasoning with which there can be no cavil,
save at the very first step. If we agree that the measurement
equals the thing measured, there's no turning back from the
conclusion; for the conclusion is subsumed in the first assumption. Let me offer a counter-proposal to Poe's. Edgar
says next to nothing about another dimension in which in-
finitude is imaginable. Indeed, it is not only imaginable, it is
doubtless extant. I mean *weight*. How *heavy* is the universe?
By constructing a seamless mesh of argumentation I could
propose that weight and distance are identical. Or, since we
measure the far-off by light years, the light being analyzed
spectroscopically to determine the elemental content, thus
the weight, I could as readily maintain that weight=time.
But Poe has naught to do with considerations of mass, I suppose because the atomic theories of over a century ago did
not as yet take account of it.

Poe's atomic theory, like Humboldt's, like Leibnitz's, like
Lucretius's, makes much of the combinations of atoms into
matter, but does not explain how matter is differentiated.
The idea of atomic weight, of the exact structure of molecules,
had not yet been defined. Even in its lack, Poe is able to
come up with an ingenious intuitive explanation of the nature
of matter, one which does indeed anticipate modern theory.

For what is *matter?* An atomic theory would seem to pre-
suppose that matter consists of atoms. But then, that answer
only enfolds a further question: What are atoms? Poe intuits
a solution to this dilemma:

> We are fully justified in assuming that matter exists only
> as attraction and repulsion—that attraction and repulsion
> *are* matter.

Or, as we in our century would say, matter is a form of energy.
But knowing nothing of atomic reactions, how did Poe arrive there ahead of us, as far ahead of us in exploring the
nature of the universe as was his Hans Pfaall in exploring
the craters of the moon?

By intuition. Early on in *Eureka* Poe has already arrived
at that point beyond which conscious intellectual inquiry cannot go.

> We have attained a point where only *Intuition* can aid
> us:—but let me recur to the idea which I have already sug-
> gested as that alone which we can properly entertain of
> intuition. It is but *the conviction arising from these induc-
> tions or deductions of which the processes are so shadowy
> as to escape our consciousness, elude our reason, or defy
> our capacity of expression.*

This has the look of those conceptions which hitherto in
Poe's work have been all but indefinable, as, say, the great
Ideas which Ligeia's husband attributed to her gigantic intellect. Such an intuition is the means by which Poe now
arrives at the indemonstrable but uncontradictable conclusion, 'that what God originally created—that that Matter
which, by dint of his Volition, he first made from his Spirit,
or from Nihility, *could* have been nothing but matter in its
utmost conceivable state of—what?—of *Simplicity*. This will
be found the sole absolute assumption of my Discourse.'

It will be seen that this conclusion, the sole assumption
underpinning everything else in *Eureka* (including the propositions I have already advanced), is the result not of scientific or mathematical speculation but of metaphysical induction. For the rest, Poe has marshalled all the evidence he can
from his scientific confrères to buttress the plinth upon
which his demonstrations rest. He has worked out his line of
argument with such cunning totality that the plinth is supported by the arguments and theories of which it is itself
the supporting assumption.

It is Poe's contention that 'simplicity' equals Unity, and
that the entire Universe has been constituted from a 'primordial particle,' willed by God. Both the unity and the resulting universe are the results and embodiments of God's
will. 'This constitution has been effected by *forcing* the originally and therefore normally *One* into the abnormal condition of *Many*.' Notice how covertly a judgment of value has

been inserted into the descriptive prose. Multeity is abnormal, unification normal, and the many is evoked from the One by *forcing*. 'An action of this character,' Poe continues, 'implies rëaction. A diffusion from Unity . . . involves a tendency to return into Unity—a tendency ineradicable until satisfied.'

There it is. That's the double motion of the universe, an expansion from the primordial particle to the outer limits of infinity, and a simultaneous tendency of all matter from that outermost limit to return inward to that simple, natural, unity from which the nature of the atoms themselves has exiled them. 'Their source lies in the principle, *Unity. This* is their lost parent. This they seek always—immediately—in all directions . . . thus appeasing, in some measure, the ineradicable tendency, while on the way to its absolute satisfaction in the end.'

Of this double movement in all creation I shall have more to say, but first it must be mentioned that Poe equates the attraction of atoms for one another with gravity, their repulsion with electricity. He claims that 'The former is the body, the latter the soul: the one is the material; the other the spiritual principle of the Universe. No *other principles exist.*'

Spiritual? The soul? How do these conceptions come into play in a universe comprised exclusively of matter which is a manifestation of energy? If we are more conventional metaphysicians, and less rigorous logicians, than Poe, we tend to think of the soul as an individuated consciousness, a portion of the self—the immortal portion. A quality or essence which survives death and enjoys or suffers in an afterlife the wages it has earned by its conduct in this world. Not so. For Poe, the soul is no such vehicle of individuality. As rigorously as in his aesthetic theory, in his metaphysics Poe separates morality from truth and truth from beauty. In point of fact he doesn't do much with morality. He is not concerned with conventional moral issues. This is not to say he has the amoral character of a fiend; after all, he does indeed acknowledge 'Conscience, That spectre in my path.' But he remains true to his faculty psychology, and in pursuing truth he has dropped moral questions in a pigeonhole marked 'File and Forget.' His theory, however, is not *completely* true to the tripartite divisions of his aesthetics. For in pursuing truth, he discovers beauty. Truth and Beauty are one. Just as Space and Time are one, and matter and energy are one. There is an irresistible charm, a fascination, in these unifications. But we must not forget that they express the 'one *First Cause*—the truly ultimate *Principle*—the Volition of God.' It is this 'Thought of God' which 'is to be understood as originating the Diffusion—as proceeding with it—as regulating it—and, finally, as being withdrawn from it upon its completion. Then commences Rëaction.'

Thus the Creation is explained. The sun and planets were created by nebular expulsion and condensations, nebulae begetting sun, suns begetting planets, planets begetting moons. The rotations of the planets result from the simultaneous attraction-repulsion of atoms.

> That the Universe might *endure* . . . it was required . . . that the stars should be gathered into visibility from invisible nebulosity—proceed from nebulosity to consolidation—and so grow grey in giving birth to unspeakably numerous and complex variations of vitalic development . . . *during the period* in which all things were effecting their return into Unity with a velocity accumulating in the inverse proportion of the squares of the distances at which lay the inevitable End.

This remarkably anticipates current astrophysical theory, as regards the creation of universes from nebulae of flaming gasses. But that's only half-way house for Poe, only the first part of the process, containing within it the incipient apocalyptic End, toward which all things tend. In his synoptic survey of current theories, *Nuclear Astrophysics* (Philadelphia, 1967), William A. Fowler suggests that stars and planets probably were indeed produced by the condensations of atomic diffusion. But he maintains that in each case this process is a local phenomenon—some stars even now are being flung out of galaxies, while others are expanding into 'red giants' (diffusing their heat over a larger area, and therefore rapidly dying out). According to Fowler, the entire universe is constantly expanding, not contracting, into infinity.

Poe, following the speculations of Humboldt and Herschel, hypothecates a process by inexorably logical (though not observational) steps, a process of expulsion-cum-collapse. This reciprocity, as he calls it, is the guarantee of its own validity, for, and here he gives the plot away:—

> The pleasure which we derive from any display of human ingenuity is in the ratio of *the approach* to this species of reciprocity. In the construction of *plot*, for example, in fictitious literature, we should aim at so arranging the incidents that we shall not be able to determine, of any one of them, whether it depends from any one other or upholds it. In this sense, of course, *perfection* of *plot* is really, or practically, unattainable—but only because it is a finite intelligence that constructs. The plots of God are perfect. The Universe is a plot of God.

To this stunning proposition, two corollaries. Poe the writer of fictitious literature emulates, as nearly as his finite intelligence permits, the action of God the plot-maker. And this is a reversible equation: in the proportion that Poe is like God, so God is like Poe. Because a man's intelligence is finite, the plot even of *Eureka* is imperfect, but more nearly perfect than is any of Poe's other plots because the extent of the intelligence which constructed it is more nearly freed from bondage to the body, therefore more nearly infinite. Indeed, as Poe himself says in the succeeding paragraph, he has 'reached a point at which the intellect is forced . . . to struggle . . . against its monomaniac grasping at the infinite.' He goes as far as mind can go toward encompassing the illimitable.

To accomplish this, Poe endows his own mind with pure mind. Here is intellect contemplating only the essence of the universe, freed for once from its prison, the corporeal body, freed to think as God thinks. The soul. Yes, for Poe,

if the universe is entirely material, matter being energy, then
the soul is that manifestation of energy which transcends the
destruction of the flesh: pure thought. For thought itself is
a manifestation of energy, as is the expansion of atoms from
their lost parent, Unity, and their return thence. The body
was *attraction*, the inward-collapsing of matter.

Thus it is part of this perfect plot of God that all being,
inorganic and organic alike, *desires its own destruction*. The
longing of creation for its own apocalypse! Poe was, in truth,
following, or being led by, or finding corroboration of his
own intuitions in, the theories of Humboldt and Sir John
Herschel. If later astrophysics denies that everything is plunging inexorably toward its own nihility, the question still remains, Why did this possibility so prepossess Poe's intuition?

I think the answer, or something like the answer, is suggested by the following hypothesis: If in *Eureka*, as Poe with
characteristic euphoria and sheer nerve claimed, 'What I here
propound is true,' its truth is not that of its surface narrative
(astrophysics) but of the symbolic allegory pulsing beneath
that surface. In *Eureka* Poe uses the imagery of the cosmos
to describe and embody the movement, not of the atoms
and the galaxies, but of his own mind; what he propounds as
physical laws are really psychal laws, the inexorably repeti-
tive behests of the deepest instincts not only of man but of
all living creatures.

> [The] final goal of all organic striving can be stated too.
> It would be counter to the conservative nature of instinct
> if the goal of life were a state never hitherto reached. It
> must rather be an ancient starting point, which the living
> being left long ago, and to which it harks back again by
> all the circuitous paths of development. If we may assume
> as an experience admitting of no exception that everything
> living dies from causes within itself, and returns to the
> inorganic, we can say '*The goal of all life is death*,' and
> casting back, 'The inanimate was there before the animate.'

I take *Eureka* as both explained by, and corroboration of,
this passage—it is the point of the entire treatise—from chapter V of Freud's *Beyond the Pleasure Principle*.

If, in his physics, Poe was a century behind our times, although in the projection of his own instinctual life he was a century ahead of his own time, he was also in the vanguard of that apocalyptic philosophy, so prevalent in the nineteenth century, which ended with the vulgar simplifications of Max Nordau's screed of despair. The sun in our universe is a fast-extinguishing candle, ergo our strivings are vain. Half a hundred years before *le malaise du fin du siècle,* Poe had understood, had intuited, had *felt* as true the undeniable principle that we, and our universe, contain within ourselves, intrinsic with our very being, the seeds of our own destruction—which we unconsciously *long for.*

But Poe redeems himself from the vulgar despair of those who felt that riding a doomed ball in a dying field of force gave cosmic sanction to their own pessimism. For Poe, with unprecedented courage—or is it merely his insatiable intellectual appetite to understand *everything* that lurks behind the surface of appearances—concludes,

> Let us endeavour to comprehend that the final globe of globes will instantaneously disappear, and that God will remain all in all.
> But are we here to pause? Not so. On the Universal agglomeration and dissolution, we can readily conceive that a new and perhaps totally different series of conditions may ensue—another creation and irradiation, returning into itself—another action and rëaction of the Divine Will. Guiding our imaginations by that omnipresent law of laws, the law of periodicity, are we not, indeed, more than justified in entertaining a belief—let us say, rather, in indulging a hope—that the processes we have here ventured to contemplate will be renewed forever, and forever, and forever; a novel Universe swelling into existence, and then subsiding into nothingness, at every throb of the Heart Divine.
> And now—this Heart Divine—what is it? *It is our own.*

The universe itself, like Arthur Gordon Pym, is in, or rather *is,* an endlessly repeated series of motions, alternately voyaging outward from its own center and rushing inward thither again—the universal movement of which Pym's voyagings forth and interments and escapes and plummeting passage over the whirlpool are the closest simulacra possible in an individual life. Closely approximate to this universal double motion, also, are the activities of Poe's other protagonists, those who are motivated first by their Will, which individuates them through their ambitious or criminal acts, then by their Impulse, which integrates them once more with the unity they all unwittingly seek, as their Imp of the Perverse hurries them toward self-exposure and death. But how often, in describing what Poe at the last terms the 'throb of the Heart Divine,' have I used the expression, *double motion.* A double motion, where what Poe sought, what he ached to discover and return to, was a *single* motion. Simplicity. Unity.

But the nature of existence betrayed that desire. At the deepest level of his being Poe felt, Poe *knew,* that there can be no such unitary stasis. He says so in *Eureka:* without the attraction *and* repulsion of atoms there can be no being, no universe, no embodiment of the Divine Volition. So it is the universe itself, expressing the Divine Volition, which establishes this proposition: *Being is never One.* To be is to be a part of a process. That process is the exemplification, in terms of inorganic matter, of an analogue to the cycle of life-and-death among the creatures. It is to this truth—I call it a reasonable truth—that we are led by the circular trammels of Poe's thought, a philosophy which seems to point determinedly inward toward a condition of pure solipsism.

It will be inferred that, even though his physics is outdated, his theology idiosyncratic, I take seriously what Poe expounds as *Eureka.* In *Eureka* he succeeded, as nearly as a man could, in conceiving and embodying those rhythms of instinctive thought which were to be the happy burden of Nesace's songs in 'Al Aaraaf.' His early poem was perhaps just as ambitious an effort to image forth a cosmogony, but the attempt was defeated by the faults in its strategy. Now, in *Eureka,* Poe has freed his conceptions from the limitations of *character*—there is neither man, shade, nor angel here, only the thought of the author emulating the Divine Volition, and so at last enabled to trace the rhythm of beating of the tell-tale Heart Divine.

How very strange, that this imagined world from which human suffering has been banished should beat with the rhythm of a heart *that is our own.* But is this not a conception more endurable than that of modern astrophysics, in which the universe is an unbounded field of ever-expanding force, a mechanism wholly divorced from any conceivable resemblance to the creatures who inhabit this odd globule of matter spinning with such doomed purposelessness in a space of which no center can be imagined? The very thought gives one a pain in the head. How much more attractive is Poe's presumption, and how much closer, in truth, to reality: not the inferential reality of the universe of stars and space, but the reality of that more proximate interior universe of *feeling*. For what have we found this motion to be which Poe imputes to all creation, this expulsion and impulsion, but the instinctual movement of the mind that conceives it? It is an objectification, a brilliant projection outward upon the universe of the conflict between Eros and Thanatos, between the life-wish and the will to self-destruction. Between the ego, asserting, exercising, revelling in its individuated powers, and the Imp of the Perverse, ever betraying the assertive self to the instinct that lies most deeply secreted within it. The rhythm imposed upon experience by the conflict between these irreconcilable instincts we recognize in its other manifestations too: in the impulsion and expulsion of *breathing* (so frequent a motif in Poe's tales!); it is characteristic also of the sexual act, as, metaphorically, of the entire life history of a species or individual. It is imprinted in nature in the double helix, it is reproduced in art in the shapes of forms. It is the deepest, the simplest, the most unitary truth of our natures. A double truth. The one movement to which all existence corresponds, as we experience it, is expansion and contraction, expulsion and impulsion. Life and Death. All is double.

And yet, if *Eureka* succeeds better than any of Poe's other tales in achieving the self-betraying unification toward which all his thought and instincts tend, how different it seems from such works as *Pym*, 'Ligeia,' 'The Fall of the House of Usher,' or 'MS. Found in a Bottle': how distinctive is *Eureka* in its rigorous intellectual development, its circumstantiality, its complete avoidance of the obsessional dream-states in which the characters of Poe's fictions suffer. Indeed it is unlike all of those Arabesques in its *avoidance of suffering*. Insofar as *Eureka* is a dream—and indeed it is—its dreamlike quality inheres in this very avoidance. Here is a long, coherent, rational work from which *pain is banished*. Although *Eureka* demonstrates that the universe is composed not of matter but of *energy*, there seems no place in that universe for the energy which Poe dramatizes everywhere else as the Imp of the Perverse. A Universe without an Imp of the Perverse!—what a dream, a wonderful dream.

Therefore, I think it is, Poe offers his *Eureka*, in his preface,

> To the few who have loved me and whom I love—to those who feel rather than to those who think—to the dreamers and those who put their faith in dreams as in the only realities—I offer this Book of Truths, not in its character of Truth-Teller, but for the Beauty that abounds in its Truth; constituting it true. To these I present the composition as an Art-Product alone:—let us say as a Romance; or, if I be not urging too lofty a claim, as a Poem.

All these hypotheses, diagrams, proofs, and explanations as an Art-Product alone! And who has taken *Eureka* so? Poor Edgar, he has so often played Hoaxiepoe that his readers don't know when not to be taken in. He'd be Truth-Teller, but they, who have been diddled in the matters of moon and maelstrom, of alchemist's stone and mesmerical miracle, do not heed him any more than did Aesop's peasant heed the shepherd's cry of 'Wolf!' So his systematic readers, from Margaret Alterton and Arthur Hobson Quinn to Edward Davidson and Vincent Buranelli, have tended to take *Eureka* as a scientific treatise, an effort to understand or obliterate the physical world, while his psychiatrist Dr. Bonaparte finds *Eureka* to be entirely a delusional document. For her it is a 'paranoid attack,' exemplifying Poe's 'megalomaniac narcissism,' in which 'he is equally attached and submissive to the father through the homosexual force of love.' Achone, poor Oedgar.

So ecstatic is his revelation that the reader of *Eureka* must infer that the Imp of the Perverse survives even Poe's effort to imagine a universe of stars without suffering. To do so he had resolutely to bar from his exposé any human character or characteristic—yet at the end the entire creation beats as though with a human heart. The impulse toward apocalyptic destruction—what is *that* but the Imp of Perverse, the attraction of matter, of body, triumphing over the expulsive diffusion of energy? By projecting it outward upon the universe, Poe has so universalized the destructive principle that it has ceased to menace and terrify, it has become ennobled with the divine energy and volition of which it, like everything else, is an expression.

Thus, to sum up, the Imp of the Perverse is, psychologically, that impulse which contradicts the individuation of the self: that yearning for self-destruction which expresses the soul's longing to return to the unity and primal simplicity from which it came. Salvation from suffering by suffering annihilation of the self. A paradigm of the universal dance of atoms and of galaxies.

A further word: I have tried to read *Eureka* as Poe offers it, 'as an Art-Product alone,' rather than as a treatise. That is to say, its perfect consistency, which Poe claims to guarantee its truth, also guarantees its beauty. For in *Eureka* the universe is considered as an aesthetic object, its perfection of design being the original and validation of those simulacra of perfection in which, in works constructed according to lesser plots than the plot of God, the soul's longing for a totally coherent experience is partially gratified. That Poe achieved such a degree of unification, in which space is collapsed into time, matter into energy, and life into death, required also that he unify science with art, ratiocination

with intuition, feeling with thought; and to do so he had in
the event to abandon the usual vehicles of his Art-Products,
the metrical poem and the prose Arabesque. The form of
Eureka is, for Poe, a nonce form. But the reader who has
encountered such other nonce forms as *The Enneads* of
Plotinos, *De Rerum Natura* of Lucretius, Sir John Davies's
Orchestra, and W. B. Yeats's *A Vision,* will recognize the
class of aesthetic objects to which *Eureka* belongs. As Valéry
has said, it is 'one of the rare modern examples of . . . a
cosmogony . . . one of the oldest of all literary forms.' It is
a poem whose only muse is Urania.

Such works plausibly impose upon all matter, all life, all
experience, one pattern, as compelling as a myth. Indeed
there are singular resemblances, as well as differences, between these works and *Eureka.* Plotinos, too, offers a double
motion, each ennead radiating its energy outward to the next
lower order of creation, each order so begotten in turn both
begetting a still lower and striving to return to the higher
order which was its own begettor. Lucretius, too, had made
a great poem, an 'Art-Product,' of an early form of the atomic
theory of the nature of things; a materialistic philosophy
which proved the hegemony of the everlasting conflict in the
universe between Venus and Mars.

Perhaps the closest analogue to Poe's construct is Yeats's.
And here too the movement of history, as of the soul, is
corroborated by the waxing and waning of the houses of the
moon, the double motion with all its tension represented in
the spinning of the gyres. But unlike Poe, Yeats borrowed
from science only its lust for systematization; in *A Vision*
he used, not the atomic, or any other scientific, theory, but
the pre-scientific traditions of neo-Platonism (including Plotinos) and of alchemy, astrology, and magic. These are better
adapted to the expression of human passions, of the adventures of the spirit in the body, of the self in the world of
historical fact, than is the depersonalized mechanical contraption proposed as the universe in *Eureka.* Hence *A Vision*
offered its author a greater range of subjects for his verse
than did *Eureka* to Poe. Where Yeats is a great author be-

cause, among other claims for his greatness, he dealt with a larger range of human action and human possibility than has any other modern poet, Poe, on the other hand, makes his claim to a lesser greatness by virtue of his limitations: because within the reduced confines of his obsessively restricted sensibility he delved more deeply, probed the recesses of the self with greater intensity and a more unflinching honesty than any before him, Poe must be granted the honor of a monument among those of the writers who bring us our deepest truths. His monument, for most of those who know him, is a haunted castle in a dark wood, flawed by an ominous fault zigzagging from its mouldering roof to the base of the wall, and darkly reflected from the tarn that glimmers beneath the House of Usher.

XI

The Fall of the House of Usher:
'MY HEART LAID BARE'

Was it because I could fancy a resemblance between the mock-medieval façade of New Rochelle High School, where I was then a sixteen-year-old senior, seeing its perforated towers, back-lit by streaks of heat-lightning in the heavy summer night, its turrets pointing both upwards in the sky and downwards in the dark still waters of the lake before it, and the House of Usher, that this tale of Poe's has haunted me for all these years? I remember, it was that very year that I first read it—as well as 'The Raven' and 'Ligeia' and 'A Predicament' and many more, and it was with the thrill of terror and revulsion which these works shook from my soul that I had so impetuously inscribed my hatred of their author on the flyleaf of my copy of his poems. For how could I but see myself as the narrator who, riding alone on horseback through a dreary wasteland, caught sight of the House of Usher—

> I know not how it was—but, with the first glimpse of the building, a sense of insufferable gloom pervaded my spirit. I say insufferable; for the feeling was unrelieved by any of that half-pleasurable, because poetic, sentiment with which the mind usually receives even the sternest natural images of the desolate or terrible. . . . What was it—I paused to think—what was it that so unnerved me in my contemplation of the House of Usher? . . . I was forced to fall back upon the unsatisfactory conclusion that while, beyond doubt, there *are* combinations of the very simple natural

objects which have the power of thus affecting us, still the analysis of this power lies among considerations beyond our depth.

Who has not felt it, that indefinable melancholia which in adolescence seems to enshroud the very world and to defy the faltering efforts of the mind to trace its source? It seemed an evil destiny, a portion of my fate as the suffering hero of an as yet undisclosed epic, a mood as inescapable as the mists that rose from the inscrutable waters of that dark lake. And though I knew those very waters had that afternoon brightly rippled over the spillway from Paine Pond two hundred yards away, where they had glistened with the clarity of *The Rights of Man*, now they had flowed thence into this strange pool downstream in which shimmered an image made unfamiliar by the fervid electric streaks that split the sky.

Shaking off from my spirit what *must* have been a dream, I scanned more narrowly the real aspect of the building. Its principal feature seemed to be that of excessive antiquity. The discoloration of ages had been great. Minute fungi overspread the whole exterior, hanging in a fine tangled webwork from the eaves. Yet all this was apart from any extraordinary dilapidation. No portion of the masonry had fallen; and there appeared to be a wild inconsistency between its still perfect adaptation of parts, and the crumbling condition of the individual stones. . . . Beyond this indication of extensive decay, however, the fabric gave little token of instability. Perhaps the eye of a scrutinizing observer might have discovered a barely perceptible fissure, which, extending from the roof of the building in front, made its way down the wall in a zigzag direction, until it became lost in the sullen waters of the tarn.

Re-reading 'The Fall of the House of Usher' now, for the how-manyeth time I know not, it seems a thesaurus of Gothic clichés: the lonely wanderer; the dreary landscape; the decaying castle; the reflecting tarn. And once inside the House, the weird inmates—the demented genius of the arts and his sickly, spectral sister; the strange affinity between these spooks and their creepy house; the incestuous attachment so strongly hinted between them; her premature burial; the ghostly congruence between his music, painting, poem, and the snatch of a wild romance read by the narrator, and the actions—the irrevocably doomed actions—which overtake the hapless personages in their haunted house.

Yet, at the time, this bundle of as yet unfamiliar horrors caused a tingling thrill of apprehension to shake me, as though 'The Fall of the House of Usher' resounded upon some hidden string within my being. What it was I could not tell, but the feelings of fascinated excitement and loathing aroused by this tale—despite its patent overwriting, its piling-on of one ghastly thrill after another—these sensations trouble me still. Do they, as Poe's narrator maintained, admit of no analysis? Can we not answer the importunate questions which Roderick Usher dared not ask—*Why did he put his sister living in the tomb?* What is the strange doom that topples the House of Usher?

These questions I myself hardly dared ask as I watched the turrets of my high school sink into the tarn between North Avenue and the schoolhouse steps. So to identify the only old-looking building I knew with a lake before it and the House of Usher added a thrilling chill to my contemplation of the tale. But close though actuality seemed to come to Poe's narrator's dream, the way into that dream could not be through actual experience. There never was a house quite like the House of Usher, for in truth—the truth of literary convention—it is no house at all but a profound and intricate metaphor of the self. There are things for which, at sixteen, life has not yet prepared one. It took me years to recognize that 'The Fall of the House of Usher' is a terrifying tale of the protagonist's journey into the darkest, most hidden regions of himself; and the fearful tableau therein enacted is a fable of his destiny dredged up from the regions of his deepest, most archaic dreams. As was true of the mariner whose MS. was found in a bottle, he attains a secret knowledge whose possession is destruction. And yet he is not destroyed. It is Roderick Usher upon whom the toppling fungus-wreathèd masonry falls as House and the Usher line together disappear beneath the waters. But the narrator, with whose journey thither we have begun, escapes to tell the tale.

Although written in 1839, nearly a decade before *Eureka*, 'The Fall of the House of Usher' seems a thesaurus not only of Gothic clichés but also of nearly all of Poe's obsessional motifs, here joined together in a dazzling, garish, and intricately consistent pattern of concentric meanings. Because all tends toward the final annihilation, some critics have succumbed to the temptation to read the tale as a dramatization of *Eureka*. True, all of Poe's tales partake of the same fixities which he so bravely schematized there, yet I do not believe that any writer of successful fictions undertakes to tell a tale in order to demonstrate his theory of the cosmos. On the contrary, he more likely is driven by the imaginative pressure of his fictions to construct such a theory that will justify and explain them.

In *Eureka*, as we have seen, Poe at last was able to imagine mind in a condition separate and free from the body, and hence even the rhythms of his prose partake of the ecstatic revelation of an all-powerful intellectual design. In *Narrative of Arthur Gordon Pym* that design was all but concealed from view, certainly from Pym's view, and accordingly the ecstatic passages in his narrative are those which he *feels* without understanding (which is not to say that the understanding denied to Pym is necessarily denied to the reader). Such is the condition of a body unaware of the power of the mind within it. In 'The Fall of the House of Usher' Poe completes what seems to me the tripartite division of functions in his most comprehensive and compelling tales. This is a fable of the soul: the soul acting independently, insofar as it can, insofar as it must, of mind, and struggling, as best it can, to be free, or, in the end, to become free, of the body.

Edgar Poe's *donnée* was nothing if not peculiar, yet its peculiarities are expressed in an inherited vocabulary of truisms. Body, Mind, and Soul: the functions defined by Greek philosophy, by the medieval scholastics. In his use of philosophical and psychological conceptions, as of literary conventions, Poe puts clichés to startling new uses. The result is almost always *weird*. Yet his characters and their catastrophes, strange though they be, despite the narrator's claim that he 'could not, even with effort, connect [Usher's] Arabesque expression with any idea of simple humanity,' do touch our own simple humanity.

When the narrator says that the analysis of the power of the House of Usher to chill his soul 'lies among considerations beyond our depth,' what he really means is that its analysis, though not impossible, is difficult. This warning has not dissuaded many readers from undertaking it. The interpretations of this tale are multifold; mine, though it profits from some of these, differs, I think, from any. I shall not pick quarrels with critics, scholars, or scholiasts; my purpose is but to comprehend 'The Fall of the House of Usher.' Knowing how carefully wrought are Poe's effects, when, as in this tale, successful, we must closely attend to many details which are introduced as merely descriptive elements.

As is true of nearly all of Poe's Arabesques, the form of 'Usher' is that of a confessional monologue. But unlike the monologists of 'The Black Cat,' 'Berenice,' 'Ligeia,' or the rest, the teller of this tale is not its principal actor. In this he seems akin to the rather dimwit narrators of 'The Gold Bug' and the Dupin tales. By means of this contrivance Poe is enabled to endow his most subjective fiction with an air of objectivity: this is not a madman's confession, but the report, by a sensible observer, of the dire predicament of someone else.

Yet, as Richard Wilbur maintains in his brilliant but fragmentary analysis of the story, who is that other but an image, an emanation, of the narrator's own self? 'We must understand "The Fall of the House of Usher" as a dream of the narrator's, in which he leaves behind him the waking, physical world and journeys inward toward his *moi intérieur*, toward his inner and spiritual self. That inner and spiritual self is Roderick Usher.' Let me support this assertion by pointing

out how Narrator and Usher are brought together in the
tale. Narrator refers to Usher as 'one of my boon companions
in boyhood' and to himself as Usher's 'best and indeed his
only personal friend.' Nevertheless,

> Although, as boys, we had been even intimate associates,
> yet I really knew little of my friend. His reserve had always
> been excessive and habitual. I was aware, however, that
> his very ancient family had been noted, time out of mind,
> for a peculiar sensibility of temperament, displaying itself,
> through long ages, in many works of exalted art and mani-
> fested, of late, in repeated deeds of munificent yet unob-
> trusive charity. . . .

And we soon learn that Roderick Usher 'suffered much from
a morbid acuteness of the senses': he cannot abide the taste
of foods, the touch of rough cloths, the odors of flowers, or
strong lights; and only the sounds of certain stringed instruments do not 'inspire him with horror.' This Usher is a super-
sensibility incarnate. And Narrator approaches the ominous
House in which he lives, *having been summoned there by
a letter.*

Everywhere else in Poe's tales, as we have seen, the sending of a letter is a report or summons from the soul: the mariner's epistle to the world cast adrift in the bottle, the letters
sent back from the moon by Hans Pfaall or dropped into the
sea from Pundita's balloon; the letter left in a sealed bottle
atop a hill on the island of Tsalal just before Pym and
Peters set off on their voyage toward the cataract. And the
undisclosed contents of the letter which the Minister D—
first, and then Monsieur Dupin, purloined . . .

And now Roderick Usher has sent a letter summoning to
his manse the long-lost companion of his boyhood, who even
then did not know him very well. His letter is an appeal for
help—Usher spoke of illness, 'of a mental disorder which oppressed him.' 'It was the apparent *heart* that went with his
request—which allowed me no room for hesitation.' Now, although none of Poe's narrators is depicted as a child, all are
striving to recapture some dimly remembered knowledge of

which, in infancy, they were more nearly aware. That child-hood condition, banished but ever sought in the tales, is dealt with directly in some of the poems. We remember Tamerlane's painful exile from the unity of experience known in boyhood. And the speaker in the poem 'Romance,' yearns for the time when the bird of that name 'Taught me . . . To lisp my very earliest word,' and his heart longs once more to 'tremble with the strings.'

There is 'a fine tangled web-work' of fungi festooning the House of Usher, and a web-work of imagery linking the tale with Poe's *œuvre*, of which it is a culmination. The tale bears as epigraph Béranger's couplet, 'Son coeur est un luth sus-pendu; / Sitôt qu'on le touche il résonne.' We have been told that Usher can bear the sound only of *certain stringed instruments*, we recall the trembling strings of 'Romance' and the lyre of Israfel 'whose heartstrings were a lute.' These are all images of soul-knowledge; nor are we surprised that the Usher family has always had 'a passionate devotion . . . to the . . . beauties of musical science.' An inexorable consistency links these phenomena together.

Yet, to obey the summons of the boyhood friend who, in the subliminal allegory of this consistent plot represents his own unconscious, Narrator feels an overwhelming apprehension as he sees the House. Which is the House of Usher, the domain of his soul, into which he will be ushered. He feels this most keenly as he views its image, and the image of its zigzag flaw, in the dark tarn—as though Nature herself were offering an image like those proffered by art, as an exemplum of a truth more prophetic and more true than reality itself, which is apprehended only as an appearance.

Indeed, the appearance of the House, at its first glimpsing, is rendered by the narrator as though it were not an actual abode but a *picture of itself*. Brooding on the impossibility of analyzing his premonitions of woe, he says,

> It was possible, I reflected, that a mere different arrange-ment of the particulars of the scene, of the details of the picture, would be sufficient to modify, or perhaps to anni-hilate its capacity for sorrowful impression. . . .

But then he sees its 'inverted images' in the pool's reflection, and shudders yet again. So the reflection becomes the image of an image. And that image is described, with careful consistency, in terms of a human head: 'vacant and eye-like windows,' the 'web-like fungi' resembling Usher's 'hair of a more than web-like tenuity and softness.' Not surprisingly, the 'House of Usher' refers to 'both the family and the family mansion.' Once within the manse, Narrator is conducted 'through many dark and intricate passages,' reaching, at last, 'the *studio* of the master.' And this, like Rowena's bedroom, like Mentoni's apartment, is a chamber of crimsoned lights, of furniture, books, musical instruments in disorganized profusion. It is yet another symbol of the interior of a disordered mind.

Nor need we be surprised that so little happens, that all is described rather than dramatized, that all is reported by the narrator (Roderick is given only two speeches in the entire tale). For what is this tale but the dream which Narrator, at Roderick's behest, has travelled so far into the intricacy of the dreary darkness to dream? And what he reports has the fixated, tableau-like rigidity, the inexorability, of a dream. It has also a dream's unremarked surprises and omissions. Unexplained events follow one another as though in the control of an unseen hand, those to whom they happen being as blind to their consequences as they are unaware of their causes.

Thus, once Narrator has arrived he learns, as though for the first time, that this boon companion of his boyhood has a sister. He sees her only once—'While he spoke, the lady Madeline (for so she was called) passed through a remote portion of the apartment, and, without having noticed my presence, disappeared. I regarded her with an utter astonishment not unmingled with dread; and yet I found it impossible to account for such feelings.'

Does she really not notice his presence? For long, she has been sick, with an undiagnosed disease—'apathy . . . wasting away . . . a partially cataleptical character'—but no sooner does Narrator set foot in her house than 'she succumbed (as her brother told me at night with inexpressible agitation).' Now she lies dying; later, as Narrator and Roderick lay her out in the vault downstairs, Narrator notices 'a striking similitude' between Madeline and Roderick. Now, for the first time, the brother murmurs that they are twins 'and that sympathies of a scarcely intelligible nature had always existed between them.'

Let me leave the lady Madeline lying in the vault for the moment, while I seek, with greater curiosity than is ever shown by Narrator, to ascertain just who she is and what her role is in his dream.

It was D. H. Lawrence, I believe, who first noticed the close resemblance between the description of Roderick Usher's appearance (I quoted this passage in my opening pages, since the physiognomy is also that of Edgar Allan Poe) and the adored and worshipped features of Ligeia. ' "There is no exquisite beauty," says Bacon, Lord Verulam, speaking truly of all the forms and *genres* of beauty, "without some *strangeness* in the proportion," ' says Ligeia's husband, repeating an aperçu which is strewn through Poe's reviews and *Marginalia*. Like Usher, and like Mentoni in 'The Assignation,' Ligeia possessed a pale and lofty forehead, a Hebraic nose, curling tresses . . . and those eyes.

In 'The Fall of the House of Usher' Madeline is never described—she appears only as a wraith, once while living, and once again, more terribly, when she emerges alive-yet-dead from her early inhumation. Yet what could she have looked like but her own twin brother, whose image is so close to that of Ligeia? What I am getting at in this laborious series of resemblances is, if Roderick Usher represents the *moi intérieur* of the rational, daylight self of the narrator, what does Madeline represent but the dreaded because beloved muse-figure of that inner self? By the daylight self of the narrator she is almost completely repressed: he did not even know she existed until revealed by her brother and lover and mourner, Roderick; on seeing Narrator she seems to die, as though to demonstrate the incompatibility between the self that meets the workaday world and the figure who, like Helen in Poe's poem, 'is Holy Land.' (We must not forget that Helen, too, resembles Ligeia.)

No sooner does Madeline seem to be dying than Roderick becomes inconsolable, and he then commences—strangely—the only actions he instigates himself in this chronicle of the fall of his House. These actions are his artistic creations, for Roderick is a polymath of creative genius. The instruments which had lain disused upon the floor, the books scattered unattended in his studio, are suddenly put to use. Hitherto, Usher had been unmanned by his terrors—'I dread the events of the future, not in themselves, but in their results'; he was immobilized by a superstitious conviction that the House, from which he never ventured forth, held an influence over his spirit; and by the thought of 'the evidently approaching dissolution—of a tenderly beloved sister, his sole companion.' Now that Madeline at last is dying, what does Roderick do but burst forth with painted images, with song, with poetry!

Usher the painter is an artist of pure abstraction. 'If ever mortal painted an idea, that mortal was Roderick Usher.'

A small picture presented the interior of an immensely long and rectangular vault or tunnel, with low walls, smooth, white, and without interruption or device . . . this excavation lay at an exceeding depth below the surface of the earth. No outlet was observed in any portion of its vast extent, and no torch or other artificial source of light was discernible; yet a flood of intense rays rolled throughout, and bathed the whole in a ghastly and inappropriate splendor.

Next he turns to that ancestral preoccupation of his House, the beauty of music, and plays wild and fanciful improvisations on his guitar. These strains are indeed the resonances of his lute-like heart, which, like Israfel's, renders the spiritual tones of that which touches it—in this case *the death of a beloved and beautiful woman.* This, no reader of Poe will have forgotten, is the decreed subject of true poetry. And indeed, in his phrensy of creativity Roderick 'accompanied himself with rhymed verbal improvisations.' His ensuing

poem is called 'The Haunted Palace.' (It is also published
in *The Raven and Other Poems*, by Edgar A. Poe, along with
Ligeia's 'The Conqueror Worm' and Mentoni's 'To One in
Paradise,' somewhat revised.) 'The Haunted Palace' is not
overtly *about* the death of Madeline, but it is assuredly *inspired* by Roderick's contemplation of her death, or her dying.
And as is the case with the other poems which Poe's characters interpolated into their tales, it is the center of significance in the story, a distillation of the tale which surrounds
it. In Usher's rhymed rhapsody, says Narrator, 'I fancied
that I received, and for the first time, a full consciousness on
the part of Usher of the tottering of his lofty reason upon
her throne.'

The Haunted Palace of course *is* the House of Usher, for
it too is described, in extended metaphor, as a human head.
Original poet though Usher is (the only other like him is
Edgar Allan Poe), among those scattered volumes on his
studio floor must have been copies of Tennyson and Coleridge. For 'The Haunted Palace,' like Tennyson's 'The Palace
of Art,' is 'a sort of allegory . . . of a soul' exiled from its
own Great Good Place by the fatal division between 'Beauty,
Good, and Knowledge' (as Tennyson lined out his theme
in the 'Introduction' to the first printing of his poem). The
House of Usher itself is a palace of art; like the pleasure
dome of Kubla Khan, it is an architectural metaphor for the
soul. But in Usher's lurid poem there is no milk of paradise;
the atmosphere is more nearly that of 'Christobel.'

Not for the first four of its six stanzas, however. The
haunted palace, which is so like Usher's head, is, at first 'radi-
ant . . . In the monarch Thought's dominion.' There, wan-
derers

> Through two luminous windows saw
> Spirits moving musically
> To a lute's well-tunèd law;

and the ruler of the realm ('Porphyrogene'—born to the purple) sat surrounded by 'A troop of Echoes whose sweet duty
/ Was but to sing.' This lyric is reminiscent indeed of Nes-

ace's songs in 'Al Aaraaf.' It is the poetic celebration of the
cerebral principle regnant, as in *Eureka*. In the last two
stanzas all is changed, changed inexplicably:

> But evil things, in robes of sorrow,
>   Assailed the monarch's high estate
>
> .   .   .   .
>
> And travellers now within that valley
>   Through the red-litten windows see
> Vast forms that move fantastically
>   To a discordant melody;
> While, like a rapid ghastly river
>   Through the pale door
> A hideous throng rush out forever
>   And laugh—but smile no more.

Narrator must be right; Usher's 'lofty reason' has already
tottered upon her throne. For this conclusion is a dying fall.
The reversals of 'luminous windows' (the eyes) as 'red-litten,'
of the 'lute's well-tuned law' to 'a discordant melody,' of
blithe spirits to 'a hideous throng,' are all accomplished mechanically, and without motive. What are those 'evil things'?
How vague and weak a word is *'things'!* It looks as though
Usher is losing artistic control as his reason weakens. Or does
he really know who and what are those 'things,' things too
terrible for his 'lofty reason' to control or even name?

'The Haunted Palace' begins as a lyric—that is to say, a
poem which, according to Poe's own dictum, has no other
end than itself—but in fact it ends as something other than
this: as a dramatic monologue whose end is the representation of Usher's tottering sanity. The poem is flawed, but
this is by no means true of the larger art-product, the tale,
of which it is a part, the effect of which is actually strength-
ened by the imperfections of the poem. Now, his reason tottering, Usher, with seeming inconsequence, babbles an
'opinion . . . of the sentience of all vegetable things.' Here
follows an extraordinary paragraph in which we learn how
'in his disordered fancy, the idea had . . . trespassed . . .
upon the kingdom of inorganization.' (This is the kingdom
of inorganic being.) What Usher is saying is that there is

direct connection, invisible though it seem, between his own destiny and the very arrangement of the stones, the fungi which festoon them, the decayed trees, and 'above all, in the long undisturbed endurance of this arrangement, and in its reduplication in the still waters of the tarn.'

Such connections between inorganic and organic, between reality and image, foretell the hypothesis in *Eureka*, a decade later, of the interchangeability of all matter because all is composed of radiation and impulsion. But these connections had already been foretold in Poe's 'Ligeia.' What was it the adoring husband perceived in his wife's deific eyes but intimations of the oneness of all sublunary things? This doctrine, no doubt originating in the Neoplatonic chain of being, is apprehended by the sensient soul as the unity of Being. But to 'Usher's' Narrator, the quotidian workaday, conscious self, 'Such opinions need no comment, and I will make none.'

After some time spent in reading (Usher's 'chief delight' is the perusal of the rites for the dead), one night the host tells Narrator 'abruptly' that Madeline 'was no more.' With precipitate haste he plans to inter her in a vault downstairs. Narrator assists as Usher places his sister's body in this deep vault, which in feudal times had been used 'for the worst purposes' (doubtless as torture-chamber). It seems an image of the vault whose image formed the idea of Roderick Usher's eerie painting. At last Madeline is laid out, the lid of her coffin screwed down, and the heavy door grates into place.

This vault, lined with copper, deep in the bowels of the House so interchangeable with its inmates, cannot help but suggest at once a family tomb and an ancestral womb. In the event, Madeline is to rise again and reappear, as in a horrible travesty of rebirth. But we well know how strangely intercommunicable, for Poe, are images of suffering one's death and dying into life. No wonder the vault in Roderick's painting glowed with self-begotten light.

Now that Madeline is consigned there, Roderick's composure disintegrates. 'Some imaginary sound' afflicts him. There is in the air a terror which reason cannot dispel. Narrator, too, is affected by 'an incubus of utterly causeless alarm.'

Outside the House of Usher, Nature or supernature lends
to the hysteria within the agitation of a whirlwind and the
weird 'glowing in the unnatural light of a faintly luminous
and distinctly visible gaseous exhalation which hung about
and enshrouded the mansion.' Narrator dismisses these as
'merely electrical phenomena,' and to divert the terrified
Roderick, commences to read aloud from one of his favorite
romances, 'The Mad Trist' by Sir Launcelot Canning (an
author invented by Poe). The passage he reads is

> that well-known portion of the story where Ethelred, the
> hero of the Trist, having sought in vain for peaceable ad-
> mission into the dwelling of the hermit, proceeds to make
> good an entrance by force.

And here, in a style of 'uncouth and unimaginative prolixity'
so little adapted to 'the lofty and spiritual ideality' of Usher,
follows the action of Ethelred, advancing through the storm
to bash down the door and slay the dragon, which expires
with a horrible shriek. While Narrator is reading this, Roderick becomes transfixed; for with his hyper-acute ears he is
hearing a door being burst apart and a howling shriek echoing up the stairs from the vault below. With a preternatural
conjunction between the text of the romance and the actions
of the avenging shade downstairs—a conjunction which imposes the armor of allegory upon the *dénouement* of the tale
—while Ethelred is hacking his way *in* to the blessed place,
Madeline is scratching her way *out* of her premature entombment. Yet the analogy is both obverse and exact, for, as
will be seen, Madeline too is crossing the threshold of beatitude, escaping premature burial to enter the doorway, at last,
of death, blessed death.

Usher sits and sways, entranced, still listening to those
sounds which Narrator as yet cannot detect. Narrator bends
close to hear Usher's anguished murmurs:

> Now hear it?—yes, I hear it, and *have* heard it. Long—
> long—long—many minutes, many hours, many days have I
> heard it—yet I dared not—oh, pity me, miserable wretch
> that I am!—I dared not—I *dared* not speak! *We have put
> her living in the tomb!*

With his supersensitive hearing Roderick has heard everything—heard her vain scratchings of the copper sheaths, her
feeble movements in the coffin, and now, intermingled with
the heroic actions of Ethelred, her bursting from her coffin
and thrusting apart the iron doors.

> Have I not heard her footstep on the stair? Do I not dis-
> tinguish that heavy and horrible beating of her heart? . . .
> *Madman! I tell you that she now stands without the door!*

Most readers think it odd that Usher, who is as crazy as
a bedbug, should call Narrator a madman. But then, mad
though he is, Usher knows more of the truth than Narrator,
with all his common sense, could possibly guess. And, seeing
that Narrator *still* has no idea of what is happening, or of
what *has* happened, or of what *will* happen, Usher, with the
impatience of the visionary as well as with the terror of the
hysteric, assails his imperceptive companion as 'mad.'
     What is it that Narrator has failed to perceive? He has set
down without comment some rather strange goings-on. For
instance, while Madeline is sick, but not yet thought to be
dead, Roderick is already busily composing *dirges*. The beloved sister is still on her sickbed while Roderick finds solace
in one of his favorite books, a Latin office for the *dead*. His
visionary painting is of a vault exactly like the vault in which
he will inter her, a vault illuminated by that eerie light cast
by the energy of the dead which we have seen to shine upwards from ruins of the City in the Sea. No wonder, then,
that Usher's aborted poem foretold the dissolution of his
'lofty intellect.' He could not become an artist *until he had
wished his sister dead*. All along, having laid her in the vault,
he knew her to be yet alive. But he had not rescued her. The
Roderick we see in Narrator's story has not enough will,
enough strength, enough resolution, to do this, or to do anything, save to create those ideational and visionary strains,
images, and rhymes evoked from his soul by the thought of
his sister's dying. What his helpless irresolution reveals is
that he *wanted* to bury Madeline even as he knew her not
yet to be dead. He has repressed this self-incriminating in-

formation but it will out, with the tell-tale beating of her heart.

He cannot escape her vengeance now, as under 'the potency of a spell,' the panels of the door swung open 'their ponderous and ebony jaws.' There, with blood upon her white robes, stood 'the lofty and enshrouded figure. . . .' We are reminded, momentarily, of that white and lofty and enshrouded figure of the whiteness of the snow who stood above Pym's cataract; but no, this is Madeline Usher, who, 'with a low moaning cry, fell heavily inward upon the person of her brother, and in her violent and now final death-agonies, bore him to the floor a corpse, and a victim to the terrors he had anticipated.'

I must try to gather up some loose strands of this eerie web-work. In the design of this fable, just as Roderick Usher is a double of Narrator—unconsciousness as an emanation of the conscious self—so is Madeline Usher the double of Roderick. Of these duplicate Ushers there is yet a further split, for the House itself is both the Usher family and its manse, as the bodily parallels and metaphors make plain.

Roderick, from the depths of a morbid depression brought on by doubts of his sanity, has summoned Narrator to his remote House, riddled with intricate subterranean passages. Of the lofty Madeline, Narrator, or consciousness, is, save for Roderick's presence, wholly unaware. Now, enacting his desire to murder his beloved double, Usher inters her in a vault from which she forcibly bursts free, as though in a ghastly travesty of rebirth, in order to fall upon him, dead at last. The House collapses inward upon its inmates as inorganic matter dissolves with organic.

Madeline is Usher's twin, his sister, his lover, and—but this is true *only when he can think of her as dying*—his muse. It is as though her dying is a precondition for the exercise of his creative impulse. The notion that the artwork outlives its subject is indeed an old one, but Poe makes the artist a cannibal or vampire whose subject *must die* so that there may be art.

This theme is stated less equivocally in a later tale I take to be a pendant to this one: 'The Oval Portrait' (1845). There, too, a narrator enters a Gothic castle which exists only as a museum of, or monument to, art. He discovers an oval portrait of a beautiful woman whose artist-husband was able to endow his painting with life—with her life, for his art fed upon her vitality. The touch that completed the portrait transferred the glow of life from the cheek of his wife to that of her image, and the subject died. In this way the death of a beautiful woman, Poe's prescribed theme for poetry, makes necessary that the beautiful woman die. And in Usher's case it inspires first the wish, then the act which leads the artist to become the murderer of his muse.

Not even the unconscious self can cope with such knowledge, for which there is no forgiveness. Once Roderick has interred his sister beyond, as he thinks, hope of escape, his 'lofty reason . . . totters' and his creative spell is shattered. From this point comes the equivocal ending of 'The Haunted Palace' and his wild despairs. Unacknowledged guilt has broken him. Meantime, deep below in her sealed and cuprous vault, the body of his soul prepares to avenge herself by bursting forth to carry him with her into the final release of actual death.

'The Fall of the House of Usher,' then, is both a testament to the autonomy of the unconscious, by whose inexorable powers are revealed the deepest truths of the soul, and, like 'Ligeia,' a fable of the one strange love story which was Poe's doom and gift. A love story in which incest, murder, and necrophilia are inescapable. To love one's twin sister is but a double displacement for the ultimate narcissism, self-love, and the ultimate incestuous desire, possession of one's mother's body. But in this strange domain from which all thought of ethics is banished as though by law—by an aesthetic law—there is yet, despite all, the sway of a moral law. There is even here the invisible reign of that most ancient tabu, inspiring guilt and terror. In the archaic memory of

the author, from which these terrible fantasies have risen,
the image of the beloved is so inextricably enshrouded with
the image of her death that his figure of the unconscious
must doubly punish himself, imagining not only that his
beloved twin and sister is dying or dead, but *making himself
responsible* for her dissolution. His guilt is doubled, too, for
not only does he become her murderer, he has done this terrible thing in order to make her 'lofty and enshrouded figure'
the more completely correspond to his own desire. His erotic
needs are subsumed in his art-products. His guitar rhapsodies,
his poems, his paintings, all these can come into being only
when his love-object exactly fits the imperious demands of
his deepest wish. But that wish makes him the committer
of both incest and murder, and his 'lofty reason' must topple
from her throne.

Accordingly, with the inexorable justice and logic of the
unconscious life, the injured beloved, whom the artist has
treated as an object, as the object of his own irrepressible
need, must arise from her entombment and claim her due.
What is her meed? Is it merely vengeance upon her murderer? Or is that very vengeance the consummation of their
terrible, all-devouring love? Obedient to the supersensual and
prophetic promptings of still another art-product, the 'romance' of 'The Mad Trist' (see how the title suggests dementia, a preordained reunion, and melancholy), Madeline
totters across the threshold of which the ebony doors are
'jaws' and falls *inward* upon Roderick, carrying him with her
to death.

From that chamber, and from that mansion, I fled
aghast. . . . Suddenly there shot along the path a wild
light. . . . The radiance was that of the full, setting, and
blood-red moon, which now shone vividly through that once
barely discernible fissure. . . . While I gazed, this fissure
rapidly widened—there came a fierce breath of the whirlwind—the entire orb of the satellite burst at once upon my
sight—my brain reeled as I saw the mighty walls rushing
asunder—there was a long tumultuous shouting sound like

the voice of a thousand waters—and the deep and dank tarn at my feet closed sullenly and silently over the fragments of the 'House of Usher.'

This seems akin to the apocalypse discussed by Monos and Una, by Eiros and Charmion, rendered through the sensibility of a single, living character. At the same time its movement anticipates that of all matter in *Eureka,* leading, as Geoffrey Rans remarks, to a sense of 'catastrophe without tragedy.' I have but to underline the obvious source of Roderick Usher's self-immolating course of action: What caused him to put his sister living in the tomb? What but his inescapable Imp of the Perverse, willing his own destruction on the instant and through the mechanism of making him will hers. As she falls inward upon him, their House, whose zigzag fault may represent the inorganic impulse toward self-annihilation, falls inward upon them both, and the entire House of Usher, the living, the dead, and the unliving, sink beneath the primal waters of the tarn in a landslide like that of the City in the Sea. A total apocalypse, from which but one character—Narrator—escapes to tell the tale.

Narrator is usually taken to be a blockhead, for he seems stupid indeed to accept so unquestioningly so many strange doings in the household of his host. I began this inquiry by accepting Mr. Wilbur's proposition that Narrator is the consciousness of the single character whose personality is figured forth among the other split personages of the tale. Poe seems to me to be telling us that consciousness alone cannot understand the inexorable *donnée* of the unconscious, but also that the unconscious, if unaided by consciousness, is the victim of the very forces among which it dwells. Why else does Roderick at the outset *send for Narrator to join him,* but that Usher fears he is losing his reason? What Poe further tells us is, those forces which the unconscious knows but cannot control are so strong that the conscious mind, even when made aware of them, cannot do much to direct them either.

This latter inference is both borne out and belied by Narrator's tale, for what is the effect of his telling his tale but to control these very forces which, the tale says, overwhelm Roderick Usher? The tale begins by proposing that the harmonious collaboration of Narrator-plus-Usher, i.e. of the conscious *and* the unconscious, will have a therapeutic effect upon the latter in its extremity. By the end, we have, not, I think, 'catastrophe without tragedy,' but *a tale* of the personal apocalypse of the unconscious, as told by the conscious mind. Now it is true that Narrator is a bit dim, that in the eerie *monde intérieur* of Usher's House he functions with the insight of a Prefect of Police. But in his own house how does he function? He tells the tale in which we learn all this. I take that tale itself to be the result of the collaboration between the Narrator-portion and the Usher-meed of the author's own mind. It is the result of a harmonious collaboration between his conscious and unconscious mind.

Thus Narrator is both inside and outside the catastrophic events of which he speaks. By separating the body that dies from the soul that suffers and creates, and the suffering soul from the mind that ratiocinates, Poe has managed to escape the fate that overtakes Roderick Usher as a result of this same division of functions. For Poe, as Narrator, is outside the apocalypse, observing that in which he took a part, as did God in Ligeia's poem 'The Conqueror Worm,' or in Poe's own *Eureka*.

Thus just as the several art-works within the tale are epitomes of the whole, so Roderick's action in creating them are epitomes of the author's in creating the tale of which they are among the parts. I speak now of Poe as author, no longer of Narrator, the character who tells the story, because I must rejoin those faculties in Poe which Poe has separated in Narrator and Usher: consciousness and intuition. These two qualities are exhibited in Roderick only while he functions as an artist. Before his creative streak, which the presence of Narrator and Madeline's attendant sickness instigated, he was distraught. After reciting 'The Haunted Palace' he is overpowered by the 'evil things' the poem foretold—his own destructive impulses. Narrator, for his part, has no tale at all to tell save for the materials which his trip to Usher's domain

had made available to him. Little though he consciously understands those experiences, in his telling of the tale we see
the collaboration of Usher's intuitive power with Narrator's
conscious mind. Like so many other of Poe's tale-tellers, his
art-product transcends his own limitations to exhibit a design
of which he is scarcely aware. The art-product which proceeds
according to the principle of the economy of the means, and
toward the predetermined end of exciting the beholder's soul,
is *imputed* to Roderick Usher's improvisations. But it is enacted in the tale of the Fall of the House of Usher.

Creative intelligence, then, the fusion of intellect-cum-
intuition, is, in the artist, the musician, the poet, a power
which transcends the materials upon which it exercises its
will and imposes its design. Like God, the artist is both embodied in and apart from the destruction of the creatures
of his will. Like God, he outlives the annihilation of his self-
created universe and can at will construct another plot containing yet again the necessity of its own destruction. Solipsism, in thought, in art, in life or death, can go no further
than this.

I have tried to be just to Poe's tale, yet the self-contained,
hermetic, consistent pattern of meanings I have extracted
from (or imposed upon) the story cannot, I am sure, account
entirely for the fixated fascination with which the tale has
been read by uncounted persons over the years. There must
be other, less Poe-defined, less intricate reasons for its power.
I do not doubt that there are very few readers who are so
simpatico with Poe's unusual requirements and demands that
they wittingly take the tale as I believe he ultimately requires
it to be taken. Some of its filiated meanings may not even
have been intended by him, but nonetheless they exist.

Was it Harry Levin in *The Power of Blackness* who first
suggested the congruence between the flawed manse and the
plantation aristocracy, and saw the fall of that House as a
prophetic paradigm of the self-destruction of the class to
which Poe longed to belong? Surely it isn't likely that Poe

intended his tale primarily as a commentary on the class structure of the ante-bellum South; but just as surely this ripple of meaning shivers the image of Usher's House reflected in the tarn.

Taken another way, the story offers Usher as a paradigm of the hero as artist, of the artist as *isolato*, of art as prophecy, of prophecy as burdened with doom. All this, though elaborated from Gothic clichés already tired by Poe's own time, strikes the thoughtful reader today as peculiarly modern. It is a form of our own anguish which is limned in these outlandish pages.

More generally, it is the grip this tale has upon the emotion of the uncanny which chills us. However repulsive one finds Poe's Gordian knot of incest, inhumation, murder and madness, his plot yet touches some unadmitted chord deep within us. It is akin to that almost forgotten knowledge toward which Poe's mariner rushed on his spectral ship, that nearly-recollected wisdom enshrined in Ligeia's eyes. Basing his investigation of 'the uncanny' upon an analysis of a tale by E. T. A. Hoffmann, whose work was among Poe's models, Freud proposed

> that we are able to postulate the principle of a *repetition-compulsion* in the unconscious mind, based upon instinctual activity and probably inherent in the very nature of the instincts—a principle powerful enough to overrule the pleasure-principle. . . . Whatever reminds us of this inner *repetition-compulsion* is perceived as uncanny.

Unusual as are Poe's particular obsessions and compulsions, the attachments of which they are variant forms and the instincts which they embody are the common properties of our human inheritance. Thus Poe, out of the very peculiarity of his psychic makeup, speaks to us not as a psychotic but as a man. Few writers have lived with their unconscious pulsations so close to the surface of their skins. Few have been as able to summon these images, or been as unable to escape them, as was Edgar Poe.

XII

The Haunted Palace

What sort of a man was Edgar Allan Poe, the narrators of whose tales dreamed such terrifying dreams? Whatever the envy and the malice with which Rufus W. Griswold blackened Poe's fame, it is a fact that a vast public was both able and willing to believe him. Poe, whose characters were so often drunkards or immoderate eaters of opium, and whose plots fulfilled their deepest dooms in acts of inadmissible savagery or dwelt with a tingling relish upon the most perverse forms of self-torture, or whose tales told either of revolting improbabilities such as the survival of the mind after the putrescence of the body, or of outrageous impositions upon the credulity of his readers,—such a man, nearly all who have read his works seemed willing to believe, must have been a fiend, a lunatic, a debauchee, a soul in damnation.

I have alleged, as an explanation for Griswold's unprincipled revisions of Poe's letters to make us so regard him, Poe's further sin in denying the validity of any religion, any resurrection, any saving spiritual grace but the hegemony of an Art which claimed to imitate the plots of God. Yet surely there is more to it than that. Surely what inspired Griswold's defamations of Poe and made them plausible to Poe's readers is their own unbending need to repress the horrible desires which Poe has revealed to them as possibly their own, or like others of their own. To do this they deny him any portion of the humanity they claim for themselves.

318 THE HAUNTED PALACE

In fact, however, Edgar Poe did not ever murder his wife, or his cat, or any benevolent old man or beautiful woman. His crime was more infamous than that. It was to tell us that the desire to do such things lurks, perhaps, in the soul of each of us.

> Tu le connais, lecteur, ce monstre delicat,
> —Hypocrite lecteur,—mon semblable,—mon frère!

To overcome such hypocrisy and acknowledge oneself a member of such a brotherhood required less cant and greater courage, and more intelligence, than could be found in these States in the nineteenth century. Poe had tried to protect himself from any such imputations as Griswold's canards attached to his name by endowing Art with an autonomy which separates it from life. The conception was his of the poem which has no motive whatever save the fulfilment of its own internal consistency. The tale—the Arabesque—also he conceived as having no design upon its reader save the excitation of his soul in the recognition of its inferential allegory, operating beneath the surface of the tale. But it is just that allegory which Poe's detractors resisted while they claimed to be repelled by the surface under which it operated. Such distinctions as Poe requires between art and life appeal only to the critical, not to the popular taste, much though he tried to address himself to both at the same time.

What sort of a man was Edgar Allan Poe? Those who knew him in his daily work attested to his considerate manners, his courtly bearing. He walked with all the courtesies of a Southern gentleman. His one besetting vice was a total inability to hold his liquor. Poe had an abnormal allergy to alcoholic toxicity. When one considers the openhanded drinking characteristic of his time and place, and the fact that journalists and litterateurs were a convivial lot, the wonder is that he was able to function at all.

To his wife Virginia, Poe, according to all responsible contemporary accounts, was devoted to the point of idolatry. Her mother Mrs. Clemm, who lived with them, after Virginia's death continued to care for 'poor Eddie.' I do not doubt that Poe had terrible thoughts about his invalid wife, whom he could not make enough money even to feed, and whose natural desires may have instigated an insupportable psychological blockage in her husband. In his life, however, Edgar Allan Poe tried to be a good man. It was in his art that he released the demonic energies which in life he, like all civil beings, had to repress. And since an art-product has only its own truths in view, in his art he was able to set those energies free within the discipline that art requires of them.

So it would seem that the violence, the passion, and the perversity characteristic of Poe's stories resemble his own actions no more than do the haunted palaces, luxurious chambers, and festooned interiors of the tales resemble the bare unheated cottages and skimpy hovels in which Poe, Virginia, and her mother Mrs. Clemm huddled and shivered during those cold winters in Baltimore, New York, and Philadelphia while Eddie was writing the tales, the poems, the reviews and treatises we still read today. With his knack and his need to turn every image of the physical world into a manifestation of the psychical, Poe's haunted palace is an image of his own head, the head where the monarch Thought should reign but for the inexorable ghosts by which it is haunted.

I have made only occasional allusions to the fact that all of Poe's writings were composed for immediate sale and constitute the output of an incessantly busy professional writer at a time when the state of letters in America made literary journalism a precarious living indeed. Poe's work has been carefully studied in the contexts of the magazine traditions in which he wrote: Edd Winfield Parks investigated Poe's debt to American magazines, and more recently Michael Allen has surveyed *Poe and the British Magazine Tradition*. Mr. Allen after his informative searching-out of parallels and predecessors for Poe's plots and theories, concludes, 'I have at no point allowed to Poe the "greatness" which Baudelaire ascribed. . . . a sense of the European magazine tradition

in which Poe was working . . . suggests, in writers like De
Quincey and Bulwer, more accurate and modest parallels for
the kind of "inquiring and versatile mind" that Poe possessed.' Nevertheless I should like to re-ascribe to Poe the
'greatness' claimed for him by Baudelaire, and recognized
also, inter alia, by such other poets as Mallarmé, Valéry, Lawrence, Eliot, Tate, Auden, and Wilbur. 'Greatness' has to do
not necessarily with departures from the conventions of one's
time, but rather with the degree of originality to which are
put the conventions that other, lesser writers, are using for
only conventional purposes.

Every writer must accept the given conventions of his day,
if only as a basis for his rejections. In Poe's case there could
be no such luxury as rejection of the popular forms of enter-
tainment. Instead, with the cleverness typical of his ratiocinating and intuitive genius, he bored from within, taking over
and re-making to his own needs the forms which the public
would tolerate. As it happens, there proved to be a correspondence between the limited attention-span of the
magazine-reading public of ante-bellum America and Poe's
own capacities to sustain a plot or a poem. Accordingly he
justifies as the only possible vehicles for the exploration of
truth the short poem and the brief tale, spurning the novel
and attacking 'the epic mania.' This quite accidental congruence between what Poe was most capable of writing and
what the public would actually put up with saved him from
being an American Chatterton. Precarious though his living
was, at least he did not starve to death before reaching his
majority.

It is self-evident that Poe's most impressive works do in
fact derive from four traditions of popular fiction: the Gothic
horror story, the tale of exploration, the science-fiction story,
and the detective tale. It is also true that Poe so rationalized
the detective story and so boldly adapted the appearance
of scientificism in fiction that modern practitioners of these
popular arts regard him as their virtual inventor.

The Gothic conventions inherited from Mrs. Radcliffe,
Walpole, Beckford, Hoffmann, Tieck, and the contributors

to magazines like *Blackwood's* were used by Poe's contemporaries for purposes other than his. Wilkie Collins exploited them for their inherent sensational effects. Hawthorne moralized them. Dickens, and later James, interlaced such Gothic themes as the haunted house, the ancestral curse, the ghost, the double who represents the unlived life, with a realistic imitation of widely varied characters and situations in a believable society. Such novels as theirs were as far beyond Poe's capacities as they were foreign to his intentions.

Poe is perhaps the more purely Gothic writer than any of these, since for him the conventions which others used as a convenience become the substance as well as the method of his fictions. For Poe the attributes of Gothicism open the way into the murky interiors of encrimsoned light, they lead through the narrow and dank passageways of the self, making available to his imagination, and to the control which his method required of a work of art, those energies, those attachments to numinous objects, which in reality we try, with as great success as we can, to repress. Such total honesty, such uncompromising knowledge of the self, is so wounding to our own esteem that we do not usually seek it with any expectation of pleasure. Poe, baring his own heart, shows us his inescapable truths, in tales (and a few poems) whose design is so consistent with their ends that we, despite ourselves, take pleasure in what appalls us. Perhaps a part of that pleasure is the reflected knowledge of our own selves which, but for Poe, we might not have had the means or the courage to confront. I would do him just that honor which requites his terrible gift.

Poe represents an extreme instance of that condition, typical of the Romantic movement, which T. S. Eliot diagnosed and attacked as 'dissociation of sensibility.' In Poe the man who thinks and the man who feels seem, at least superficially, to direct the reader toward mutually exclusive responses. Poe in his thinking-cap is the contriver of a rationalistic theory of poetic composition, the setter and solver of such puzzles as engage the attention of Monsieur Dupin, Legrand, and, in *Eureka*, of God. He is also the clever inventor of a strato-

spheric balloon, and the exposer of Maelzel's chess-man. Poe
in his procrustean bed of sensation of course takes us somewhere else—into the haunted palace, the haunted house, the
haunted mind, of such obsessed miscreants as Usher, Ligeia's
husband, Egaeus, the murderers of wife, cat, old man, Fortunato, and William Wilson.

So, to recapitulate, we can infer that one side of Poe is
devoted to the Enlightenment's faith in reason, while the
doppelgänger of this rationalist is incessantly undermining
that faith with his recourses to the Gothic machinery of horror and his appropriation of the explorer's tale, which he
turns into the exploration of a psychic soulscape.

But no, these doubles of Poe's aren't *always* engaged in
mutually exclusive enterprises. For reflect how frequently
they collaborate. When Ratiocinator is doing his best, he becomes exalted with the sensation of being at one with the
covert workings of the soul of the universe. When Sufferer
achieves the enactment of his self-destructive impulse, the
author who so contrived his nearly perfect plot attains that
intellectual consistency—the production of a predetermined
effect upon the reader and the working-out of his character's
destiny according to rule—which is a function of the artist
as plot-maker, or in imitation of God thinking.

Indeed, what lends Poe's enterprise its garish grandeur is
his heroic effort to rejoin those faculties which in himself
he felt so fatally to be sundered. If he represents, as I have
just proposed, the dissociation of sensibility *in extremis*, at
the same time he offers us his heroic effort to unify those
fatal flaws in the ramparts of his being. His own understanding of his state reflects his unquestioning debt to the facultative psychology of the preceding century, from which he drew
the categories of his own thought—body, mind, soul; the perception of beauty, knowledge of truth, knowledge of good.
These he accepted as independent entities the consequences
of whose separation from a hypostasized primal unity formed
the theoretical basis of all of his desperate ratiocinations.

Although his major works all seem (at least to me) to be
tightly wound upon the spindles of his unconscious conflicts,

there are yet aspects in which his writings seem epitomes of his nation and his time. Abstruse though *Eureka* seemed then as now, is it not deeply attuned to one side of the character of the American people in its worship of energy, in its projection of a mechanistic universe impelled by a determinism inexorable in its operation? Such views, in the rather different vocabulary of modern physics, comprise a philosophy of nature to which we are still struggling to adapt ourselves.

There is of course another side of the American character or outlook—one of many others—which Poe spurns. That is our sublime commitment, despite all our experience, to the notion of progress. As will be seen from the concluding pages of *Eureka*, Poe's cosmogony rests on a cyclical process; not, as was true of Yeats's cycles, a historical process, but a process enacted simultaneously by all creation and in the sensibility of the individual man. History is irrelevant to this process, and progress is inconceivable. 'I have no faith in human perfectibility,' Poe wrote to Lowell in a letter I have already quoted (2 July, 1844). 'I think that human exertion will have no appreciable effect upon humanity. Man is now only more active—not more happy—nor more wise, than he was 6000 years ago.' No more could Poe agree 'to lose sight of man the individual, in man the mass.' A screed less calculated to win the admiration of that earnest New Englander would be hard to devise. As though to cinch the fact, Poe, ever responsive to his Imp of the Perverse, ends his letter to Lowell by attacking Longfellow once again for 'the grossest plagiarisms ever perpetrated.'

Nor would I be understood to claim too much for Poe as a Representative American. I hope to have shown how unique, and at the same time, how general, are Poe's very peculiarities, his overriding themes, techniques, theories, and practices as a literary artist. Strange and lonely as he and his work appear, he nevertheless had his *semblables* in his own time, though not, to be sure, among his neighbors in the United States. 'So far from having nothing in common with the spirit of the first half of the nineteenth century, Poe is certainly one of its most typical figures; that is to say, he is a

thorough romantic, closely akin to his European contemporaries,' wrote Edmund Wilson in 1926 (*The Shores of
Light*, p. 183), pointing to kinships few later scholars have
had the wit to know what to make of: the resemblance of
his 'nightmarish vein of fancy' to Coleridge, the debt of his
early poetry to Shelley, and of his 'dream fugues' to De
Quincey. His themes, Wilson suggests, are like those of Byron
and Chateaubriand, and he adds that each of these European
writers seems as anomalous in his own country as does Poe
in the United States. They are all among the founders of a
convention long since taken for granted, the alienation of the
artist. There is yet a further irony in this; for the artist's
alienation has become the condition of all men of feeling,
and the artist himself, in his isolation and suffering, a type
of modern man.

Convinced that Poe's *donnée* was such that a web-work
of consistent imagery overspreads the whole, in which there
is the exploration and elaboration of his given themes, I have
treated that body of work as though all were coterminous,
paying little heed in my arrangement of the tales and poems
to the actual order of composition. Nor have I been concerned
to trace his motifs to their sources, for it in no way impugns
either Poe's originality or the uses to which he put his plots
and motifs in his own writings to discover that E. T. A. Hoffmann's tales of doppelgängers preceded his, or that the horrors of 'The Pit and the Pendulum' or 'Monsieur Valdemar'
were perhaps borrowed from forgotten tales in *Blackwood's
Magazine* (whose excesses Poe set out to spoof with excesses
of his own, as in 'A Predicament'). Nor does it detract from
the integrity of his work to find that before *Eureka*, De
Quincey had published an analytical and rhapsodic sketch,
'System of the Heavens.' When taxed in his own day with the
charge he levelled so persistently against Longfellow et al.,
that of plagiarism, Edgar Poe replied, with Mephistophelean
truth, that the terrors in his tales 'were not of Germany, but
of the soul.'

In all literature there is a polarity between accident and
archetype, between the representation of the particulars of

reality and their subordination to some recurrent and eternal pattern of experience. Poe, whose tales are abstracted from reality, and whose poems are sometimes abstracted yet again from those abstractions, is an artist who tends toward the expression of the pure archetype with as little as possible of the texture of actuality in his work. Thus in 'The Black Cat,' 'Ligeia,' 'The Fall of the House of Usher,' he has created unreal persons—wraiths—in impossible situations without reference to any 'real' place or time. Yet from these conditions so willed, contrived, and unactual, he succeeds in evoking real terror, real love, real hatred, real guilt, the real Imp of the Perverse.

If his copious writings are all the elaborations of a set of limited archetypes, so it may be said that his life itself enacted one of the most cherished plots of his time. Rather, because that life was Poe's, we must more truthfully say it enacted the *reversal* of a cherished fairytale. That plot is told in its proper sequence in *Oliver Twist*. It is retold and Americanized in *Huckleberry Finn*. It is what my daughter, then aged nine, said about the stories she had read: 'They all begin with the child in poverty and he has lost his parents, then they find him and he ends in richery.'

Poe's own life began as though it was to be the plot of a romance by Dickens or a fairytale by George Macdonald. The orphaned son of wandering players is taken into the family of a merchant prince in Richmond. But, as we have seen, John Allan betrayed the role of savior, benefactor, patron, and father. He became instead the pseudosavior, the evil king, the ogre. What can the boy Eddie do but play Jack the Giant Killer, as in 'Hop-Frog' or 'The Purloined Letter' or 'The Tell-Tale Heart'? But in Poe's tale, as in his life, there was no ministering tutelary figure, no goodwife in the kitchen to tell him how to slay the giant. Nobody to help him but Virginia, herself dying, and poor dim Mother Clemm. Any friend who might appear in the wings with good intentions—John Pendleton Kennedy, James Russell Lowell,

Nathaniel Parker Willis—would soon enough think better of
his good offices after an encounter with Edgar's Imp of the
Perverse. In Poe's life none of the compensations came true
by which the authors of fairytales, in their folk wisdom, arranged to avenge the hapless seventh son against the circumstances which made him the least likely suitor for the maiden
who dwelt atop the mountain of glass.

So Poe was driven himself to avenge those circumstances
which life made seem irreparable. His chosen means, the
only one available to him, the one he used with such per-
tinacity and resolution throughout his life of sufferings, was
the imagination. Of this he wrote, in *Marginalia* 'The range
of Imagination is unlimited. Its materials extend throughout
the universe. Even out of deformities it fabricates *Beauty*
which is at once its sole object and its inevitable test.' Recalling that by 'beauty' Poe means, not the conventional attributes of that term, but an all-embracing *consistency* among
the constituent parts of the experience in a literary form,
we can appreciate the magnitude of Poe's accomplishments
in the brief forms to which he committed his strange genius.
The deformities from which he fabricated beauty were the
unbearable tensions, the horrible desires, the sublime apoth-
eoses of his own being. From these usually unacknowledged
motives, from these lusts and savage impulses which few
have had the courage to admit or to reveal, Poe made those
consistent and self-contained *designs*, whose symmetry is appreciable only to the reader whose sensibility, like the
author's, combines intuition with ratiocination.

Poe's art and his philosophy, like his life itself, comprise
the reversal of our expectations. It has always seemed to me
that the first appearance of metaphor in English literature
is one of the most profound. I mean that passage in Bede's
Ecclesiastical History in which an unnamed advisor to King
Edwin, speaking in the year 627 to the question of whether
or not the kingdom should be converted to a new faith, described the human lot in these words:

> The present life of man, O king, seems to me, in compari-
> son of that time which is unknown to us, like the swift

flight of a sparrow though the room wherein you sit at supper in winter, with your commanders and ministers, and a good fire in the midst, whilst the storms of rain and snow prevail abroad; the sparrow, I say, flying in at one door, and immediately out at the other, whilst he is within, is safe from the wintry storm; but after a short space of fair weather, he immediately vanishes out of your sight, into the dark winter from which he had emerged. So this life of man appears for a short space, but of what went before, or what is to follow, we are utterly ignorant.

King Edwin's hope was to be 'cleansed in Christ, the Fountain of Life,' but for Poe there is no such hope. Accordingly Poe's view of the present life of man is not to consider the flight of the sparrow while within the sight of human eyes a welcome relief from the storms of the great unknown outside. It is from that outer world, beyond the seeming comforts of mead hall, hearth, and company, that Poe, too, in his haunted palace has received an avian messenger, who for a space of time reminds him of the contrast between that realm and this one. Poe's raven tells us that this, the known life, is an unmitigated disaster, a spell of suffering, loss, horror, and sorrow, of longing almost unbearable for the bliss he can almost remember, for the obliteration he yearns for as much as he dreads. Were Poe to adopt precisely the simile of the sparrow's flight, either by pretending to have read it in an ancient author, or, like the Venerable Bede himself, by plagiarising from a Celtic myth the legend of the bird as the human soul, the flight of that soul would veer from the unity of its origin into the disorder of our passionate, fleshly and corruptible world, leaving, at last, through the wind's eye of death to fly once again to the primal unity of its happier star.

Index

Allan, Frances, 25–26, 254, 255
Allan, John, 25, 33–35, 122, 325
Allen, Michael, 84, 319
Alterton, Margaret, 290
Auber, Daniel-François-Esprit, 72
Auden, W. H., 14, 63–64, 210, 273–74, 320; 'The Guilty Vicarage,' 129

Basler, Roy, 253
Baudelaire, Charles, 13, 15, 16, 22, 47, 147–48, 159, 175, 191, 320; 'Au lecteur,' quoted, 318
Bede, *Ecclesiastical History*, 326–27
Béranger, Pierre Jean de, 52, 301
Blackwood's Magazine, 9, 84, 97, 205, 214, 321, 324
Blake, William, 33
Bonaparte, Marie, 26, 27, 46, 150, 155, 157, 233, 236, 247, 254, 264, 291

Bonnefoy, Yves, 47
Bradbury, Ray, 151
Bulwer, Edward, 320
Buranelli, Vincent, 290
Burton, William, 183
Byron, George Gordon, Lord, 29, 35, 53, 97, 210, 324; 'Hebrew Melodies,' 52; *Manfred*, 32

Campbell, Killis, 52
The Castle of Otranto (Horace Walpole), 159
Chateaubriand, François René, Viscount de, 324
Chesterton, G. K., 113
Chivers, Thomas Holley, 37, 175
Clemm, Maria Poe, 26, 319, 325
Coleridge, Samuel Taylor, 35, 45, 66, 81, 97, 324; *Biographia Literaria*, 45, 84–85; 'Christobel,' 305; 'Kubla Khan,' 38, 187, 305; 'The Pains of

ABOUT THE AUTHOR

Daniel Hoffman's work on Poe was begun while a Research Fellow of the American Council of Learned Societies. He is professor of English at the University of Pennsylvania and has taught also at Swarthmore College and Columbia University.

BOOKS BY DANIEL HOFFMAN

POE POE POE POE POE POE POE

BROKEN LAWS

STRIKING THE STONES

BARBAROUS KNOWLEDGE

THE CITY OF SATISFACTIONS

FORM AND FABLE IN AMERICAN FICTION

A LITTLE GESTE

THE POETRY OF STEPHEN CRANE

AN ARMADA OF THIRTY WHALES

PAUL BUNYAN, LAST OF THE FRONTIER DEMIGODS

As Editor

AMERICAN POETRY AND POETICS

THE RED BADGE OF COURAGE AND OTHER STORIES